An Illustrated History of Siesta Key

The Story of America's Best Beach

Philip M. Farrell

and

Thomas Philip Farrell

Pineapple Press, Inc.
Sarasota, Florida

Inquiries should be addressed to:

Pineapple Press, Inc.
P.O. Box 3889
Sarasota, Florida 34230

www.pineapplepress.com

All photographs not otherwise credited are by the authors, or in some cases by non-copyrighted and/or anonymous sources.

Library of Congress Cataloging-in-Publication Data

Names: Farrell, Philip M., author. | Farrell, Thomas Philip, author.
Title: An illustrated history of Siesta Key : the story of America's best
  beach / by Philip M. Farrell and Thomas Philip Farrell.
Description: First edition. | Sarasota, Florida : Pineapple Press, 2018.
Identifiers: LCCN 2017052177 | ISBN 9781683340164 (pbk.)
Subjects: LCSH: Siesta Key (Fla.)--History. | Siesta Key (Fla.)--Description
  and travel.
Classification: LCC F319.S54 F37 2018 | DDC 975.9/61--dc23
LC record available at https://lccn.loc.gov/2017052177

First Edition

Design by Symbiosys Technologies
Printed and bound in the USA

Contents

Foreword

Jeff LaHurd

Long before Dr. Beach proclaimed Siesta Key "the best beach in the country"—validating what locals already knew—Siesta Key enjoyed a reputation as a picturesque attraction for locals and snowbirds alike.

My earliest memories extend to the early 1950s and include the single-lane, hand-cranked swing bridge on Stickney Point Road—the very narrow Siesta Key Bridge, barely wide enough for two cars to pass without trading paint—and vast stretches of undeveloped, blindingly white, sugar-sand beaches.

The village in those days offered only a handful of shops, including Davidson's Drugs, with many thinking John B. Davidson was foolish for opening in such a sparsely settled area. At the other end of the island was Nancy Connelly's perennially popular Crescent Beach Grocery Store.

The scenic isle became a magnet for renowned artists, writers, architects, and others seeking its lovely solitude—a verdant tropical island a short drive from the Sarasota mainland.

It was much later that I delved into its colorful history. I discovered the stories of "Uncle" Ben Stickney, beloved by all for his cheery hospitality and community picnics on his property. I also learned of the tragic story of Harry Higel, "Sarasota's indefatigable booster," who served on the town council, platted the north end of the key, and built the Higelhurst Hotel. When the hostelry burned to the ground, his son recalled watching the blaze and the tears streaming down from his father's eyes. He vowed to rebuild, but never did. In the end, Harry Higel was murdered, so badly bludgeoned that he was unrecognizable, and the murder case was never solved.

There are the stories of Captain Lewis Roberts and his pioneering family, the Mira Mar Casino with its huge spotlights for night-time swimming, Roberts Casino, and the Tropicana Supper Club; and more recently the iconic Summerhouse restaurant, the Magic Moment, and numerous other popular gathering places; and today's Beach Club and the never-changing Crescent Club—a refreshing throwback to the quieter 1950s.

In the long-ago day, way before rampant development, driving on the beach was not only tolerated but encouraged, as it still is on Daytona Beach.

As with the rest of Sarasota—and the state of Florida for that matter—development on Siesta came to a halt after the hurricane of September 1926, which tore through Miami. Development remained suspended through the Great Depression and World War II, and began again with the post-war boom. Today's tidal wave of development has forever washed away the tranquility for which Siesta was previously appreciated.

In *An Illustrated History of Siesta Key: The Story of America's Best Beach*, Philip M. Farrell, M.D., Ph.D., and his grandson, Thomas Philip Farrell—who fell in love with a Siesta Key vastly different from the one I recall—have ably drawn on the historical and social themes of this unique sliver of land to document its singular past as well as its current place as the "best beach in America."

The duo covers all the bases, from the Indian settlements to the Spanish influence to the influence of barrier islands on tourism, including a chapter on the little-known Mennonite community's relationship to Siesta. They continue with the "spring breakers" and the expansion of the village to present a complete look at contemporary Siesta Key.

Well documented and ably written, this volume is a welcome addition to the histories of Sarasota and will be appreciated as much by future generations as today's readers.

The Farrells have done a remarkable job.

Note on Sources

During the two years of research for this book, we read the books referenced in the text and/or bibliography and over two hundred articles in well-archived newspapers such as the *Sarasota Herald Tribune* and *Pelican Press*. We consulted even more websites, studied the files of the Sarasota County Historical Resources Center, and conducted countless interviews with a variety of experts and knowledgeable Siesta Key residents. Our inquiries were very informative, but it also became clear that we could not rely completely on any single source in the discovery process focused on the history of Sarasota County and its barrier islands. The recollections of individuals about dates, in particular, did not always agree with those of other interviewees or with authoritative sources such as the newspapers. On the other hand, stories told by individuals about events and cultural changes on Siesta Key were generally more revealing than information we found in books, newspapers, and websites. These stories may have been occasionally biased, but they were rich and colorful, if not dramatic. Because of the variations in information we discovered, our *modus operandi* was to seek at least two and often three or more sources to confirm each important historical development—similar to a journalist seeking multiple sources for a story or a scientist applying the scientific method to confirm experimental results through repeated experiments. If we have erred in describing some aspects of Siesta Key's history, readers should be assured that we did our best and look forward to hearing from anyone who has an alternative view.

Preface

This book is the product of two years of research and ten years of observations on Siesta Key during annual visits. There were several reasons to embark on this project, but the major motivation was to learn more about this unique barrier island. To quote Elie Wiesel, "I write to understand as much as to be understood." His philosophy has always applied to my scientific reports of medical research data. When my curiosities on Siesta Key led to systematic research, however, I recognized that many long-term residents were surprised to learn these historical details and the advantages of recording what was uncovered through my inquiries became clear.

It all started with an interest in Gulf of Mexico barrier islands that dated back to the early 1950s. Then, in 1957 our family vacation included a trip to Sarasota. The area at that time was obviously much less developed than it is now, and its tropical beauty was striking. Later, more visits to gulf barrier islands such as Marco and Sanibel, as well as vacations in Destin, made it clear that the sand on all those beaches was similar. I didn't understand why until I read with great pleasure a fascinating and inspiring book entitled *Barrier Islands of the Florida Gulf Coast Peninsula* by Richard A. Davis Jr. Dr. Davis explains how the sand on all these gulf beaches has come from the same source, the Appalachian Mountains. Yet the sand of Siesta Key is special. When my wife, Alice, and I first strolled along Siesta/Crescent Beach in March 2005, we were both struck by the fact that this was the whitest and finest sand we had ever seen. It looked and felt like powdered sugar to us. We had to come back, so when my post-deanship sabbatical arrived, we returned for our first stay at Coquille Condominiums on the mid-key.

During that three-month sojourn and our subsequent annual visits, I've enjoyed riding my bicycle almost daily on routes that covered ten to fifteen miles. These rides raised many questions in my mind, such as: Why is the most prominent road named Midnight Pass when there is no Midnight Pass on any of the maps we were using? Why is Ocean Boulevard so named even though it is not along the ocean? Why do so many streets have Spanish names near the Siesta Key Public Beach but nowhere else? Lastly, who was the Higel of Higel Avenue and the Roberts of Roberts Point Road? One day while riding with my biking buddies Trent Robinson and Bill Hasbrook, we pedaled past a Higel house and then a Harry L. Higel plaque. Returning solo, I read the plaque and learned the tragic history of Mayor Harry Higel. I was thirsty for more knowledge of his role on Siesta Key.

These curiosity-provoking bike trips were important sources of inspiration, but discussions with Coquille residents were even more stimulating. I'm especially grateful to Joan and Jim Mangan. Joan was always kind as she answered my naïve questions and described the "good old days" when the beach was deserted and the Summerhouse was a magnet. Almost as stimulating were my many strolls to the Crescent Beach Grocery—not just to buy provisions but also to gaze at the old Siesta Key photographs Nancy Connelly displays on the walls there. I became convinced that a rich history permeated Siesta Key.

Perhaps none of these curiosities would have led to a shift away from medical/scientific writing toward this book. But then I recognized an opportunity to collaborate with my grandson, Tom, who was finishing undergraduate studies in history and anthropology at the University of Wisconsin in Milwaukee. We both were also aware of the talents and creativity in computer graphics of my granddaughter, Julia Farrell Patton. Julia's training at the University of Minnesota made her essential in creating the cover and other graphics for the book. Fortunately, Tom and Julia's visits to Siesta Key also stimulated their interest. Next, Tom and I found the Sarasota County Historical Resources Center and the single most important resource in the creation of this book, Larry A. Kelleher. His skills as a digital preservationist, as well as his incredible memory and appreciation of the local history, gave us the confidence that an original and, we hoped, significant contribution could be made by a book such as this. Larry not only taught us; he also guided our research and kindly corrected our misunderstandings.

This history of Siesta Key reaffirms the two axioms that make knowledge of the past essential in planning for the future. As Mary Anne Evans (a.k.a George Eliot) stated: "History repeats itself." And, to quote George Santayana: "Those who cannot remember the past are condemned to repeat it." Those statements apply well to an uncertain future as Siesta Key celebrates its present status as having "America's Best Beach."

Tom, Julia, and I hope that you enjoy the story.

—Philip M. Farrell

Acknowledgments

It is impossible to recognize and thank everyone who contributed to making this book a reality. We embarked on this venture because our family has had the privilege to live for a few months annually on Siesta Key in the Coquille community, whose owners have been more than supportive. Early in the research Joan and Jim Mangan were both inspirational and informative, while throughout the process Hunter Barney advised us well. We thank them and Coquille President Trent Robinson, who led the senior author toward the path of discovery. We are likewise deeply grateful to Lance Smith and Sally Luce for their guidance and encouragement, as well as Sally's expert critique of some chapters.

After the Coquillers inspired us, Richard Davis published *Barrier Islands of the Florida Gulf Coast Peninsula,* a lifetime-achievement book that deepened our commitment as we read it. Although repeated readings of the book by us could have sufficed, Richard did much more, teaching us about coastal geology and serving as an outstanding adviser while showing great patience with our questions. Richard shares with the authors a history of educational experiences at the University of Wisconsin where he was a postdoctoral fellow in 1964–65. Three other geologists were also helpful: Tom Stafford, a longtime research colleague; Ron Blakey, an expert in paleogeography who clarified Florida's origin for Chapter 2—both of whom also have been connected with the University of Wisconsin—and Stephen Leatherman, a.k.a. "Dr. Beach," whose annual swimming beach ratings/rankings have brought fame to Siesta Beach. Lastly in this category of scientific advisers, we want to recognize and thank Professor Chin Wu, Department of Civil and Environmental Engineering at the University of Wisconsin College of Engineering, who provided information on beach nourishment.

The authors next benefited enormously by being able to engage the great historian/anthropologist Barbara A. Purdy, Professor Emerita at the University of Florida, who was introduced to us by our colleague and friend, Tom Stafford. Barbara is a superstar we hardly deserved to have guidance from when we most needed her help, but she was always generous with her time and full of valuable information and advice. She also connected us with her outstanding colleague, William Marquardt, who advised us on the Calusa and arranged tours and meetings at Pine Island's Randall Research Center; there we met and were well informed by the program coordinator, Cindy Bear. Our task of understanding the Amerindian era, however, was only possible because of the great archaeologist, George Luer, who welcomed us into his home at the historic Old Oak Site of Sarasota and taught us the essentials; we admire and thank George. Another historian/anthropologist who knows Siesta Key history better than anyone, Nancy Connelly, made extraordinary contributions to this book, for which we are forever grateful. John Davidson likewise played a key role informing us through discussions and, more importantly, by making his *Pelican Press* archives available for study—a gold mine for discovering the past half-century of Siesta Key history.

A larger treasure trove was found at the Sarasota County Historical Resources Center. There, the most important person in creation of this book, Larry Kelleher, has been invaluable throughout the project and will always have our gratitude. His colleague, Sarasota County Archeologist Steve Koski, enlightened us and led us to George Luer. Sarasota County's former historian and undoubtedly most knowledgeable authority, Jeff LaHurd, was extremely helpful in clarifying difficult topics and is deeply appreciated for having contributed an insightful and generous Foreword.

In addition, we are deeply grateful to Laura Campbell-Burns, great-great-granddaughter of Frank Higel Sr., for sharing stories and many documents about her ancestors. The interviews with Laura were critical in our arduous but fascinating efforts to write the Higel chapter, as were the notes from her colleague, Judie Bauer. Similarly, Laura's "Uncle Harry" Higel was very informative and appreciated. We also thank Sally Luce and Mark Lefebvre, who critiqued the Higel chapter and offered valuable suggestions. Our study of Amish and Mennonite settlers and tourists was revealing because of a wonderful expert, J. B. Miller, who teaches this topic in courses for Sarasota County Schools (Adult Community and Enrichment Program) and taught us about the special population we regard as Siesta Key's first spring breakers. He is responsible as much as the authors for Chapter 11, which Sally Luce also reviewed and helped us revise. Chapters 13 and 14 would not have been possible without the many informative and pleasant communications with Cyrus Gregg, Carl Abbott, and Paul Mattison; we are deeply indebted to them.

We thank most sincerely several people who provided invaluable information during interviews and tours. These include Al Milner at Jamaica Royale; a wonderful group living at Tortuga (Paula and Larry Krambeer, Martha and Maury Kramer, and Linda Conway); Rob Steinmetz at the Sanderling Club; Averill Babson at the Gulf and Bay Club; Gary Kompothecras of "Ask Gary" fame; Brad Stewart at Captain Curt's and his good friend, Howard Partain; Stan McGowan, owner of the Butcher's Block; Catherine and Bob Luckner, who have led the Siesta Key Association; Lisa Dean and Gary Roberts for information on Captain Lewis Roberts; Rhonda Rogers at the Venice Museum & Archives, and Kenneth Milano for providing rare photographs; Emy Stein (Island Visitor Publishing, LLC) for information and photographs; Betsy de Manio for information and key referrals; John McCarthy and John McIlroy for details on Siesta Beach land acquisitions; Walter Rothenbach, Sarasota County Parks and Recreation Director from 1966 to 1998, who more than anyone is responsible for creating "America's Best Beach" and summarized the land acquisitions for us; Tracy Fanara, program manager at Mote Marine Laboratory, who provided information on Florida red tide; Mike Solomon, who provided invaluable information on his parents, Syd and Annie and their controversial home, as well as photographs; William Hasbrook, a good friend and lawyer, who analyzed and advised us on legal issues, and his wife, Sally, who critiqued Chapter 17; Jovanka Ristic at the American Geographical Society Library, University of Wisconsin-Milwaukee; and two typists who were both excellent and cheerful, Diane Daspit in Sarasota and Angie Schulz in Three Lakes, Wisconsin.

Last but not least, we are eternally grateful to members of our family who patiently contributed a variety of efforts to make this book possible. Julia Farrell Patton has been awesome throughout the process, designing the cover and creating all the graphic illustrations, as well as reviewing chapters with her husband, Steven. Others who advised us and/or reviewed chapters include Stephan Farrell and Michael Farrell, as well as Roberta Farrell, who was critically important during the final phases of editing. All of the Farrells have appreciated Alice's role in this project and tolerance of her husband's obsessions.

CHAPTER 1

Introduction to Siesta Key and Its Beaches

No day is a bad day if you've watched the sun set on the beach. It's the one experience you can count on time and time again to reliably clear your head, give you perspective, and make you appreciate what you've got.

—M. C. Coolidge, *Sideways in Sarasota*

Siesta Key is a three-thousand-year-old barrier island just west of Sarasota. According to the U.S. Census Bureau, it has a total area of 3.5 square miles, of which 2.4 square miles are land and 1.1 square miles are water. Its coordinates are 27°16′31″N, 82°33′9″W. The island has had numerous names including Clam Island, Mussel Island, Palm Island, Sarasota Island, and either Sarasota Key or Little Sarasota Key. The northern section has been labeled Fishery Point and Woodruff Point and is now known as Bay Island.

The origin of the name Siesta Key can be attributed to one of Sarasota's first mayors, Harry Lee Higel, who established the Siesta Land Company with two partners in 1907 and platted the northwestern section of the island as the Siesta subdivision. Higel later opened the first Siesta post office on Big Sarasota Pass. It was not until 1952, however, that the U.S. Board of Geographical Names officially recognized Siesta Key as the name of the barrier island situated between Roberts Bay and the Gulf of Mexico.

Sections of its gulf beaches were also renamed from time to time. They have been known as Sandy Hook, Sarasota Beach, Mira Mar Beach, Crescent Beach, Siesta Beach, and Siesta Public Beach. The beaches at the southern end were called Azar Beach, Waverly Beach, and finally, Turtle Beach.

As of this writing, the Siesta Key Chamber of Commerce website describes three beach segments: "Siesta Key has three wonderful beaches on this 8-mile stretch of 'the world's finest, whitest sand' along the Gulf of Mexico, each one of our beaches offers a slightly different beach experience, but they all share the same azure gulf waters, picture-perfect sunsets, and soothing breeze that melts away your troubles so you really can't go wrong with any of them." The website continues:

Siesta Beach. In 2011 Siesta Beach was rated as the #1 beach in the United States by "Dr. Beach," a.k.a. Dr. Stephen P. Leatherman... In 2004 the Travel Channel named it "The Best Sand Beach in America" because of its 99% pure quartz sand that stays cool under your feet... Its shallow water near the shoreline and year-round lifeguard protection make it a great beach for the whole

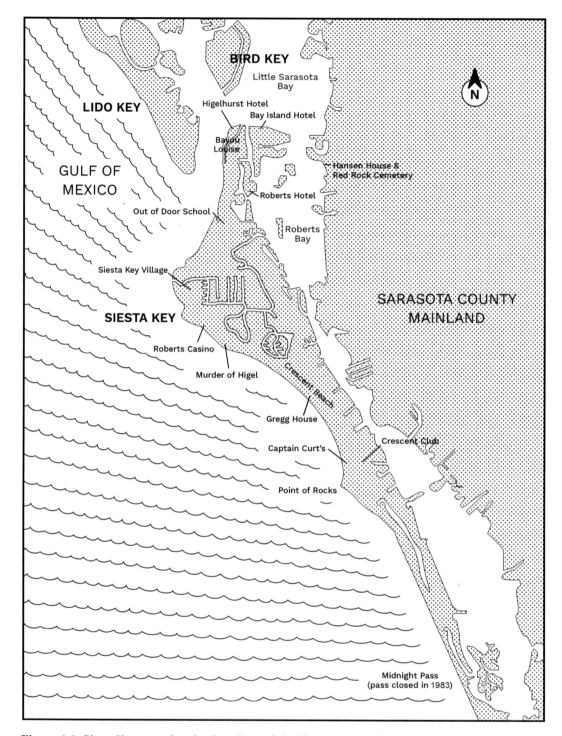

Figure 1.1 Siesta Key map showing locations of significant sites and events

family. Whether you enjoy playing tennis or volleyball, fishing or boating, or a Drum Circle on Sunday evening to mark the end of another perfect weekend on Siesta Key, there's always something to do on Siesta Beach and it is all within walking distance of the many shops and restaurants in Siesta Key Village.

Crescent Beach. Located just south of Siesta Beach and with only one public access road, you can enjoy the same azure gulf waters and picture-perfect sunsets in a quieter, more secluded setting. At the southern tip of Crescent Beach, you'll find Point of Rocks, an area rich with coral formations… The sand at Crescent Beach was rated as "The World's Finest, Whitest Sand" at the Great International Sand Challenge in 1987, beating more than 30 entrants.

Turtle Beach. Located on the southern tip of Siesta Key, Turtle Beach offers a

Figure 1.2 Aerial view of Siesta Key in 1948 showing multiple beach-dune ridges as a result of sediment accumulations and the Point of Rocks protrusion at the south end of Crescent Beach. (Courtesy of the University of Florida George A. Smathers Libraries, with thanks to Suzanne Stapleton and Pamela Handley)

"sportier" beach experience with its picnic areas, playground, volleyball court, and horseshoe pit. Turtle Beach has a boat launch area and fishing is permitted in the adjacent Blind Pass Lagoon...

It is noteworthy that the website does not mention the half-mile-long Siesta Public Beach and does not distinguish Siesta Beach from Crescent Beach as to their precise location. The same is true of most maps. Moreover, aerial or drone photographs and Google Earth views do not identify any separation of two beach segments. In fact, Siesta Beach and Crescent Beach are essentially the same strand of

Figure 1.3 Signs proclaiming that Siesta Beach is the #1 Beach in the USA are attached to most bus stops on Siesta Key as a reminder that what was once a "hidden treasure" is now "America's Best Beach." This sign is at the famous intersection of Roberts Point Road and Higel Avenue near the sites where tourism began on the barrier island

snow-white sand extending from Sarasota (Sandy Hook) Point to Point of Rocks. Nearby, at the end of Avenida Messina lies the last remaining groin (a structure built out from shore to protect a beach from erosion) extending to Point of Rocks, which was the outermost boundary on the western side of the key when it was formed three thousand years ago. In this book, we will refer to this beach as Siesta/Crescent Beach.

The history of Siesta Key provides a fascinating account of how the small barrier island transformed during the past century from a sleepy community into a crowded, internationally renowned vacation destination. Many sites and events shown on the map on page 2 contributed to a rich and complex history. In our research, it became obvious that understanding and explaining the development of Siesta Key required not only an appreciation of Sarasota County's history over the last two centuries but also a broader analysis, especially in the context of Florida's evolution as a tourist destination. From in-depth study and many hours of interviews, we recognized distinct periods of development that transitioned either gradually or quickly into new phases with entirely different features. The chronology summarized below is based on our interpretation, which has been confirmed by local experts. To clarify each period's prominent feature, we have provided distinctive names, such as the Interlude, the Beach Cottage Era, and the Condominium Era.

Summary of Chronology According to Periods of Development

Prehistoric Era: Period leading to formation of barrier islands and the "birth of a beach"

Amerindian Era: Visitations and transient habitation of Amerindians as an estuary society

Spanish/Cuban Era: Period driven by estuary fishing

Pioneer Era: Settlement of Siesta Key by homesteading pioneers

Land Boom and Bust Era: Initial phase of real estate development and its failure

Interlude: Fishing Shack Era with innovations

Beach Cottage Era: Launch of sustained tourism

Condominium Era: Development of high-rise residential condominiums

Tourist Boom Era: A larger population supports the and development of entertaining villages

"Best Beach" Era: National recognition as "America's Best Beach" is followed by large spring break crowds

Several of these periods overlapped and generally emerged during transitions driven by commercial development of different lodging types and tourist opportunities. Siesta Key's development resembles what has occurred on many other gulf barrier islands, but there are many unique features as well. Most significantly, Siesta Key's history is replete with colorful characters, regional differences in evolution, and certainly its unique status as "America's Best Beach"—a beach that is expanding in size while more than half of Florida's beaches are experiencing critical erosion. The explanations for Siesta/Crescent Beach being an accreting rather than eroding strand are provided in Chapter 16 and illustrated on color page 1, bottom photo.

CHAPTER 2

Birth and Development of "America's Best Beach"

To be ignorant of what came before you were born is to remain always a child. For what is the worth of human life unless it is woven into the life of our ancestors by the records of history?
—Marcus Tullius Cicero (50 BCE)

A gulf coast beach beautiful enough to receive international recognition and stimulate a book deserves to be fully understood, especially its history in the context of global events. The gulf coast beaches of Siesta Key have been enjoyed for recreation over a relatively short time. In fact, their prominence as a vacation destination did not develop until after World War II. In general, visiting seaside beaches for vacations is a relatively modern phenomenon that can be traced to nineteenth-century England. Popularized as a health and pleasure destination in the Victorian era, the beaches at Brighton became not only a magnet for Londoners taking advantage of inexpensive railway transport, but also the catalyst for the British tourist industry. Soon thereafter, America's first beach holiday resort was developed as Coney Island's Brighton Beach Hotel became a British cultural export and seaside attraction for nearby New Yorkers.

On a larger scale, Florida, with its more abundant beaches and warmer water, began to play a central role in the development of tourism as a major international industry. Among the countless coastal beaches in Florida, one has stood out repeatedly in competitions, namely the crescent-shaped gulf beach on Siesta Key shown on color page 6 during its evolution over the past eight decades. Moreover, based on many competitions, including rating systems with objective criteria as described in Chapter 12, as of this writing Siesta Beach is considered "America's Best Beach."

Siesta Key is part of Florida's gulf coast barrier island system, an essential component of the state's fragile ecology. Described as "the most complicated barrier island system in the world" in the analysis by Richard Davis in *Barrier Islands of the Florida Gulf Coast Peninsula*, these thirty gulf coast islands have created a tourist haven that contributes significantly to the more than 100 million tourists visiting Florida annually. Yet few of these visitors and probably only a small fraction of Florida's 20.5 million residents seem to be aware of the origin and colorful history of the gulf barrier island system and its unique sand. Indeed, it is doubtful that many Floridians appreciate the geographical origin of their state, its geologic uniqueness, and the fact that its sand—with greater than 95 percent quartz content—is actually a gift from the Appalachian Mountains of present-day Georgia and the Carolinas. Nor are they likely to recognize, or at least acknowledge, that in the perspective of geologic time, the barrier islands of Florida's gulf coast and their current tourist boom era may be short-lived.

The long and unique history of people in Florida is intertwined with stories of exploration, entrepreneurism, and adventure. Yet its ancient past is even more fascinating, although it is largely a "hidden secret," according to Albert Hine in his book, *Geologic History of Florida*. The goals of this chapter include summarizing Florida's geologic history leading to the formation of the gulf barrier island system with its Appalachia-derived treasure; explaining its ecological importance; and describing the vast reservoir of subterranean and submerged resources within the Florida peninsula. These resources, which have accumulated over millions of years, include a seemingly limitless volume of quartz sand, limestone, and phosphates sufficient to support multi-billion dollar industries, and the freshwater aquifer system that accounts for the state's famous springs. After covering the ancient history of Florida, the chapter will focus on its gulf coast barrier islands and especially those of Sarasota County. Their formation, recent struggles with beach erosion, and overdevelopment will set the stage for the stories that follow about human occupation and entrepreneurism.

The Geographic Migration of the Florida Platform: How Florida Joined North America

The Florida peninsula is the youngest and most geographically prominent component of the North American continent. But it was not always part of North America. The illustrations on color pages 2 and 3 summarize the chronologically critical events in the incredibly long journey by which Florida joined what became the United States

geographically—millions of years before it joined the country politically as a state in 1845. Here is a simplified summary.

Peninsular Florida is essentially a large landmass of granite-based rock that broke off from Africa during an ancient super-continental collision, migrated toward and became attached to North America. Then, it was covered with locally produced limestone followed by purified quartz sand transported from the southern Appalachian Mountains. After environmental stresses reduced its size by the equivalent of its current acreage—that is, by half—the result is a distinctively shaped and uniquely covered platform appendage of the eventual United States.

Unlike the rest of the United States, peninsular Florida was originally embedded 700 million years ago within the African and South American continents as part of the supercontinent *Gondwana*. At that time all of the rest of what became the United States and the Florida Panhandle were part of the future North American continent on another supercontinent known as *Laurasia*. Peninsular Florida's bedrock foundation was located at approximately the present-day South Pole when its nearly 8,000-mile-long migration via plate motion began about 650 million years ago. Thus, most of peninsular Florida's original surface, now its rock basement, is similar to the foundation of northwest Africa with a composition of granites, sandstones, and shales, but with no sand. By approximately 475 million years ago, a series of continental collisions began to form new landmass aggregations, creating Earth's last supercontinent, *Pangea*, while suturing the eventual Florida peninsula to ancestral North America, which already included the panhandle region.

During the long period of collisions from about 450 to 250 million years ago, the Appalachian Mountains—undoubtedly the source of Florida's quartz sand as well that of the Georgia and Carolina coasts—also formed.

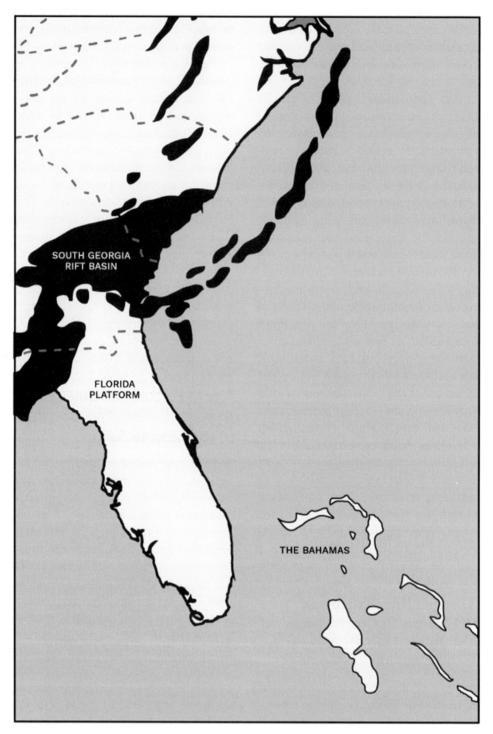

Figure 2.1 The South Georgia Rift Basin, located over the *Laurasia-Gondwana* suture zone, and other rift valleys shown in black along the eastern region of the present-day United States that formed approximately 200 million years ago. Eventually, the rift filled with water to form the Georgia Seaway Channel—60 miles wide and approximately 1,000 feet deep—which in turn eventually filled with Appalachia-derived sediment

The original Appalachian range was massive, similar in size to the present Himalayas, with peaks as high as 15,000 feet up to 25,000 feet. This geologically valuable mountain range was named *Apalchen* by Spanish cartographer Diego Gutiérrez in 1562 following the explorations led by Hernando de Soto. The name, later changed to *Apalachen*, recognized the Amerindian tribe, referred to as Apalachee, that earlier Spaniards had encountered in a village near present-day Tallahassee.

By about 250 million years ago, peninsular Florida's landmass was located more than a thousand miles inland, with no ocean contact and thus no distinctive shape. Next, however, a breakup of *Pangea* occurred from 200 to 160 million years ago and initiated creation of Florida's peninsular profile and the surrounding seas. From about 150 to 100 million years ago, Florida's *Gondwanan*-derived rock was separated from North America by the South Georgia Rift Basin, a 60-mile-wide canyon over the *Laurasia-Gondwana* suture zone. At that time, while covered with warm, shallow water, peninsular Florida's surface was altered by formation of a 3- to 4-mile-thick calcium carbonate (limestone) layer resulting from biochemical reactions involving the over-layered plant, microbe, and animal ecosystem. In essence, these environmental conditions and ingredients created a "carbonate factory" producing a thick layer of limestone and ultimately the Florida Platform, a wide plateau—extending east of the modern shoreline for a few miles and west for over 100 miles—upon which the peninsula rests.

A global warming period ensued, the result of volcanic eruptions causing very high carbon dioxide levels and a "greenhouse effect," similar in nature to but much greater in magnitude than today's warming climate trend. This environmental change caused the previously shallow west margin of the Florida Platform, shown on color page 2, to be dramatically altered by interruption of the "carbonate factory" and severe erosion to create the very deep West Florida Escarpment. This "signature ramp," a 10,000-foot underwater cliff, begins about 100 miles west of the present gulf coast and is further distinguished by enormous 25,000-foot-deep carbonate canyons. Interestingly and relevant to modern Florida, those multiple environmental stresses beginning about 100 million years ago initiated formation of the spectacular and invaluable Florida aquifer system with its extensive subterranean water channels, large caverns of fresh water, and countless sinkholes that are being used to learn more about Florida's history of human occupation through underwater archaeology. In addition, the rising sea levels converted the South Georgia Rift Basin to the Georgia Seaway Channel as it filled with water.

Florida's Debt to the Appalachians: The Origin of the Quartz Sand

Perhaps the most surprising aspect of Florida's famous beaches in general, and the gulf coast barrier islands in particular, is that the sand is not indigenous. Not long after the Appalachian Mountain range was created, it began to experience an inexorable erosion through chemical and physical weathering, reducing the chain's peaks from as high as 25,000 feet to their present maximum height of 6,684 feet, and generally much lower. The composition of the Appalachians, in retrospect, was favorable for the southeastern United States because its igneous and sedimentary rocks were enriched in quartz, one of the hardest and most durable minerals on Earth. Chemical weathering combined with physical weathering, abundant rainfall, and huge rivers led to an enormous volume of quartz-rich sediment being transported for more than 100 million years to the

Atlantic shore through the Georgia Seaway Channel. This long-term process filled that ancient rift to create a land bridge, southern Georgia's coastal plain, and eventually carried the sediment to Florida beginning about 15 million years ago. In other words, when the Georgia Seaway was no longer available for the flow of sand from the Appalachian Mountains, and Florida was visibly attached to North America, the route to the panhandle and peninsula was open. Sediment transported by the 167-mile-long Apalachicola River and numerous other large rivers then brought the sand to the Florida panhandle, Florida Platform, and ultimately the barrier islands. The implications of these geologic/geographic developments were fortuitous for Florida and eventually became the seminal events that catalyzed the tourism industry.

While the quartz sand transport continued, Florida's first clash with Cuba,

a land mass collision that occurred 56 to 40 million years ago, caused about 100 miles of its carbonate-covered southern margin to combine with Cuba and be donated to the island. This led to Cuba's scenic, agriculturally valuable western region while also creating the Straits of Florida. By about 30 million years ago, Florida's sand from ongoing southern Appalachian Mountain erosion began to cover much of the limestone platform via a process of river, stream, and longshore transport—the movement of sediment along the shoreline through the action of wave-generated currents. In fact, until 4 million years ago, delivery of Appalachia-derived physically weathered and purified quartz sand from north to south continued along the gulf coast by longshore transport processes. These processes effectively disseminated the sand while purifying it and clearly account for the white sandy beaches predominantly

Figure 2.2 The snow white, high quartz content sand of the gulf coast barrier islands—typical appearance on Siesta/Crescent Beach in the mid-key region

composed of the same hard silicon dioxide mineral. Very little new sand, however, has been delivered from regions north of Florida since then.

Emergence of the Gulf Barrier Island System and Development of Siesta Key

After the last Ice Age effects were complete and glacial melting began, sea levels rose and literally drowned the westernmost 100 miles of Florida's west gulf coast. Thus, the true size of Florida—that is, the Florida Platform—is about twice what is available today for habitation. A dramatic change in the marine geography took place around 3,000 years ago. Through longshore transport processes combined with wave and tidal energy effects, a system of barrier islands began rising out of the Gulf of

Mexico. Thus, beginning in about 1000 BCE and extending over decades to centuries, the Amerindians saw the chain of islands emerging progressively and very close to their villages—literally swimming distance away. It is no wonder that they considered this line of new islands sacred territory and used it as burial grounds for their elite. With the enhanced fishing opportunities provided, their impression must have been that the gods were sending them a gift to be cherished, exploited, and incorporated into their culture.

The age of the gulf barrier islands has been determined by radiocarbon dating of carbonate-rich sediments. The original estimates were done on Sanibel Island during the 1970s. These studies provided consistent estimates and led to the conclusion that they formed approximately 3,000 years before present. On Siesta Key, the radiocarbon

Figure 2.3 Vintage postcard from approximately 1950 showing the Point of Rocks protrusion (bottom) and beach cottages of the era

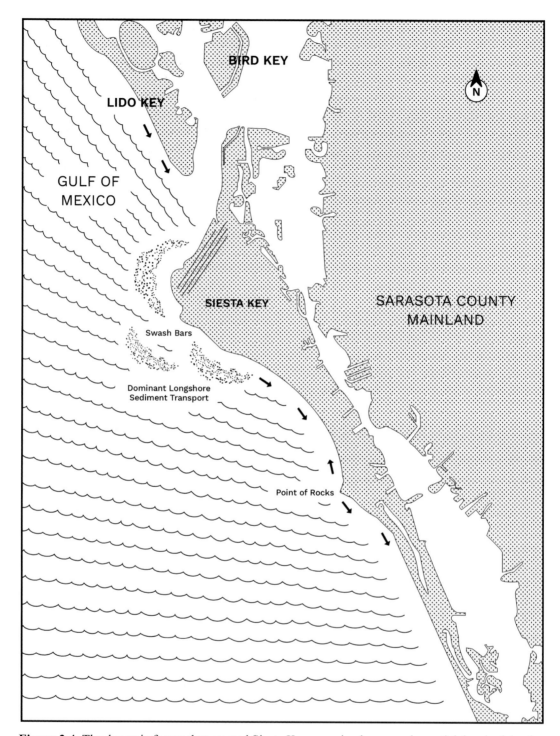

Figure 2.4 The dynamic forces that created Siesta Key—a mixed-energy drumstick barrier island—and that continue to contribute to its beach expansion. (Illustration created by Julia Farrell Patton based on Figure 12A in "Barrier Island Morphology as a Function of Tide and Wave Regime," by M. O. Hayes.)

dating research was done by Darren Spurgeon for his master's degree in geology from the University of South Florida. The details are reviewed by Richard Davis in *Barrier Islands of the Florida Gulf Coast Peninsula* and include a summary of data that demonstrate that the distinctive gulf-side midpoint of Siesta Key known as Point of Rocks is about 3,000 years old and, interestingly, is about 1,000 years older than the prominent northwestern section where human settlements began. The comparative data, in fact, suggest that the Point of Rocks component was part of an earlier barrier island that became submerged for a period and perhaps resurfaced as the point of origin for all of Siesta Key. This protrusion accounts in part for the crescent-shaped beach profile.

The marine forces promoting creation of the barrier islands have been debated, but the key factors accounting for their origin and various configurations were clarified through observations, analyses, and interpretations reviewed by Davis. Of course, as mentioned above, the seminal event facilitating gulf barrier island formation is well known and attributable to the same phenomenon so dramatic today, namely the melting of glaciers. In fact, around 25,000 BCE, when the Laurentide ice sheets of North America were up to two or three miles thick, ocean levels were about 350 feet lower than today. Next, around 18,000 years ago, progressive melting of glaciers began in the Northern Hemisphere and was followed about 6,000 years later by the same gross melting phenomenon in Antarctica. Concurrently, rising sea levels led to major geographic/geologic changes, such as creation of the Great Lakes and a shrinking of the Florida Platform. Then, about 7,000 years ago, the rise in sea level slowed enough for barrier islands to emerge on the Texas coast but not on the west coast of Florida. By 3,000 years ago, however, the combination of marine forces and abundant sediment moving by longshore transport established conditions favorable for barrier

island formation on the gulf coast of Florida. More specifically, the barrier island creation process involves an interaction of waves, tidal currents, and longshore sediment transport as sand is being deposited by a process known as *upward shoaling* to create multiple beach-dune ridges. Siesta Key is classified as a mixed-energy drumstick barrier island. A mixed-energy barrier island is defined by Davis as an "island that is wide at one end due to sediment accumulation and progradation but narrow at the other end, indicating sediment-starved conditions." These features give it a characteristic drumstick shape. Siesta Key also has a significant tidal inlet, i.e., Big Sarasota Pass, which contributes to sand deposition. The tidal inlet also promotes the creation of swash bars, which are accumulations of sediment developing as a result of incoming waves that can then transport the sand landward through wave-generated currents. In other words, the formation of swash bars actually captures the sediment that otherwise might be transported away. Other factors considered important by M. O. Hayes include the influence of "medium wave energy" (2- to 5-foot mean wave height) and coastal conditions that create "barriers that are short and stunted with a characteristic drumstick shape." In addition, Hayes emphasizes that "large end-tidal deltas that are common on mesotidal coasts play an important role in shaping the morphology of the barriers by storing large volumes of sand which become available to the island from time to time and by strongly influencing wave-refraction patterns." These factors seem to be important for Siesta/Crescent Beach. Certainly, large volumes of sand are being stored at the Big Sarasota Pass tidal inlet.

The upward-shoaling mechanism for barrier island formation was actually discovered by a sequence of observations and deductions in France during the nineteenth century by Élie de Beaumont, a geologist born in Normandy near the beaches that supported the 1944 D-Day invasion during World War II. He proposed that barrier islands formed as a result of sand accumulations emerging parallel to the shore as a consequence of upward shoaling associated with repetitive wave action (see Figure 1.2, page 3). This mechanism was confirmed by the research of Richard Davis in his studies of Shell Key, which is located just north of Tampa Bay. In addition, the multiple beach-dune ridges seen with aerial photographs of Gulf barrier islands in their pre-development stage are consistent with barrier island formation through repeated upward shoaling. This mechanism is relevant today because upward shoaling effects are limited or even impossible when seawalls and large shoreline development construction projects become extensive.

Stars of the Florida West Coast: Gulf Barrier Islands of Many Types

Many residents—and most spring break tourists, living for the moment as they do annually—seem to take for granted the most complicated barrier island system in the world. These gems of the gulf coast, however, are unique and ecologically invaluable as well as fragile. As found elsewhere in the world, barrier islands usually occur in linear arrays consisting of anything from a few islands to the chain of thirty found along the gulf coast. Beyond their important role in Florida's tourist industry, they are critically important in shielding the mainland from the turbulence of the seas and inevitable storms, thus protecting the coastline, and for supporting maintenance of the intracoastal waterways on the mainland side of the barrier island. Other ecologically important wetland systems such as lagoons and marshes are created by barrier islands. Their presence effectively supports a special environment of relatively calm, brackish water where

an estuary can exist—mixing fresh and salt water and creating a rich habitat for a variety of plant and animal life. Indeed, the fishing potential of such waters is what must have attracted the successive waves of settlers to Sarasota County and other Gulf coast communities, starting with the Amerindians, followed by Spanish and then Cuban fishermen, and finally Americans from other parts of the country.

Sarasota County is blessed with four substantial barrier islands, namely Longboat Key, Siesta Key, Casey Key, and Manasota Key. In addition, Longboat Key is contiguous with Anna Maria Island to the north in Manatee County, and the human-made Lido Key is twinned with the smaller, also human-made Bird Key to its east. These barrier islands display varying geography/morphology and levels of development, although some would argue that they are all overdeveloped. Certainly, none of Sarasota County's keys are pristine. To experience and enjoy a pristine gulf barrier island, one needs to visit Cayo Costa Island near Boca Grande and the Charlotte Harbor Estuary, where more than 95 percent of the land is owned by Florida and preserved as a state park.

Sarasota County's barrier islands illustrate the two prominent categories of the Davis classification scheme that explains both island structure and varying stability, namely wave-dominated and mixed-energy types of islands. The wave-dominated keys are long, narrow barrier islands in which the primary energy leading to their formation is produced directly or indirectly by waves combined with longshore currents. The various kinds of keys in Sarasota County are also attractive for study because they are so close together and are somewhat interdependent. The most southern of the barrier islands in this group, Casey Key and Manasota Key, are wave-dominated, moderately developed barrier

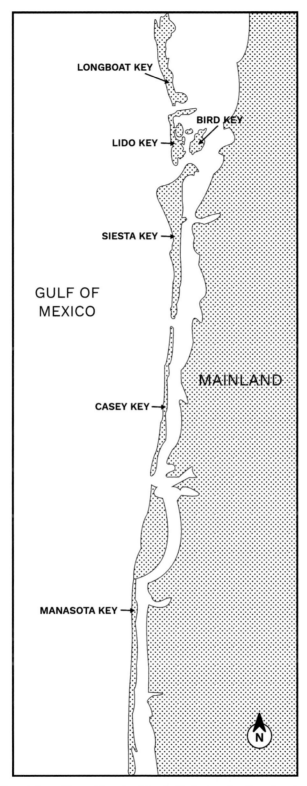

Figure 2.5 Sarasota County's gulf coast barrier islands featuring the four developed keys of substantial size: Longboat, Siesta, Casey, and Manasota (which extends into Charlotte County)

islands, whereas to the north, Longboat Key is a wave-dominated, densely developed barrier island. Between Longboat/Lido and Casey Key, and related to how it was formed, Siesta Key has the advantage of being a mixed-energy barrier island that has become densely developed during the past fifty years. This results in a characteristic drumstick shape—an important factor. Siesta Key is a particularly good example because Siesta/Crescent Beach is wide and abundant with sand, and actually expanding, whereas two miles south at the narrow end of the island Turtle Beach is sand-starved enough to show continuous erosion and a need for regular nourishment, as described in Chapter 16. One of the interesting features of Siesta/Crescent Beach is that it has been expanding significantly while the island is being developed. This is one of the reasons it has become "America's Best Beach."

CHAPTER 3

The First Floridians

The Amerindians die so easily that the bare look and smell of a Spaniard causes them to give up the ghost.
—German missionary in 1699, as quoted by Michael Crawford in *The Origins of Native Americans*

Among the many incredible aspects of Florida's past, the history of the very early arrival and ultimate decimation of the Amerindians stands out uniquely as both heroic and terribly tragic. When the discovery that Paleoindians lived near Tallahassee at least 14,550 years ago was reported in 2016 AD, questions arose about how and why they traveled to Florida. Much information has been published from archaeological and genetic studies to provide reliable insights. Many Native Americans show physical and genetic similarities to Asians, but reviewing those data and the controversies surrounding various interpretations are beyond the scope of this book. On the other hand, there have been several archaeological discoveries about their way of life that are relevant to Sarasota County in general and Siesta Key in particular.

The First and Greatest Diaspora from Africa

After exiting Africa sometime between 60,000 and 100,000 years ago, *Homo sapiens sapiens* moved into Europe, Asia, and eventually into the Americas, where they were challenged by Ice Age glaciation. The prevailing theory is that humans crossed the Bering Land Bridge and arrived on the North American continent about 16,500 years ago, and traveled south of the Canadian (Cordilleran) ice sheet by 15,000 years ago. It is also suspected that these Paleoindians would have not traveled on foot initially, but instead voyaged along the western coast of North America in small canoes and rafts. This would have allowed them to reach a more favorable southern climate much sooner than if they had traveled overland. Later, an ice-free passage was found in western Canada to allow entry to the present United States east of the Rocky Mountains.

It is well known from archaeological studies and radiocarbon dating of many ancient burials in Oregon, Texas, and Wisconsin that humans were occupying the western, southwestern, and midwestern regions of North America around 14,000 years ago. They were probably also exploring areas of Pennsylvania and Virginia by then. In addition, these hunter-gatherers, likely traveling the longest distances by boat, reached South America about the same time. Thus, the Paleoindians were similar to their European and Asian relatives in being able to travel long distances. From century to century, these tribes explored for food sources while following herds

Figure 3.1 George Luer, Ph.D., doing archaeological fieldwork at Palmetto Lane Midden in Sarasota, near Whitaker Bayou. Dr. Luer has devoted most of his career to discoveries about the ancient tribes who once inhabited Florida after being inspired at Siesta Key's Out-of-Door School in the 1960s and by trips with his parents to ancient sites such as King Tut's tomb. He advanced his scientific career in the yard of his parents' home, which was built on a very large ancient shell mound (midden) overlooking Siesta Key near the north bridge—the "Old Oak" site where Amerindian and Spanish inhabitants preceded the Luer family

of migrating large mammals over large tracts of land, hunting big game such as mastodons, catching small animals, and gathering plants.

Traveling to Florida Beginning at Least 14,500 Years Ago

As for the question of why the Paleoindians migrated to Florida, it is likely that these habitual travelers were seeking a combination of better living conditions—just like the many retirees moving to the Sunshine State in recent decades—and food. Their journey to the southeastern region of North America must have involved a combination of overland and waterway migration. The plains provided meat and vegetables, and they could readily catch fish when traveling by water. The routes that the first Floridians took is unclear and may never be known, but they had a few alternatives. In keeping with the coastal travel theories, it is conceivable that they crossed the Midwest on foot, reached the Atlantic coast, and boated south. Or perhaps they reached the Gulf of Mexico first from Texas or by traveling south on a river such as the Mississippi, and then followed the gulf coastline until reaching the Florida landmass.

When the Paleoindians arrived in Florida, it was cooler, sea level was much lower, and the climate was dry enough that groundwater levels in the interior of the state were much less than they are today. More arid conditions meant that different groups of animals and plants were present. Some of those animals, like mammoths, mastodons, and bison, had proliferated during the Ice Age but would disappear as the climate warmed and they fell prey to human hunters. The Paleoindians, needing drinking water nearby, tended to camp close to watering holes. When the Paleoindians first arrived, rivers such as the Aucilla

were not flowing streams, but rather consisted of a series of small limestone catchment basins or watering holes. Those catchment basins were good sources of drinking water, and so the Paleoindians tended to camp near them. They attracted animals as well, and so these became the hundreds of sites where animals were ambushed, butchered, and eaten, and their remains discarded along with other debris. The sites now contain evidence, particularly Paleoindian stone tools and bones of butchered animals, that can be discovered by underwater archaeologists and subjected to radiocarbon dating.

The largest of these underwater Paleoindian projects, the Aucilla River Prehistory Project, has yielded Ice Age animal bones such as "Bertha," the mammoth on display at the Florida State Museum of Natural History in Gainesville; a bison skull with a broken stone point in it, providing dramatic evidence for Paleoindians killing now-extinct animals; and a variety of seeds and rind fragments from gourds that Paleoindians ate. In addition, carved wooden stakes for temporary tent-like structures have been discovered there. The Page-Ladson site, a 30-foot sinkhole in the Ancilla River, has been particularly valuable, revealing evidence of human occupation 14,500 years ago just seven miles from the current shore of the Gulf of Mexico. Specifically, stone tools and evidence of a butchered mastodon were identified there, clear evidence that Paleoindians were living along the gulf coast and hunting large mammals 2,000 years before those animals became extinct.

Closer to Sarasota, two other important Florida archaeological sites show strong evidence for very early human presence in the southeastern region of the United States: the Little Salt Spring and Warm Mineral Springs sites, both of which have

Figure 3.2 Wooden throwing stick carved at right-angle for hurling at game in the Paleoindian period about 7,000 years ago

excellent preservation due to the low oxygen content of deep water. In the case of the Little Salt Spring site, the sinkhole has been a treasure trove for artifacts, and it contains human burials dating between 6,000 to 8,000 years ago. Impressive finds include purposefully carved wooden throwing sticks—right-angled weapons that could be hurled at small game such as rabbits. Thus, we can conclude that early Amerindians were inhabiting an area within thirty miles of Sarasota thousands of years before the barrier islands formed in the Gulf of Mexico.

Periods of Amerindian Evolution in Florida

The period of Florida history from 10,000 BCE until 3000 BCE was a time of climate change for Florida. With worldwide temperatures rising, the glaciers in the northern half of the continent began to melt and cause large amounts of fresh water to flow down through the southern United States as seawater levels rose. The interior of Florida also changed as new lakes and streams formed in the previously dryer interior part of Florida, and the land began to become far swampier over several thousand years.

The interval between 7000 BCE and about 500 BCE is designated the Archaic period in Florida. The Native Americans were generally wanderers at that time, using hunting-gathering strategies after arriving at an area during the season that was best for certain kinds of foods. The Florida Native Americans were quite different from many other western Amerindian cultures because they had access to abundant marine resources that provided excellent nutrition, most notably the rich seafood that could be found off either the Atlantic or gulf coast. By about 5000 BCE, the Amerindians began to settle down into villages near the swamplands.

By 3000 BCE, the Florida climate and sea levels were becoming similar to present-day conditions, and the human populations began to thrive and grow, relying on saltwater and freshwater food supplies. Shellfish were an easy and reliable source of nutritious food for these people and as a result, large shell middens began to form. These shell middens are very complex deposits of shells, artifacts, animal and plant remains, and interesting features such as fire pits and spent tools. The contents are found in layers and pockets where they provide invaluable sources for modern archaeologists like George Luer to sort through and discover more information about the people of the past. (George can describe the type and origin of every shell fragment found in one of these middens.) According to Steve Koski, there were at least eleven of these archaeological sites on Siesta Key at one time, three more on Casey Key, and another twenty-four along the

Figure 3.3 Shell midden approximately 20 feet high by 70 feet wide in the Tampa Bay region. This is the type of midden that Juan Ponce de León may have seen on the east coast of Florida on April 2, 1513, and Frank Higel saw in 1881while sailing past present-day Venice

shore on the mainland to the old Midnight Pass, i.e., just before Spanish Point. Camps on the bayside of Siesta Key were used intermittently for fishing and shell-fishing excursions. Tall middens there and elsewhere functioned not only as camps and burial sites, but also to provide access to sea breezes, visibility, protection from insects and human invaders, and as the foundations of villages.

Estuary Societies with Distinct Regional Cultures

By about 500 BCE, the Archaic lifestyle advanced into more distinct regional cultures with larger, more organized populations, such as the Calusa tribes described by the Spanish explorers. These Amerindians were skilled estuary fishermen and occupied an area around Charlotte Harbor south to Estero Bay, including Sanibel. The Calusa caught most

of their fish with nets that were woven from durable natural fibers in different mesh sizes used seasonally to catch the most abundant fish available. They also made bone and shell gauges used in net weaving to assure uniform mesh sizes in whatever net they were making. Cultivated gourds were used as net floats, and sinkers and net weights were made from mollusk shells. Early settlers of Sarasota later used similar techniques of fishing for mullet with nets as a source of revenue, as described in Chapter 5. It is noteworthy that the successful Amerindian techniques used for subsistence later became the basis of the commercial fishing industry.

Relying on abundant marine resources, the Calusa built well-engineered villages and evolved into a powerful and fierce chiefdom with a stratified society consisting of "commoners" and "nobles," in Spanish terms. At the Pineland site, thirty miles west of Fort Myers, the Calusa built high mounds,

Figure 3.4 Calusa village chief with his wife in about 1500 (From the website of the University of Florida Museum of Natural History, Gainesville, FL)

canals, and graded terraces in a village that was one of the centers of their empire. Their ferocity and fighting skills were sufficient to defeat the first wave of Spanish invaders, as described in the next chapter, but they had no defense against invasion by viruses causing Old World diseases.

Manasota Culture Discoveries in Sarasota County

Earlier in time and north of the Calusa empire, distinctive differences began to form in the traditions of the area of present-day Sarasota and Manatee Counties, which archaeologists George Luer and Marion Almy named the Manasota culture. These Amerindians practiced many of the same fishing and building techniques as the Calusa, but they were influenced by the burial and ceramic practices of northern Florida. From about 500 BCE to AD 800 the Manasota culture thrived between Tampa Bay and Charlotte Harbor. To quote Luer and Almy, "Archaeologically, the Manasota

culture is characterized by... sites that yield evidence of an economy based on fishing, hunting, and shellfish gathering... burial practices involving primary flexed burials... (and) shell tools" rather than stone tools. They lived on coastal sites spread linearly and parallel with the shoreline, with some covering several acres and featuring shell midden ridges and ramps that supported nearly year-round settlements. They were able to feast on whatever fish or shellfish was abundant and to supplement their diet with deer and other game they hunted inland. Barrier islands such as Siesta Key were sources of clams, oysters, and other shellfish from the bay, as they camped on the bayside.

Each Manasota settlement appears to have contained a few related families. When people died, they were buried near their home or in cemeteries located near the settlement. The absence of grave goods suggests that Manasota society was relatively egalitarian. Leadership in the community was probably based on individual ability. Villages in a region might

Figure 3.5 British map from 1765 found in London and showing the Spanish geographic names for gulf coast sites such as Tampa Bay, which was designated *Bahia del Espiritu Santo* (From the American Geographical Society Library, University of Wisconsin-Milwaukee Libraries)

have been integrated through marriage or trade networks.

By about 100 BCE, Manasota peoples had begun to adopt some of the religious, ceremonial, and mortuary practices of neighboring cultures to the north. The primary archaeological manifestation of this new ceremonialism was the use of sand burial mounds and, later, the placement of ornately decorated pottery with the dead. They continued to have a sedentary existence as an estuary society whose lifestyle evolved by AD 1000 into a Safety Harbor culture. That culture is named for the site discovered in Pinellas County where the historic *Bahia del Espiritu Santo* ("Bay of the Holy Spirit," the Spanish name for Tampa Bay) was "discovered" in 1539 by the Spanish explorer Hernando de Soto. Safety Harbor practices developed throughout the Tampa Bay to Charlotte Harbor area under the influence of Mississippian cultures of the American Midwest and Southeast—evidence for the extensive travel along the gulf coast. Safety Harbor society was highly stratified with a noble class, warriors, slaves, and common folk such as the tribe fishermen. Politics and religion were closely related, and political rulers were often believed to be gods who demanded respect and tribute in return for ensuring peace and prosperity.

The Spanish Invasion and Decimation of Florida's Amerindian Tribes

The Spanish explorers arriving in 1513 posed the threats of violence and warfare to the first Floridians, but the lethal viruses they brought with them were much more devastating. When smallpox invaded this population, which had no immunity to Old World diseases, repeated epidemics killed the majority of those infected. It has been estimated that Florida in 1513 had at least 200,000 Amerindian inhabitants and possibly as many as 700,000 Native Americans living in the region, but this number was probably reduced to less than 10,000 within two centuries. Moreover, H. F. Dobyns, in his book *Their Number Became Thinned,* concluded that throughout the Americas, an estimated population of 25 million natives was reduced to 750,000.

For advanced societies like the Calusa and Safety Harbor tribes, the Old World diseases were not only lethal, but also had a demoralizing effect. It is known that a Spanish ship arriving with just one or two sailors having even mild cases of smallpox with exposed blisters or pustules could decimate an entire village in a matter of weeks. The catastrophic impact of smallpox was nearly matched by successive waves of other lethal viruses in epidemics occurring for two to three hundred years. Measles was the second Spanish-borne killer that was often fatal to Amerindians. Again, they had no immunity and succumbed rapidly. Influenza also took its toll, as did bacterial disorders such as cholera. Thus, the Florida Amerindians became "The Lost Tribes," as shown on color page 4.

CHAPTER 4

Influence of the Spanish

El imperio en el que nunca se pone el sol. ("The empire on which the sun never sets.")
—Sixteenth-century boast of Spanish Kings Charles I and his son, Philip II

Sarasota County was significantly influenced by Spain and the name *Siesta* Key itself evokes thoughts of Spain. Here are some of the ways Spain and Spanish culture influenced the development of Florida, the Sarasota area, and Siesta Key.

Top Ten List of the Spanish Impact on Florida and the Gulf Coast

1. First discovery by Europeans of the "island" (peninsula)
2. Named peninsula La Florida and claimed the Panhandle ("West Florida")
3. Discovered Gulf Stream, its impact, and potential for transatlantic voyages
4. Discovered and described the "First Floridians," especially the Calusa tribe
5. Created informative maps, variably accurate but functional and inspiring
6. Named Gulf coast waterways, islands, and communities, including Sarasota
7. Initiated citrus and cattle industries with Valencia orange seeds and Andalusian cows
8. Introduced smallpox and other European viral diseases, which decimated Amerindian tribes
9. Responsible for North America's oldest continuous community, St. Augustine
10. Inspired an architectural "Spanish craze" as Florida "discovered" Spain in late nineteenth century

Timely Opportunity to Discover, Exploit, and Colonize

Exploration and exploitation of the New World created the greatest empire since ancient Rome as Catholic monarchs of the Trastámara and Habsburg families led Spain to become a global power during the sixteenth and seventeenth centuries.

The Spanish-influence story begins with Italian Christopher Columbus who, during the pivotal year of 1492, when the last of the Moors were conquered in Granada, persuaded Queen Isabella and King Ferdinand II to sponsor a modest, uncertain three-ship exploration for Asia. The expedition set sail on August 3, 1492. Columbus returned to Seville in March of 1493 with dramatic reporting of the "New World." The resulting second voyage was more ambitious, with the objectives of exploitation and colonization. It reflected the new Spanish policy of "Gold, God, and Glory"—expanding territories while creating settlements and establishing missions dedicated to converting the natives to Catholicism. On his second voyage, Columbus left Cádiz on September 24, 1493, with a fleet of seventeen ships carrying 1,200 men (priests, farmers, and soldiers),

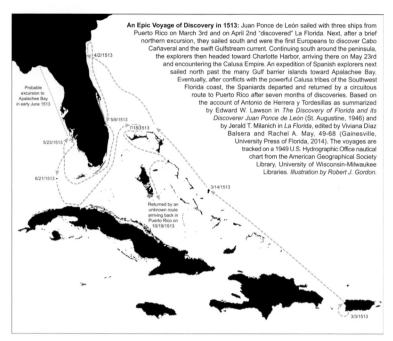

An Epic Voyage of Discovery in 1513: Juan Ponce de León sailed with three ships from Puerto Rico on March 3rd and on April 2nd "discovered" La Florida. Next, after a brief northern excursion, they sailed south and were the first Europeans to discover Cabo Cañaveral and the swift Gulfstream current. Continuing south around the peninsula, the explorers then headed toward Charlotte Harbor, arriving there on May 23rd and encountering the Calusa Empire. An expedition of Spanish explorers next sailed north past the many Gulf barrier islands toward Apalachee Bay. Eventually, after conflicts with the powerful Calusa tribes of the Southwest Florida coast, the Spaniards departed and returned by a circuitous route to Puerto Rico after seven months of discoveries. Based on the account of Antonio de Herrera y Tordesillas as summarized by Edward W. Lawson in *The Discovery of Florida and its Discoverer Juan Ponce de León* (St. Augustine, 1946) and by Jerald T. Milanich in *La Florida*, edited by Viviana Díaz Balsera and Rachel A. May, 49-68 (Gainesville, University Press of Florida, 2014). The voyages are tracked on a 1949 U.S. Hydrographic Office nautical chart from the American Geographical Society Library, University of Wisconsin-Milwaukee Libraries. *Illustration by Robert J. Gordon.*

Figure 4.1 The voyage of Juan Ponce de León's three ships in 1513 leading to the discovery and naming of *La Florida*

supplies (about 500 horses, as many hardy Andalusian cattle, 400 black Ibérico pigs, some sheep, countless chickens, and plants or their seeds, including the Valencia orange), and an ambitious veteran of the Moor wars, Juan Ponce de León.

Courageous Spanish explorers/conquistadors fortified with the Pope's blessing and authority, succeeded efficiently in their mission, especially between 1492 and 1521. Their conquests and exploitations in Central and South America enriched Spain with precious metals and territories in the New World. The area claimed as Spanish Florida was much larger than what eventually became West Florida (the panhandle) and East Florida (the peninsula), as it extended to the current states of Georgia, the Carolinas, Alabama, and parts of Mississippi and Arkansas. When Spanish explorers returned to their destination building in Seville along the Guadalquivir River, the *Torre del Oro* ("Tower of Gold") built by the Moors in 1220 to guard their harbor, they brought more gold and silver during the sixteenth century than was found in all the rest of continental Europe.

Then, the returning conquistadores reported to the king's representatives and met with the *Casa de Contratación* ("House of Trade"), officially called *La Casa y Audiencia de Indias*. Established by Queen Isabella, it had broad powers over all matters related to the voyages of discovery and operated a navigation school for new pilots, or navigators.

Discovery and Naming of *La Florida*

Juan Ponce de León took advantage of his learning experiences on Columbus' second voyage and became one of Spain's most formidable Indian fighters, leading successful battles against the tribes of Hispaniola, Haiti, Puerto Rico, and the Bahamas. His warrior reputation, and growing conflicts with the Columbus family, especially Christopher's son, Diego, led Ferdinand II to award Ponce de León an important charter in 1512: to discover, conquer, and settle at his own cost an island north of Cuba which was known then as Bimini. Although his goal was to find and explore that island, Ponce de León actually discovered not just Florida but the entire North America continent, although he and his crew failed to recognize the magnitude of their discovery.

Information in historical records on Ponce de León's voyage of discovery provides a clear picture of the peculiar route taken by his brilliant navigator/pilot Antón de Alaminos. Leaving from Puerto Rico on March 3, 1513, his three ships (*Santiago, San Cristóbal,* and *Santa Maria de la Consolación*) sailed to the well-known, friendly Bahama Islands to use them as a staging area to guide them in their search. After taking on water, the small fleet sailed northwest along the eastern margin of the Bahamas, followed by a "can't miss" more westerly heading toward the southeastern coast of the peninsula. The adjustment of their course to a west-northwest track brought them toward central Florida. Ponce de León sighted land along the east coast of Florida on April 2, 1513, during Easter Holy Week. He named the beautiful, flowery "island" *La Florida* for the season Spaniards call *Pascua Florida* ("Feast of Flowers") or "Flowery Easter." Although it is not known exactly where the fleet made landfall, most scholars currently agree it was somewhere between Daytona Beach and Cape Canaveral at a prominent site such as Turtle Mound. Next, after a brief northerly excursion for unknown reasons, the expedition sailed south, where they discovered and named *Cabo Cañaveral* (Cape Canaveral or "Cape of Canes")—a distinctive protrusion of land jutting into the Atlantic and featuring many reeds resembling wild sugarcanes.

During the first week of May, the fleet reached Biscayne Bay and took on water at an island they named *Santa Marta* (now Key Biscayne). On May 15, they left Biscayne Bay to explore the keys and west coast of the Florida peninsula. Eventually, they found a gap in the reefs near Key West and sailed northeast until on May 23 they reached numerous barrier islands in the vicinity of San Carlos Bay and Charlotte Harbor. There they discovered the Calusa tribe—probably first on either Sanibel Island or in the relatively large, well-developed village on Pine Island referred to as *Tampa*. (Mapmakers later confused the two large bays along the peninsula's gulf coast, moving the name "Tampa" north, where it stayed. The great city of Tampa is actually a misnomer due to a cartographical error.) The Calusa tribe, outnumbering the Spanish by 10-to-1, initially welcomed the explorers. They proceeded with trading activities and attempts to communicate as the Amerindians apparently said there was gold nearby that was used to make adornments for their chief. From late May to early June, some Spaniards stayed in the Calusa territory while others sailed north, past the numerous barrier islands, including Siesta Key, to the panhandle, terminating the exploration at Apalachee Bay.

After the return of the explorer subgroup, the Spanish and the Calusa clashed over some unrecorded conflict. The well-led, fierce Calusa Amerindians refused to trade and eventually drove off the Spanish ships, surrounding them with warriors in swift sea canoes armed with bows and arrows. Within a week, there was another hostile sea encounter with Calusa near Sanibel Island, but the Spaniards sank several canoes before sailing away. They were looking for a chain of islands farther southwest that had been described by their Amerindian captives taken aboard from sunken canoes. This island chain, seventy miles west of Key West, was discovered on June 21, 1513, and named *Las Tortugas* ("the Turtles"). The name is noteworthy as the second oldest surviving European place-name in the United States, although it was later modified to "Dry Tortugas" to signify the lack of fresh water there. For the expedition, this discovery was a godsend because the islands were peaceful and a great source of food; their log records 170 giant sea turtles captured and eaten. From *Las Tortugas* they sailed southwest, reaching Puerto Rico on October 19, 1513, after being at sea for seven months.

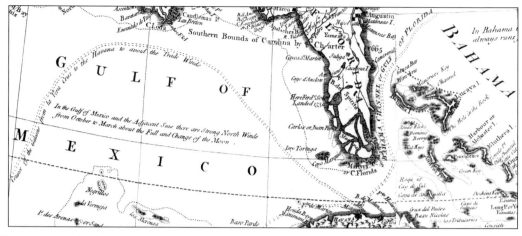

Figure 4.2 Map from 1763 showing the Gulf Stream (From the American Geographical Society Library, University of Wisconsin-Milwaukee Libraries)

Discovery and Significance of El Cabo de Corrientes

Antón de Alaminos discovered the 5 mph Gulf Stream current probably near Jupiter on April 22, 1513. He named it *El Cabo de Corrientes*. In translation, Ponce de León's logbook says: "...although they had great wind, they could not proceed forward... at the end it was known that the current was more powerful than the wind." Ponce de León's smallest ship, *San Cristóbal*, was swept northeast in the Gulf Stream and lost from his fleet for two days. The Gulf Stream is as wide as 50 miles, as deep as 2,500 to 4,000 feet, and has maximum current speed of 5.5 mph, which can be greater than the wind velocity. It is no surprise that a small sailing ship could get caught in the current and swept away.

No one could have appreciated in 1513 that the Gulf Stream's effect on the climate of the Florida peninsula would be one of the most important factors in tourism. Its influence maintains average water temperatures at or above 75°F. Winds passing over this warm water blow warm air inland in winter, keeping temperatures milder than elsewhere, including the cooler Florida panhandle and nearby southern Georgia.

Returning to Spain and Then to the New World

After returning for a six-month stay in Puerto Rico to defeat a Carib tribe uprising, Ponce de León sailed to Spain for the obligatory presentation to the *Casa de Contratación*. As a hero of the Moorish Wars and successful explorer, he was warmly received in Seville by King Ferdinand II and Queen Isabella, knighted, and given a personal coat of arms, thus becoming the first conquistador to receive such honors. *Casa* bureaucrats and cartographers were increasingly interested in the New World's geography and wealth potential, particularly since Amerigo Vespucci, their former *piloto mayor de Indias* ("chief navigator of Spain") and director of the Seville school of navigation, had already asserted that the newly discovered "islands" were not isolated land at all, but part of a new continent eventually named for him. After a long interrogation of Ponce de León, the bureaucrats and cartographers added their conclusions to the *Padrón Real*, a master map that served as the basis for official navigation charts provided to Spanish sailors. Having no direct evidence of an alternative, they displayed *La Florida* as an island.

During Ponce de León's stay in Spain, a new royal contract was drawn up, confirming his rights to settle and govern *La Florida*. In 1521 Ponce de León organized a colonizing expedition of two ships with two hundred men, including priests, farmers, and artisans; fifty horses and other domestic animals; and farming implements. The expedition landed on the southwest coast of Florida—probably in the vicinity of the Caloosahatchee River or Charlotte Bay. Immediately attacked by Calusa braves, Ponce de León was injured by an arrow or spear that embedded in his thigh. After this lost battle, Ponce de León and the would-be colonists sailed to Cuba, where he soon died of the wound. Some have speculated that the Calusa weapon was poisoned with the sap of the manchineel tree ("tree of death"), but it's as likely a bacterial infection and sepsis (blood poisoning) took the life of the Spanish monarch's favorite warrior who had killed hundreds, if not thousands, of Amerindians in the New World, as well as countless Moors.

Naming Many Florida Waterways, Islands, and Communities, Including Sarasota

As required by the *Casa*, Spanish explorers identified, charted, and named important geographic features such as waterways, islands, and distinctive coastal landmasses. Many of these are shown in Figure 3.5 on page 23. Most relevant to this book is the name "Sarasota." Its origin has provoked lively discussions, disputes, and uncertainty, as well as good publicity for tourism. Sarasota appeared on maps in the eighteenth century with various spellings such as "Zara Zota," "Zara Zote," "Sara Zota," "Sarazota," and "Sarasote". No evidence of an Amerindian origin exists, and as described in Chapter 3, the area was more of a visitation site than habitation site for the Manasota natives. "Zara Zota" may have been derived from a

Spanish term meaning "a place of dancing." Others recognize that "Zara" or "Sara" may be derived from "caesar" or "czar," while "Zota" might imply a fortification. Interestingly, there is an important city and province in central Spain called Zaragosa. Settled by a Celtic tribe of Iberians during the Iron Age, it was conquered by the Romans under Augustus Caesar in 25 BCE, developed as a peaceful *oppidum*—a retirement settlement for army veterans as a reward for service to Caesar—and named *Caesaraugusta*. In 1018, after occupation by the Moors, the Islamic capital city of the Taifa caliphate was called Saraqusta.

An early Spanish map found in London in 1763, when Florida became British, shows the word "Zarazote" across present-day Sarasota County. When the Many of these are shown in Figure gulf coast was charted in the mid-nineteenth century, *Boca Sarazota* was the name given to "Sarazota Pass" in its correct location. Soon, thereafter, the adjacent barrier islands, including present-day Siesta Key and the bay, were both labeled "Sarasota" on maps.

Spanish Priests Initiated the Citrus Industry in Florida

Oranges were brought to Spain through trade with China and cultivated by Roman settlers. Unbeknownst to the ships' captains, the availability of oranges on Spanish ships provided a diet with sufficient vitamin C to prevent scurvy during transatlantic voyages—a connection that ships' captains were unaware of and that was not discovered by the British for another 250 years. By the time of these voyages of discovery, Spain was producing a vast amount of oranges. The Valencia orange was favored as the sweetest while the Seville orange was considered bitter.

Records indicate that priests brought Valencia orange seeds on the transatlantic voyages. The first orange trees were planted around St. Augustine between 1513 and 1565. Nearly four hundred years would be required before production became a profitable business venture, but peninsular Florida was a wilderness until after the Civil War. With expanding agricultural opportunities, Florida's annual commercial citrus production increased from one million boxes shortly after the Civil War to more than five million boxes by 1893. Then, the Great Freeze of 1894-95 destroyed many orange groves, especially north of a line from Tampa to Melbourne, causing a devastating decrease in production to 147,000 boxes in 1895. Consequently, the citrus industry began a gradual move to locations farther south where by 1910 production had recovered to pre-freeze levels. Production had reached 10 million boxes by 1915, 100 million in 1950, and more than 200 million boxes of oranges and grapefruit by the early 1970s. Presently the citrus industry generates more than $10 billion for Florida's economy. Arguably, the creation of the citrus industry is the greatest lasting influence the early Spaniards have had on Florida.

Responsible for North America's Oldest Community

St. Augustine, the oldest continuously occupied settlement of European origin in the United States, was founded in 1565 by the Spanish admiral Pedro Menéndez de Avilés. This religious fanatic was often in conflict with the *Casa,* but had the support of King Philip II, the long-reigning second Hapsburg monarch who gave Pedro Menéndez an *asiento* on March 20, 1565. This royal designation provided Pedro Menéndez not only the permission but also a monopoly to sell slaves in the Spanish colonies and granted him various titles, including that of *adelantado* (governor) of Florida. Philip II sent Pedro Menéndez to make a permanent colony and fort to protect Spain's claimed territories as a buffer for the Spanish treasure fleet returning from Latin America. It would also be a place from which to attack the French because he was aware that Huguenots, under the command of Captain Jean Ribault, were exploring Spanish territory. Pedro Menéndez de Avilés sighted land on August 28, 1565, the feast day of St. Augustine of Hippo, and so he named the colony *San Agustín.* In a battle against the French, the Spanish soldiers succeeded in a weather-assisted slaughter, and *San Agustín* survived.

Although numerous French and English attacks followed, threatening Spain's buffer colony, *San Agustín* survived under five successive flags and eventually rediscovered its Spanish heritage during the late nineteenth century.

Establishing *Ranchos* with Introduced Breeds of Cattle and Pigs

Early Spanish explorers' attempts to develop settlements were dependent upon developing a plan for food production. Ponce de León recognized this in 1521 and so did Pedro Menéndez de Avilés and the later arrivals. But the sixteenth century Spanish diet, largely defined by traditional Moorish foods such as wheat, olive oil, lamb, and wine, was not readily transferrable to *La Florida* due to the humid climate that precluded cultivation of vineyards, wheat fields, and olive groves. Moreover, sheep simply could not survive the unrelenting heat of peninsular Florida. Although *San Agustín* became the entry point for the majority of the imported cattle, many of the *ranchos* and *rancheros* (smaller cattle ranches) were inland. Hardy Andalusian cattle became a mainstay, proliferating in a feral existence in the interior, where grasslands were abundant for grazing. Similarly, once introduced to

La Florida, wild Ibérico pigs seemed to proliferate everywhere. Spanish *ranchos* were home to North America's first cowboys (*vaqueros*) and brought us the Spanish words *lariat, lasso, bronco,* and *rodeo.* As we will see in the next chapter, the readily available Spanish cattle during the nineteenth century played an important role in the settlement of Sarasota.

The Spanish learned much from the Calusa and other Amerindian people who had established fishing camps along the southwest gulf coast estuaries, such as Charlotte Harbor and Sarasota Bay. These camps were another type of Spanish ranchero. Although not enamored with eating fish, the Spanish were imbued with the Roman Catholic faith. Among other religious burdens, they were required "under pain of mortal sin" to abstain from meat on certain days as penance, which as a practice was proclaimed to save one's soul. Abstinence days included forty days of Lent, every Friday, and a peculiar set of days known as "Ember Days." During the eighteenth and nineteenth centuries, Spaniards coming from Cuba used the Florida estuaries to catch and preserve, by salting, enormous quantities of fish from November to March. Rancheros devoted to commercial fishing were common along the gulf coast and generally developed on sites with shell middens previously occupied by Amerindians. The Old Oak site on the Sarasota mainland near the north bridge to Siesta Key is a good example.

The Spanish Florida Mission System and Its Collapse by Unintentional Genocide

The best-organized attempts to develop Spanish settlements in *La Florida* were efforts by priests, especially Jesuits. The Amerindians who originally occupied the Florida peninsula but disappeared with devastating diseases and became the "Lost Tribes" (color page 4) were important to the Spanish explorers/conquistadores and settlers. They initially provided information on geography and agriculture, fishing skills, tantalizing but misleading stories about gold and silver deposits, and were also a source of women/wives and slaves. The most compelling quest the Spanish envisioned was fulfilling their mandate from the Pope to convert the natives to Christianity. Their plan was to create a series of missions in the expanded territory of *La Florida*—similar to the California mission system that was developed quite successfully later, from 1769 to 1833. Missions facilitated control of the area and prevented colonization by other countries, such as England and France. Missions were predominately in northern Florida and present-day southeastern Georgia. Efforts to establish missions farther south were more challenging due to hostile populations, especially the Calusa and Tocobaga tribes. Even in central and northern Florida the efforts were risky. The first attempts in 1549 by Father Luis de Cancer and three other Dominicans in Tampa Bay ended in failure after six weeks with de Cancer's death at the hands of the Tocobaga natives. Afterwards, Spanish missions were attached to presidios—strong forts with conquistadores available for protection. Between 1565 and 1567, ten presidios were established at major harbors. These missions were initially organized and managed by Jesuits, but as many of them were murdered, they were replaced by 1573 by Franciscan friars.

Most missions were unsustainable due to poor supply lines, Amerindian attacks, lack of leadership, and English raids. Most significantly, when the Florida Amerindians continued dying by hundreds and thousands due to smallpox and other European viral diseases, the Franciscans simply lost their conversion "targets" and the conquistadores

Figure 4.3 Ponce de León Hotel in St. Augustine during approximately 1900

lost their labor supply. Estimates suggest that from a maximum population of about 200,000 Amerindians throughout *La Florida* in 1513, there were fewer than 10,000 natives by 1700. Along the southwest gulf coast, the previously thriving and combative Calusa tribes were depopulated from an estimated 20,000 people when Ponce de León visited to fewer than 2,000 by 1697.

When the Spanish mission system lost its *raison d'être*, the unintentional genocide dooming their ambition to colonize, coupled with the conclusion that no gold or silver was forthcoming, it was gradually abandoned—another failed Spanish effort to establish viable settlements in *La Florida*.

Florida Discovers Spain Through Architecture

Two centuries after Spain exited Florida and despite conflicts associated with the Spanish-American War in 1898, Floridian developers dedicated to tourism brought back the Spanish culture and triggered national interest

in Spanish architecture and heritage. This rekindling of historical interests was directly linked to architectural ingenuity promoting tourism, making the Atlantic coast of Florida a destination for affluent easterners.

Recognizing the European discoverer of Florida, the seminal winter resort for northeastern elite "snowbirds" was the Ponce de León Hotel, known as "The Ponce," completed in 1888 in St. Augustine. The genius of multi-millionaire Henry Flagler, the railroad magnate, led to the magnificent building that, more than any single development, triggered the "Spanish craze." The Ponce was the first-ever building constructed entirely of poured concrete and was unique in being wired for electricity at the outset, with power supplied by generators from Thomas Edison. Its design, known as the Spanish Renaissance style, was influenced by treasured buildings in Seville, especially the Muslim Giralda and adjacent Christian/Muslim constructions. Other buildings in the United States inspired by the Giralda include the clock

Figure 4.4 El Vernona Hotel in Sarasota around 1930 (Courtesy of Sarasota County Historical Resources thanks to Larry Kelleher)

tower of the Ferry Building (1898) in San Francisco, the Wrigley Building (1920) in Chicago, the Freedom Tower (1920) in Miami, Florida's Biltmore Hotel (1926) in Coral Gables—all tributes to the Moorish architectural genius.

The Ponce, just like the man whose name it bears, launched a new era for *La Florida*. Other Spanish-style hotels with towers followed in St. Augustine, such as the Alcazar, mimicking the Castilian kings' palace in Seville, and the Hotel Cordova. In 1968 the Ponce de León Hotel was transformed into Flagler College, as Florida expanded higher education. In 1975 it was added to the National Register of Historic Places and in 2006 it was designated as a National Historic Landmark. The search for a combination of a distinct identity

and tourist destinations during 1888–1926 culminated in efforts to celebrate all things Spanish, as the railroad barons, Henry Flagler on the east coast and Henry Plant on the west coast, with the Tampa Bay Hotel, as well as others selected elaborate Spanish architecture for their distinctive resort hotels.

The "Spanish craze" came to Sarasota thanks to Owen Burns and John Ringling. It began with the El Vernona Hotel, described as "the most perfect example of Spanish architecture in Florida." It was designed by architect Dwight James Baum, who was responsible for many of the most significant buildings constructed in Sarasota in the 1920s, including John Ringling's palatial home, Cà d´Zan (although it is modeled after a Venetian mansion and not representative

Figure 4.5 Mira Mar Casino on Siesta Key around 1935 (Courtesy of Sarasota County Historical Resources thanks to Larry Kelleher)

of the "Spanish craze"), the Sarasota County Courthouse, and the four Mediterranean Revival Style buildings in the arts and culture district. Mr. Baum studied examples in Southern California of both the Mission Revival style and the Spanish Colonial Revival style, applying these concepts in 1925 to design the Sarasota Times Building on 1st Street, which was added to the National Register of Historic Places in 1984. Spanish-inspired towers would also have adorned the ill-fated 235-room Ritz-Carlton on Longboat Key in Sarasota County, begun during 1926 but resulting in a "ghost hotel."

Figure 4.6 The Gulf View Inn during the 1930s (Courtesy of Sarasota County Historical Resources thanks to Larry Kelleher)

Figure 4.7 Gregg's Spanish Cottage at 6100 Midnight Pass Road

On Siesta Key, the Mira Mar Casino was the most significant representation of the "Spanish craze." Built in 1925 on Siesta/Crescent Beach just north of the public beach, it was advertised as "Sarasota's Exclusive Night Club" and became a local hot spot during the Roaring '20s. Also on Mira Mar Beach, the northern section of Siesta/Crescent Beach, the Gulf View Inn was built in 1924 in the Spanish Mediterranean Revival style to house prospective buyers of property in a nearby eight-hundred-lot subdivision being developed by the Crescent Beach Development Company, bordered now by Ocean Boulevard, Avenida Del Mayo, and Avenida Del Mare. The subdivision's use of numerous Spanish street names reflected the "Spanish craze," and the names persist today as a reminder of the Spanish influence on Siesta Key. The Gulf View Inn functioned as a hotel for almost sixty years, although it was almost swallowed by the Gulf of Mexico. As a final expression of the Spanish architectural influence, there were beach cottages built in the Spanish style. A good example at 6100 Midnight Pass Road is the most prominent of eight beach cottages in the Gregg's Cottages complex.

CHAPTER 5

Pioneer Settlers Display Early Florida Hospitality and Leadership

True hospitality consists of giving the best of yourself to your guests.
—Eleanor Roosevelt, a frequent visitor to Siesta Key

From the arrival of de Soto in 1539 to the end of the Second Seminole War in 1842, the Sarasota area was sparsely inhabited. The only attraction was the excellent fishing, which was productive enough to draw fishermen from Cuba, about two hundred miles away, and to feed the descendants of Spanish explorers. In particular, the plentiful mullet easily caught in nets was an ideal commercial fish when salted for preservation, just as one finds today in Mediterranean European countries such as Spain, France, and Italy. According to the 1946 book *The Story of Sarasota,* one fisherman bragged, "You could hardly row your boat to one of the keys without ending up with a dozen or so fish in your boat. The fish were so thick you'd hit them with your oar and into the boat they'd flop."

But much more than mullet could be readily caught in the Intracoastal Waterway estuary between the mainland and the keys of Sarasota County. There was abundant pompano, trout, red snapper, and numerous other species. Moreover, the shellfish supply seemed limitless, and all species were delicious and nutritious, including oysters, clams, shrimp, and stone crab. In fact, until the past half-century, the estuaries around Sarasota provided more than enough seafood for the inhabitants and commercial fishermen.

William Whitaker: Sarasota's First White Settler

In 1842, the potential for settlers in South Florida was recognized, but a federal stimulus was needed to facilitate occupation. Thus, on August 4, 1842, Congress passed the Armed Occupation Act, which stipulated that six months of provisions and 160 acres of land anywhere south of Palatka and Gainesville would be given to settlers willing to carry firearms to defend their homes for five years. Plus, additional land could be bought for $1.25 per acre.

Stepping into history while taking advantage of this unique opportunity was William H. Whitaker, Sarasota's first white settler, who arrived in 1842 when he was 21 years old. Whitaker had run away from his home in Savannah, Georgia, at 14 years of age, working as an itinerant dock laborer, a fisherman, and then for four years as an Amerindian fighter in the Second Seminole War. In 1842, following the advice and guidance of his Tallahassee-based brother,

Figure 5.1 Siesta Key fishing success led by Captain Lewis Roberts (back row) at the dock of Bay Island Hotel in 1913. Note that Harry Higel is in the front row, third from the right. (Courtesy of Sarasota County Historical Resources thanks to Larry Kelleher)

Whitaker bought a sloop, filled it with provisions, and sailed south along the gulf coast until he "discovered" Sarasota. Nearby, a Spanish fisherman named Alzartie and several Cuban fishermen made it clear that Sarasota Bay was perfect for fishing and that wild game was also abundant. Moreover, the lush vegetation growing in the sandy soil suggested that there was also agricultural potential. While sailing within Sarasota Bay, Whitaker saw a shoreline area of yellow bluffs where a limestone surface appeared favorable for a secure homestead on elevated, solid ground.

Next, Whitaker established himself as a commercial fisherman and then, five years later, as a cattleman. He caught enormous numbers of mullet when the schools were running in the winter and entering Sarasota Bay to escape sharks. He observed that these panicked fish would leap in a frenzy out of the water to signal their presence in schools as wide as a hundred yards and more than a mile long. A fisherman as skilled as Whitaker could fill his boat with a netful in a matter of minutes. The hard labor was actually the cleaning, salting, drying, and packing of the fish for his customers. Fortunately, he had a pre-existing, reliable customer base: the Cuban traders who previously did the arduous work but were happy to pay Whitaker and return home quicker. The mullet harvests were lucrative enough by 1847 to capitalize Bill Whitaker's venture into cattle-raising. His herd, branded "47," roamed the open range around the Myakka River and brought him more profits through local sales. Whitaker also planted the area's first orange grove using seeds from his Cuban customers.

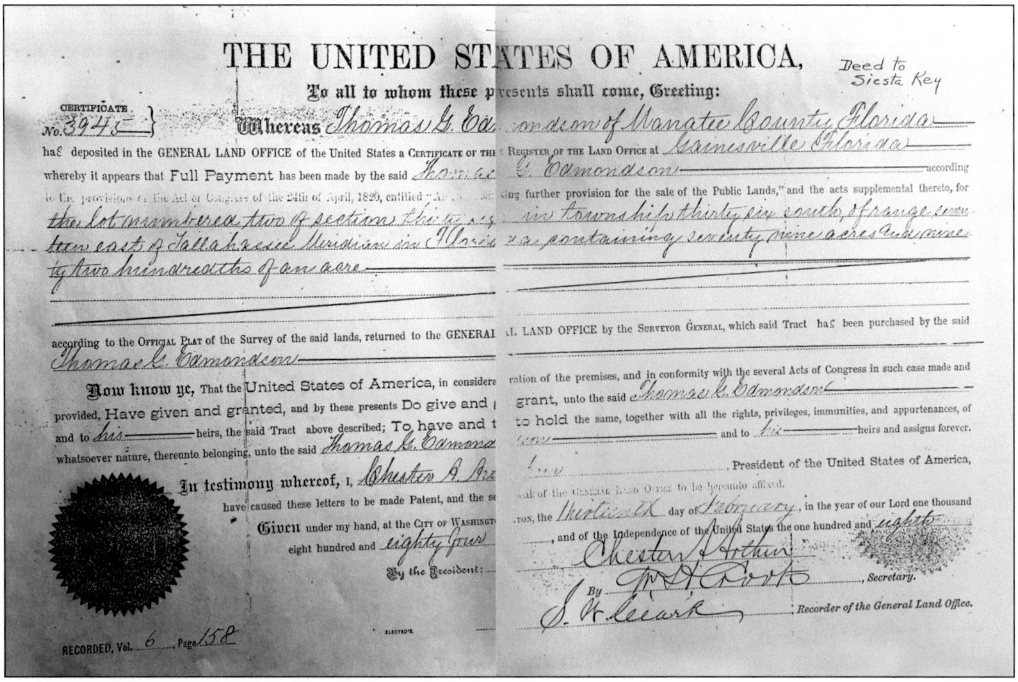

THE UNITED STATES OF AMERICA,

Deed to Siesta Key

To all to whom these presents shall come, Greeting:

CERTIFICATE No. 3945 } Whereas Thomas G. Edmondson of Manatee County Florida

has deposited in the GENERAL LAND OFFICE of the United States a CERTIFICATE OF THE REGISTER OF THE LAND OFFICE at Gainesville Florida whereby it appears that Full Payment has been made by the said Thomas G. Edmondson according to the provisions of the Act of Congress of the 24th of April, 1820, entitled "An Act making further provision for the sale of the Public Lands," and the acts supplemental thereto, for the lot numbered two of section thirty six in township thirty six south, of range seventeen east of Tallahassee Meridian in Florida, containing seventy nine acres and ninety two hundredths of an acre

according to the OFFICIAL PLAT of the Survey of the said lands, returned to the GENERAL LAND OFFICE by the SURVEYOR GENERAL, which said Tract has been purchased by the said Thomas G. Edmondson

Now know ye, That the United States of America, in consideration of the premises, and in conformity with the several Acts of Congress in such case made and provided, Have given and granted, and by these presents Do give and grant, unto the said Thomas G. Edmondson and to his heirs, the said Tract above described; To have and to hold the same, together with all the rights, privileges, immunities, and appurtenances, of whatsoever nature, thereunto belonging, unto the said Thomas G. Edmondson and to his heirs and assigns forever.

In testimony whereof, I, Chester A. Arthur, President of the United States of America, have caused these letters to be made Patent, and the seal of the General Land Office to be hereunto affixed.

Given under my hand, at the City of Washington, the thirteenth day of February, in the year of our Lord one thousand eight hundred and eighty four, and of the Independence of the United States the one hundred and eighth.

By the President: Chester A. Arthur

By ..., Secretary.

..., Recorder of the General Land Office.

RECORDED, Vol. 6, Page 158

Figure 5.2 Homestead deed of Thomas Edmondson on Siesta Key in 1884. Note that this document was signed by President Chester Arthur. (Reconstructed from pieces by Julia Farrell Patton. Provided courtesy of Sarasota County Historical Resources thanks to Larry Kelleher)

Satisfied with his progress and seemingly secure future, at age 30 Bill Whitaker married 21-year-old Mary Jane Wyatt of nearby Manatee on June 10, 1851. Well-educated and "polished" at a Louisville, Kentucky boarding school, Wyatt had become a "Lady pioneer" upon her return to Florida and could shoot wild game with the best men. The Whitaker family grew fast, beginning with Nancy Catherine Stuart Whitaker, born on April 19, 1852, and eventually expanding to eleven children. Within a year of marriage, Whitaker also had the good sense to secure his land with a U.S. government deed to 144.8 acres of homesteaded land, which he enlarged by another 48.6 acres that he bought from his close friend Alzartie. He was a model citizen as he and his wife used their mile-long Sarasota Bay frontage and associated land to take care of not only themselves but also their neighbors and visitors. For instance, he obtained and delivered mail for all the residents until a post office for the community of "Sara Sota" was operating. The Whitakers also advised new settlers, including the Webbs from Utica, New York, who developed their homestead twelve miles south, built a sugar refinery plant, and then built the area's first hotel—Webb's Winter Resort on Little Sarasota Bay.

From those eleven healthy children and a stable, successful family, it should come as no surprise that many descendants of Bill and Mary Jane Whitaker have lived in Sarasota over the years. One of the noteworthy offspring was Louise Anstie Whitaker, the second white baby born in Sarasota. She married Captain Thomas Gordon Edmondson of Baltimore soon after he arrived as a winter visitor in April 1876. They lived in Baltimore for about a decade before returning to purchase a homesteader's claim on Clam Island that eventually became important in the Siesta Key tourist industry, as described in Chapter 7.

Captain Lewis Roberts and Ocean Deep Hansen Roberts: Pioneer Settlers of Siesta Key

The names of the streets and waterways on and around Siesta Key provide historical clues to the pioneers who settled and developed this barrier island. After the first settlement boom period of 1862–1883 on the Sarasota mainland, political interventions and federal regulations limited further development using the homestead claims. Ironically, however, the politicians and speculators focused exclusively on the mainland and missed their opportunity to sequester the valuable land on the keys. Consequently, another type of pioneer emerged to capitalize on the Homestead Act loophole that excluded Florida's barrier islands from the new restrictions. For Clam Island, this leadership came from an unlikely source—a fisherman for whom Roberts Bay was named, Captain Lewis Roberts (whose name is often misspelled as Louis). This huge man who stood 6 feet 6 inches tall and weighed approximately 350 pounds had been sailing a small boat the nearly 100 miles from Key West up to Sarasota Bay since 1870 to take advantage of the fabulous fishing. Finally, in 1878, he settled in the area permanently.

The captain's success in commercial fishing was superseded by his romantic discovery. He fell head over heels for Ocean

Figure 5.3 Fishing in Sarasota Bay around 1900 on the boat of Captain Lewis Roberts (sitting)

Deep Hansen, who was memorialized by the naming of Ocean Boulevard. Ocean Deep Hansen was born on July 12, 1860, to Peter and Mary (Christensen) Hansen while these recently married immigrants from Denmark were sailing across the Atlantic from England to America—hence her name "Ocean Deep." The Hansen family had settled in 1870 on Little Sarasota Bay alongside what became known as Hansen Bayou. It seems likely that Captain Lewis was smitten by this young lady while selling fish to the Hansen family. In any event, they were married May 29, 1881, and soon thereafter filed a claim for a homestead on land across the bay from Ocean's parents. This choice property, known as Roberts Point, is located near present-day Roberts Circle, and of course is accessed today by Roberts Point Road. Back in 1881, and continuing until 1917, it was only accessible by water—primarily by Captain Lewis's boat. The couple's first child, George, arrived on April 10, 1882, after Lewis built a starter home that would be enlarged many times. Similar to the Whitaker family and typical for the time, ten more children followed, the last being born in 1902.

The first two decades on Siesta Key must have been heavenly for Lewis, Ocean, and their children. Swimming in the gulf was a daily pastime and the best way to beat the heat. Lewis loved to float on his back and was said to look "just like a little island." His children, and eventually others, called this giant "Big Daddy." He adored his wife and his children, naming Hansen Bayou for Ocean's family, Nettie Bayou for his daughter Nellie because "Big Daddy" liked to call her Nettie, and Louise Bayou for another daughter. Not surprisingly, the captain's fishing business thrived. Big Daddy also cleared the land on Roberts Point for Ocean's large garden—actually a small farm. As

Lewis enlarged their dwelling, it became a hospitable boarding house for fishermen who were catching anything they wanted from the bay.

Ocean and Lewis Roberts became famous for the delicious meals they served to guests and Sarasota residents who ferried across Sarasota Bay just for dinner. Naturally, fresh fish was the usual entrée. But the most spectacular meal was the clam chowder—a delectable dish that became known up and down the gulf coast. Big Daddy, likely with help from his children, dug up the fresh clams, while Ocean adjusted her recipe for whatever ingredients were available. The two of them next assembled everything together in a huge iron kettle. Lewis then stirred the soup with a wooden oar while it simmered for hours, acquiring a fabulous flavor. Nothing comparable was served on Siesta Key until a century later when Captain Curt's restaurant began featuring an award-winning clam chowder…but that's another story for Chapter 15. By 1900, the fishing, food, and lodging on Siesta Key began attracting winter guests from the north. The potential for tourism became apparent to the two congenial hosts with their extraordinary talents.

Transformation to the Roberts Hotel

In 1906 Big Daddy enlarged the house again and transformed it into the Roberts Hotel. This marks the beginning of the hospitality industry on the island and is a milestone for Siesta Key. Recognizing the opportunity to capitalize on a new venture, Captain Lewis joined forces with Harry Lee Higel, mayor of Sarasota and an entrepreneurial landholder on the key, and E. M. Arbogast, to form the Siesta Land Company. As described in

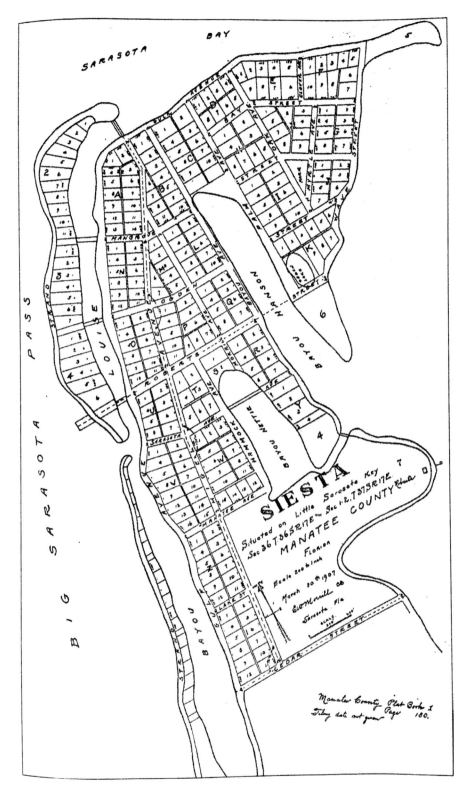

Figure 5.4 Plat of the Siesta subdivision in 1907. Note that this document was filed with Manatee County prior to Sarasota County being established

Figure 5.5 Siesta post office in about 1915 (Courtesy of Sarasota County Historical Resources thanks to Larry Kelleher)

Chapter 7, Harry Higel brought vision, resources, and political clout to the trio of partners. Arbogast, who visited the Roberts Hotel from West Virginia in 1906, brought investment capital and ambition. The trio organized a sequence of island developments that included platting a Siesta subdivision, dredging canals from bayous, and eventually planning for good roads. The Roberts family then changed the name of their resort to the Siesta Hotel. Not long thereafter, Harry Higel renamed the island Siesta Key as he promoted a tourist destination distinctly different from what was offered in Sarasota: "A wondrous place to rest." After Mayor Higel developed the island's first post office in 1915, the name Siesta Key became more popular.

Figure 5.6 Roberts Casino near the intersection of Beach Road and Ocean Boulevard in about 1930 (Courtesy of Sarasota County Historical Resources thanks to Larry Kelleher)

The Siesta Hotel enabled Captain Lewis to retire from commercial fishing and work full-time in the hospitality business. He not only ran the hotel and restaurant, but also operated a casino/dance hall in the early 1920s. This two-story building was located at the intersection of Ocean Boulevard and Beach Road and was said to accommodate three thousand people. Its location accounts for the naming of Ocean Boulevard when the roads were improved on the key to accommodate the increasing automobile traffic. In those days, the cars drove right onto the beaches for a day's outing. The resiliency of Lewis and Ocean Roberts is exemplified by their immediate rebuilding of their hotel, renamed the Siesta Inn, after the original burned down in 1922 due to an electrical fire.

The hotel fire, nonetheless, was a relatively minor stress for Lewis and Ocean Roberts compared to the tragedy that had struck during the third week of November in 1900. In their nineteenth year of marriage, this couple, who loved their children dearly, were just recovering from the loss of their daughter Dollie Roberts, who was born on October 20, 1888, and died on March 7, 1890. Tragically, they lost one-year-old Minnie on November 13, 1890, two-year-old Dewey the next day,

Figure 5.7 Cars parked on Crescent Beach during the 1930s (From a postcard displayed on the Sarasota History Alive website)

and both four-year-old Albert and ten-year-old Harry on November 19. Although "food poisoning" was mentioned as the probable cause of death, they probably died from yellow fever, based on our medical opinion. All of these children were buried in unmarked graves at Red Rock Cemetery in Sarasota, which was known as the Hansen Cemetery at the time. The shock of such a week would devastate most families, and it is recorded that "after Ocean buried them, her two year-old in the arms of an older child, she was never the same." How many mothers could cope with the stress of losing four young children in one week? Perhaps the hospitality business, her dynamic "bull-of-a-man" husband, and their vision to create a distinctive resort helped her survive such a horrible tragedy. Ocean Roberts carried on for thirty-six more years. She died on July 19, 1936, on Siesta Key just 249 days after the death of her husband, the legendary Captain Lewis Roberts. Both are buried in unmarked graves near her father, Peter, and the four tragically deceased children. The authors visited this cemetery at 1401 Quail Drive and were surprised to find that it looks like a jungle among houses and has only one headstone, that of Peter Hansen, even though fourteen burials occurred there from 1900 to 1969.

Hospitality Established Siesta Key's Original Culture

Lewis and Ocean Roberts launched tourism on Siesta Key and must be considered the premier pioneering couple on the barrier island. Their impact as a partnership is unsurpassed to this day, as the Roberts Hotel/Inn became widely known and attracted tourists for many years. Captain Lewis was certainly the forefather of the hospitality industry on the key. His assortment of skills as a fishing guide, lodging entrepreneur, restaurateur, and entertainer, combined with Ocean's charm and culinary talents, ensured many decades of success. They surely deserve to be memorialized by Roberts Bay and the streets named for them in an important neighborhood.

The long-term significance of the Roberts' pioneering efforts following the Whitakers' example is that Lewis and Ocean set the tone early for hospitality on Siesta Key. Others such as J. H. Faubel at the Bay Island Hotel followed in their footsteps, so that Siesta Key became known as an island that welcomed visitors with open, hospitable arms. This may seem like a minor matter in the twenty-first century, but in the context of Florida's (and Sarasota's) wild, undeveloped, and potentially dangerous environment at the time, hospitality was crucial when pioneers first settled on the key.

CHAPTER 6

Early Barriers to Florida Tourism and Settlement of Sarasota

Time is the only actual true barrier to success.
—Steven Redhead in *Life Is a Cocktail*

Although Captain Lewis Roberts and Ocean Deep Hansen Roberts set the stage for Siesta Key tourism, a combination of local, regional, statewide, and national obstacles delayed and/or limited developers and discouraged tourists. A top-ten list of these challenges is provided below. Many of these barriers had to be overcome throughout Florida and then in Sarasota County before Siesta Key could become available to and developed for residents and tourists.

Challenges for Florida's Early Settlers and Visitors

Delayed development of well distributed railway lines

Lack of good roads that could withstand seasonal rainstorms

Few bridges over inland and Gulf coast waterways

Intolerable weather, especially the combination of severe heat, rain, and hurricanes

Dangerous critters, especially snakes, alligators, and mosquitoes

Lack of sanitation, plus contaminated water

Ineffective medical care, particularly for acute diseases and injuries

Endemic infectious diseases such as yellow fever and malaria

Florida's economic recessions (e.g., 1890 and 1926)

The Great Depression and impact of World War II

Railroad Deficiencies in Florida

Good, well-distributed railroad lines came incredibly late to Florida, while much of the nation, particularly the northern states, had well-developed railways underway by the Civil War. All of Florida was surprisingly slow in establishing railway lines to connect with the populous cities along the eastern seaboard and Midwest. Remarkably, the completion of the east-to-west Pacific transcontinental line occurred almost thirty years before the first interconnected tracks were brought to Florida resorts by Henry Flagler. Flagler's passenger trains to St. Augustine in 1885 served primarily the eastern regions of Florida where he built hotels primarily for New Yorkers, eventually all the way to Miami.

The Flagler story is a fascinating and important part of Florida history. Henry Flagler was a wealthy industrialist and one of the visionary founders of the Standard Oil Company, but he is also considered the

Figure 6.1 The "slow and wobbly" train loading passengers for a trip from Sarasota to Bradenton around 1893

founder of both Miami and Palm Beach. Flagler first came to Florida for the weather in the winter of 1879 with his first wife Mary on the advice of her physician because of her severe and soon fatal illness. When she died, Flagler married Mary's caregiver, Ida Alice, in 1881. They honeymooned in St. Augustine and loved the city but hated the hotels and local transportation. To address the first deficiency, Flagler became Florida's first major developer while reducing his leadership role with Standard Oil. His first hotel, the Ponce de Leon, was built in St. Augustine in 1885–1888 as a 540-room palace (see photo on page 32). To bring in guests, Flagler purchased and modernized several short line railroads that eventually were consolidated to become the Florida East Coast Railway. Next, to create an "American Riviera," Flagler extended the railroad tracks south and built hotels all the way to Palm Beach, which was planned

as the terminus. However, severe freezing winters in 1894 and 1895 motivated Flager to continue south below the 1894-95 frost line. Thus, he founded "Mayaimi" (Miami), refusing to have the rapidly successful city named "Flagler." Lastly, the railroad line was extended all the way to Key West, Florida's most populous city at the time with 20,000 inhabitants.

Another successful industrialist, Henry Plant, similarly transformed himself into a railroad and resort developer. His goal with the "Plant System" became important for central and southwest Florida as he extended his Georgia and Carolina railroads south, creating fourteen railway companies and 2,100 miles of track serving his resort hotels in Sanford, Kissimmee, Ocala, Tampa, and Fort Myers. When Henry Plant died in 1890, his enormous railway empire was purchased by the Atlantic Coast Line (ACL). Its principal route was from Jacksonville to

S. A. L. Depot, Sarasota, Fla.

SARASOTA

Photo by T. F. Arnold.

Figure 6.2 The Seaboard Air Line depot in Sarasota as shown in a postcard

Tampa via Orlando, but eventually it began serving Sarasota, where a third major railway, the Seaboard Air Line (SAL), was already operating successfully by 1903, replacing the "slow and wobbly" trains and establishing an excellent depot. In a repeat of history, SAL's venture southwest was attributable to another honeymoon—that of Mr. and Mrs. Ralph Caples. In fact, Sarasota and Siesta Key should be grateful to Ellen Caples for convincing her reluctant husband to stay a few days in 1899 with her comment as she gazed on Siesta Key: "Just look at that view across the bay. I never saw anything more beautiful." Later, the Caples encouraged the Ringlings to come. Moreover, the Chicago-based couple likely played a role in the pivotal visits of the "Chicago Colony" led by Bertha Palmer.

Primitive Roads

Arrival in Sarasota by train, however, was only part of the journey. An equally important component was the road system, initially for horse and buggy travel, and later, by the 1920s, for automobiles and buses. Karl Grismer describes the problem in his book, *The Story of Sarasota:* "South of Tampa, the so-called roads were nothing but trails... Sarasota was practically isolated from the rest of the world... As for the roads, there were none...a trail wound through the woods, skirting swamps and loads of bayous... On none of the trails were there any bridges... To become civilized Sarasota literally had to pull itself out of the mud." Eventually, however, Sarasota and Siesta Key began to spend on roads, including, in 1916, a 9-foot-wide asphalt road from Sarasota to Venice, including bridges.

Crude but Functional Bridges

Even as Sarasota's roads began to receive attention and became passable for automobiles, the best beaches on the barrier islands were still remote and accessible only by boat. Although this provided reliable business for Captain Lewis Roberts and other boat operators, the emerging era of the automobile was a game changer. In fact, when Henry Ford's Model T began rolling off the assembly line at twenty cars per day in 1913, reducing the time it took to build a car from more than twelve hours to just over two hours, the handwriting was on the wall. Both middle-class and more affluent Americans simply wanted the freedom and efficiency to come and go whenever and wherever they pleased throughout the nation. And, the lack of good bridges was a troublesome limitation throughout Florida.

Horrendous Weather

Florida's weather and its consequences have always been a mixed blessing. Prior to electrification, this land of perpetual summer could be intolerably hot for settlers and visitors. Surprisingly, there were also some freezing winters that damaged crops and discouraged visitors. Plus, the almost daily rains of the summer months were equally discouraging as they often became torrential during May through August or even later. As one pioneer settler commented in July, 1886, "We are at the peak of the rainy season: rain, rain, and rain. If it rained on schedule a few hours each day, I should not object to this phenomenon, but one week ago we had rain keeping on for 36 hours... Under such circumstances I can't work and the enormous quantities of water streaming into my low clearing destroy or damage the small achievements that have been completed so far."

Yet the chief weather-related concern for many developers and tourists was the risk of hurricanes, especially after the 1926 disaster in Miami that took at least 372 American lives, left over 40,000 people homeless in Miami, and precipitated Florida's economic collapse ahead of the nation's stock market crash. Since then, many Floridians live in fear of hurricanes and with good reason. The "Great Miami Hurricane," with its 150 mph winds, not only devastated Miami after critically damaging the Bahamas,

but also traversed the peninsula to reach the gulf near Fort Myers, where it flooded Captiva and Sanibel and opened a new pass. Then it turned northwest to hit the western panhandle, Alabama, and Mississippi with nearly twenty inches of rain in twenty hours. The costs were staggering—the equivalent of $165 million in today's currency.

On the other hand, Florida's autumn and winter weather became the anchor of the tourist industry. And eventually, with electrical cooling appliances and swimming pools, the summers became enjoyable also. For North Americans and Europeans in the modern era, Florida's weather variations might be complained about, but they are managed and even celebrated.

Dangerous Pests

From the initial settlement of Florida, the region's harmful critters have proved more difficult to manage. Frightening comments about mosquitoes, flies, and snakes by the early pioneer settlers were echoed by the early tourists. They agreed with one of the original names of Manatee (and later Sarasota) County: "Mosquito Country." A settler commented in 1886 that "the terrible plague of the mosquitoes" was "enough to drive me mad." The only way to repel these billions of flying pests was to burn smudge pots in front of homes and feed the fires with "cow chips." Evidently, the awful odor was preferred to the bites. On Siesta Key, there was an abundance of dangerous critters that the pioneer settlers had to avoid or battle. Fortunately, pioneers such as Big Daddy Roberts were equal to the task.

Lack of Sanitation and Good Health Care

At the end of the nineteenth century, the towns and cities of the United States were often public health disaster areas. Consequently, the risk of severe infectious disease was high. Moreover, epidemics of potentially fatal diseases were common in every southern city. The lack of sanitation and safe water certainly jeopardized the lives of Florida's settlers and visitors. This situation was aggravated by the primitive medical care throughout Florida and most of the United States. As Sarasota's population increased, the lack of sanitation became intolerable. Outdoor privies and cesspools were inadequate, attracting flies and polluting the atmosphere. Cow and horse dung added to the horrible stench. No one can estimate how much disease resulted directly from lack of sanitation.

Originally the pioneer settlers in the Sarasota area had to self-treat the wounds, infections, and illnesses that commonly befell them in the wilderness. Generally this was the woman's responsibility—just as she assumed the primary role in educating her children and for religious upbringing. The Sarasota County Historical Resources Center provides a summary of how health care was practiced.

Each family kept a kitchen garden near the house, which included commonly used medicinal herbs such as dried palmetto berries or pennyroyal tea for colds and flu; soda and ginger for colic; honey, lemon juice or horehound for coughs; cinnamon or nutmeg for diarrhea; willow bark tea for fever; oak bark tea or a drop of turpentine on a lump of sugar for worms; chewed tobacco poultice for insect stings; and kerosene or animal fat for wounds. Colds were often dealt with by using a mustard plaster on the chest, wrapping the patient in a blanket and resting for at least 24 hours. Indeed, the warm climate itself was recommended by northern doctors for many diseases such as consumption (tuberculosis). The pioneer housewife did have access to several home health medical books for guidance, as well as advice from other women in the area. Patients with more

difficult or persistent cases might be treated by a more experienced "herb woman" or taken to a doctor.

During this era, a physician could often only make tentative diagnoses, treat injuries, and provide supportive care. The miraculous introduction of antibiotic therapy was five decades in the future and could not even be envisioned. Consequently, a sore throat, a festering wound, and even childbirth could be fatal. In fact, at the turn of the nineteenth century, as many as one-fourth of women admitted to the maternity ward of a hospital died of puerperal fever or, as it was commonly known then, "childbed fever." Imagine all the tragic experiences—first the joy of completing a pregnancy and having a baby, next two or three days later a fever develops, and then death ensues within a week following the baby's arrival. Equally tragic in retrospect, these preventable deaths were caused by the medical profession's lack of attention to cleanliness. Thus, a woman was better off delivering babies at home, which many, if not most, did at that time.

Sarasota was more than doubly fortunate to have the Whitaker family among its earliest settlers. Not only was William Whitaker the first pioneer settler and leader, his wife Mary equally impressive, but their son, Furman, was the first physician to launch a successful medical practice. Dr. Furman Whitaker began his medical practice in 1896 using his home as a clinic. Next, Dr. Jack Halton moved to Sarasota and became known as the "Singing Doctor" because of his wonderful baritone voice. Halton was born in England and graduated from the Miami Medical College of the University of Cincinnati. He opened his first office near the pier at the foot of lower Main Street, and in 1908 opened the famous Halton Sanitarium on Gulf Stream Avenue. Halton was active and prominent in the community, serving for one term as a

Figure 6.3 The Halton "hospital" on South Pineapple Avenue located in a small shopping complex next to a grocery store called Mac's. There were other retail or services in the same location. It was a narrow building that today would be called a clinic and not a hospital

councilman and establishing the American Legion's underprivileged children's clinic. Later, he served as the surgeon for the Seaboard Airline Railroad. Several years after Dr. Jack Halton came to Sarasota, his brother, Dr. Joe Halton, arrived. After establishing his practice, he opened the private Halton Hospital, which served the community until the 1950s, though it was not a full-service hospital. Dr. Joe Halton was also known for his civic mindedness and was recognized for his community service by being named Sarasota's Man of the Year for performing over 1,600 operations on needy children.

Endemic and Epidemic Infectious Diseases

The experience of the Roberts family in November 1900, losing four children in one week, was unfortunately not atypical

in the South. The risk of serious or fatal infectious disease and the lack of good acute medical care, as well as the absence of preventative or curative therapies, made traveling dangerous. This was especially true during the three- to four-month summer rainy season when vacationers might usually travel. The polio virus was always a menace during summer throughout the United States, but the South was plagued with two other deadly viral diseases, yellow fever and malaria. Although the mosquito species *Aedes aegypti* was clearly the culprit, this yellow fever-carrying vector was not identified as such until Walter Reed's definitive research in 1900 confirmed the "mosquito hypothesis" that Dr. Carlos Finlay proposed in 1881 from his experiments in Cuba. Ironically, yellow fever was brought to the Americas by African slaves and is considered by some as their revenge.

By the late nineteenth century, yellow fever had become the most dreaded acute disease afflicting southwest Florida's settlers and visitors. There were epidemics in 1867, 1887, and 1889. The settlers were shocked by the suddenness and severity of the often fatal disease, while they wondered where it had come from—just like plague victims during the Roman epidemics and the devastating Europe-wide fourteenth century reign of Black Death terror. One severe outbreak of yellow fever in the Manatee area was definitely linked to the arrival of a steamship from Havana containing a crewman with fever and violent symptoms, leading to death within a few hours. Visitors to the ship or who were exposed by just walking on the dock also developed the fatal fever. For unknown reasons, some victims had milder cases and recovered within a few weeks. Many others, however, developed the toxic phase and succumbed within hours, having suffered from severe abdominal pain, yellow jaundice due to liver failure, bleeding from the mouth, the eyes, and the gastrointestinal tract, and finally delirium. It is tragic that so many children died such violent and rapid deaths within a few days of exposure. The suddenness and violence of the illness spread terror over Florida communities. Large ports—Tampa, Key West, and Jacksonville—had the most frequent and severe outbreaks. The Tampa-to-Sarasota steamship *Mistletoe,* transporting people and goods on the dredged Intracoastal Waterway after 1895, thus unwittingly delivered yellow fever as well. Also, the captains of local ferry and fishing boats like Lewis Roberts may have brought yellow fever to Siesta Key.

Malaria, often called intermittent fever, was a scourge in all tropical environments and was thought to be caused by breathing air contaminated by rotting vegetation in swampy areas. Of course, these areas were full of swarming mosquitoes. Doctors believed that some people were disposed to certain diseases, while others could be exposed to the same disease and not be affected. The germ theory of disease did not become the basis of treatment until the late nineteenth century, and antibiotics did not appear until the 1930s.

Later, as a result of extensive travel and human contact in World War I, an influenza virus pandemic from 1917 to 1918 killed at least 50 million people worldwide—a devastating viral epidemic reminiscent of the impact of smallpox on Americans and considered "the greatest medical holocaust in history." This outbreak severely limited travel during 1918 to 1920. Its impact, however, pales in comparison to the devastating impact of endemic yellow fever and malaria viral infectious diseases in the South. For instance, more than 20,000 southerners succumbed to yellow fever in 1878.

Florida's Habit of Periodic Economic Recessions

No state has experienced as many economic downturns as Florida. From the near bankruptcy of 1881 to the real estate bust of 2008, when property depreciated 40 percent or more in many cases, one of the most predictable features of life in the Sunshine State is a future recession. Despite a variety of thriving industries, Florida's economy seems to rise or fall depending on the real estate market. In the past, however, emerging favorable events and/or business leaders have always overcome the problems and the state has recovered. For instance, when the state was deep in debt and overextended supporting railroad construction projects, along came Hamilton Disston. On May 20, 1881, he paid $1 million in cash to buy Florida land through the governor at the bargain price of 25 cents per acre.

In the 1890s, a failed railroad (the "Slow and Wobbly"), land speculation and

Figure 6.4 Hamilton Disston, industrialist and real estate developer who purchased four million acres of Florida land in 1881—apparently the most land ever purchased by a single person in world history. It saved the state from bankruptcy and initiated many Florida development projects as well as attracting more railway lines. Some consider Disston Florida's "savior"

devaluation, and the deep freezes of 1894-95 jolted the Sarasota economy. It should be not surprising, in retrospect, that when Sarasota incorporated as a town in 1902, its leaders chose the hopeful motto "May Sarasota Prosper." But another recession arrived in 1907. Next, land boom speculation together with the Great Miami Hurricane led to another collapse in the mid-1920s that ushered in the Great Depression of the 1930s. Then, World War II deprivations supervened. If nothing else, the boom-bust cycles prove that history repeats itself and that greed is a strong driving force. Ironically, Florida's experience in the 1920s was a preview of the nation's real estate bubble in the first decade of the twenty-first century. In both boom-bust cycles, the impact of outside speculators, easy credit for unqualified buyers, and incredible land appreciation created an unrealistic, unsustainable economic pseudo-expansion followed by collapse when land valuations declined precipitously.

CHAPTER 7

Harry Lee Higel

Siesta's Key's Founder of Tourism, Following in His Father's Entrepreneurial but Tragic Footsteps

A progressive citizen—that man Higel. One of the finest Sarasota ever had. It was Higel who gave Siesta Key its name.

—Karl Grismer, *The Story of Sarasota*, 1946

A Life Full of Triumphs and Tragedies

Harry Lee Higel was the founder of Siesta Key tourism and a heroic leader of Sarasota during its early development phase, culminating in the creation of a town and later a city. The life of this progressive civic pioneer and entrepreneur deserves careful study. Harry Higel was uniquely outstanding as a leader of both urban development and tourism while serving his business interests as an "indefatigable hustler," as he was praised in the *Sarasota Times* on January 6, 1921. After an initial move with his family to the developing community of Horse and Chaise, Florida, which eventually became Venice, Higel moved twenty miles north to Sarasota. Before long he became visible and successful as a businessman by purchasing the town dock, the heart of the early community. Higel then established a steamboat business and initiated his extraordinary efforts as a real estate developer.

Figure 7.1 Harry Lee Higel at 35 years of age in 1902 when Sarasota was incorporated as a town (Courtesy of Sarasota County Historical Resources, David Sallein Collection, with thanks to Larry Kelleher)

Figure 7.2 Original Sarasota dock showing its likely appearance when Harry Higel bought this strategically located structure that provided access to the town from the Gulf of Mexico

At the turn of the century, Harry Higel launched a political career, starting with election to the town council and culminating in being elected the first mayor of Sarasota when it was incorporated as a city a decade later. While successfully serving three terms as mayor, he devoted his entrepreneurial interests to developing a tourist destination on Siesta Key. At the peak of his many successes, a series of tragedies befell Higel during the last four years of his life, culminating with his brutal and tragic murder while strolling along the gulf shore of Siesta Key on the evening of January 6, 1921. Although his probable assailant was never brought to justice, we were able to shed more light on murder and alleged murderer's motivations from interviews and original documents. During recent decades, this hero of Sarasota and Siesta Key development has become somewhat forgotten. Although this

chapter is about Harry Lee Higel, to fully appreciate his talents and accomplishments in the context of the early challenges faced in gulf coast development, one must also understand his father Frank's incredible life as an adventurer, pioneer, and entrepreneur, as well as his tragic suicide.

Childhood in Alsace Leading to Immigration

Francis "Frank" Higel was an adventuresome, uncommon man from the German-speaking Alsace-Lorraine region, along the border of eastern France and southwestern Germany (also referred to as *Germania Superior*). Frank Higel's rise and fall illustrate his unique characteristics and obsessions, which are not atypical for immigrant entrepreneurs. Much of what we know about him comes from his descendants, especially their many unpublished records of comments about his activities; these were made available to the authors and elaborated during interviews with Higel's descendants. Frank Higel was born on December 20, 1839. As a child he developed a love of chemistry while learning the art and science of winemaking to produce the famous white *Vins d'Alsace.* He did so while working, like all Alsatian children, on harvesting grapes from vines that originated during the Roman occupation in the Octavian Caesar Empire.

The history of Alsace-Lorraine reveals many periods of wars and severe difficulties. Shortly before Higel's birth and continuing during his childhood, a period of rapid population growth and loss of trade opportunities involving Italian ports led to major economic problems, housing shortages, few employment possibilities, and widespread hunger in the region. Consequently, during a period of unrest in eastern France, Higel traveled to Italy, stowed away on a boat to America at the young age of twelve, and landed and settled in Philadelphia sometime in 1852. Short in stature at barely over five feet but skilled in sailing the high seas, he enlisted in the Union Navy for a tour of duty before the Civil War. With his Alsatian background and commitment to self-education through an early version of the Harvard classics, Frank Higel further developed what his descendants refer to as a "scientific mind." Indeed, he showed great talents as a chemist in Philadelphia that led to innovative experiments and eventually a move to Florida.

Philadelphia and Civil War Phase

Frank Higel married 23-year-old Adelaide ("Addie") Kirchoff, from another German immigrant family, in 1863. The young couple were relatively well off and lived in a three-story brownstone house at 1010 North 5th Street where their first child, Frank Jr., was born on December 20, 1863. Frank Higel Sr. was likely away at the time his first son was born because he had re-enlisted in the Union Navy during 1863 in the vital role of quartermaster, fought in the Siege of Vicksburg, and continued his second tour of duty until the end of the Civil War. Returning to Philadelphia, he and Addie enlarged their family with the birth of Harry on New Year's Eve in 1868 and then four more sons born from 1870 to 1877.

Figure 7.3 Francis "Frank" Higel in Philadelphia around 1870

Frank's Invention, Plans, and Adventures in Florida

Frank Higel's promising discovery that led to his journey to Florida's wilderness was a patented invention to produce starch as a source of sugar from the roots of the cassava plant, a tuber similar to a yam and currently a major source of carbohydrates in the tropics. He recognized the potential profits of this process to produce edible sugar and compete with the sugarcane industry. This was prior to the commercial cultivation of sugar beets—now a multi-billion dollar industry in the United States. It was a brilliant idea that offered great promise and deserved the patent Higel obtained. After learning that the cassava plant was being grown successfully in Florida, he obtained initial capitalization during the late 1870s from his wealthy neighbor, Hamilton Disston, a Philadelphia saw manufacturer. Disston (Figure 6.4, page 52) is famous in Florida's history for buying four million acres of state-owned land at twenty-five cents per acre as a speculative venture that saved Florida from early bankruptcy. Disston's land acquisitions included acreage in present-day Venice and Sarasota, as well as tracts in Naples, Ft. Myers, and elsewhere in Florida.

With deserted land on his hands, Hamilton Disston must have been all ears when Frank described his business development plan requiring a mild climate and long growing season—perfect conditions for South Florida.

Figure 7.4 Sarasota dock showing a moored sailing dinghy named *GERTRUDE* that provided "trips to the Gulf beach." Note the crudely repaired sail as well as the horse and buggy being held by the driver while oysters are being purchased. Assuming his height is 5 ½ feet, it may be estimated from measurements of him and the boat that the dinghy was ~15 feet long. (Courtesy of Sarasota County Historical Resources with thanks to Larry Kelleher)

Figure 7.5 The Frank and Addie Higel house in Venice that was built by Frank in about 1881 with the glass windows Addie demanded and enough rooms for their six sons. Note the elevation to protect against water damage and the front porches

He must have also been impressed with Frank's dedication to the project that amounted to an obsession. Frank's next step in 1881 was to leave his wife and six sons in Philadelphia, build a small boat, and sail solo from Atlantic City, New Jersey, more than a thousand miles to Key West, Florida, where he explored agricultural land opportunities. According to his descendants, "Frank built him an over-sized canoe with a sail, named it *Desperate*, and began a six-month journey down the east coast of Florida searching for Key West..." This incredible journey is a testimony to his courage and sailing skills, as well as his obsession. In reality, he probably constructed his boat—a sailing dinghy about eighteen feet long with a beam of nearly five feet—at Hamilton Disston's sawmill in Atlantic City. It obviously required great seagoing skills and fortitude to sail such a small craft to Florida, especially against the 5-mph Gulf Stream current.

As his descendants recorded, "... he wasn't impressed with Key West so continued sailing up the gulf coast of Florida to find an area on his map known as Horse and Chaise." He first landed on Casey Key, where he met a fisherman named Richard

Roberts, a homesteader with 121 acres of land in Horse and Chaise. Frank Higel's inspection of that land revealed an enticing site with a natural windbreak left by Amerindians: "… many shell mounds 150 feet wide and 20 feet high that would keep salt spray off his crops." Consequently, he bought 73 acres from Roberts for $2,500. Higel was further enticed by the resemblance of Horse and Chaise to Venice, Italy, with its "similar climate, same latitude, and various bays…he remembered as a child." His descendants recorded: "He wanted good soil for plantings and a rural life for his six sons… [and] he christened his holdings *Venice*."

Frank Higel grew cassava plants, determining that with the necessary equipment he could build a factory and produce the starch/sugar, a valuable product in the post-slavery era when sugarcane was more expensive. He negotiated further with Hamilton Disston for more investment capital and sent for his family. They arrived in Tampa by train during 1883, traveled by horse and wagon over two days to the Sarasota area. Higel met them there with his sailboat and transported Addie and their six sons to Horse and Chaise. The considerable capacity of *Desperate* is apparent when one takes into account the fact that he brought the entire family on board for the twenty-mile trip to Horse and Chaise. Upon arrival, as the descendants recorded, Addie Higel was "horrified…they had left their nice three-story brick home in Philadelphia for this miserable wilderness!" Obviously and not surprisingly, Addie Higel was shocked by the mosquito-infested, snake-filled wilderness, despite the fact that "Frank built her a house with glass windows," as she had requested—in fact, it was a large and luxurious house for 1880s Florida. Although her descendants emphasize that Addie Higel was a "city girl," she made a

gallant effort. With his wife and six sons, Frank Higel initiated the sugar production process successfully as a pilot project—growing cassava plants and producing starch. He then invited Hamilton Disston to come to Florida with the equipment required for his sugar-producing plant.

Tragedies Follow the Successful Start-up Phase

When Disston arrived in Tampa in December 1885 to equip and fully capitalize the cassava-to-sugar business, a bitterly cold spell greeted him, the "Great Freeze of 1885-86"—the coldest period on record in Florida as of this writing—which devastated almost all of Florida's fragile crops. Consequently, Disston, staying in a hotel with no heat and frozen pipes, decided that the primitive and cold conditions of Florida made the joint venture with Frank undesirable. He withdrew his support and shipped the equipment for the sugar-production plant back to Philadelphia. Financially jolted by two consecutive years of great-freeze winters, Disston began to sell off his Florida land assets after the financial panic of 1893—a major economic depression throughout the United States.

Undaunted by this unexpected downturn, Frank Higel and his family stayed on what his descendants describe as "the 1,000 acres he had acquired" and pursued other ventures in an entrepreneurial spirit. He developed and sold cane syrup and many other products desired by homesteaders, including jellies, canned fruits, lemon juice, and orange wine. As a marketer, Higel was successful in promoting the medicinal value of his products, a common practice in the South at that time, but only locally due to limited boat and railroad transportation options. Higel then helped establish a post office and with the first postmaster, Darwin Curry, the community's name was changed in 1888 from Horse and Chaise to Venice—a name Frank Higel had suggested to the thirty inhabitants who had settled there because of the network of creeks and bayous that reminded him of Venice, Italy.

In 1891, however, because of the harsh lifestyle in Venice, the failed businesses, and the stress of raising her children in the wilderness, Addie Higel took the two youngest sons and returned to Philadelphia, where she moved in with her sister. Frank Higel was apparently furious. He traveled to Philadelphia to meet with his wife on October 22, 1892, demanding that she come back to Florida. When she refused, as his obituary stated, "Frank Higel of Florida shot his wife and committed suicide here today. Higel came to this city a month ago in pursuit of his wife. The latter left him a year ago…" According to the Higel descendants, when "she refused, he then drew a revolver and fired as she darted past him. The 'ball' struck the right side of her neck and she screamed in terror. Higel fired again with better aim and she dropped to the floor with a wound in her rite (*sic*) temple…seemed to be dead… The murderer walked to the rear of this apartment and fired a third shot into his brain, bringing him instant death." Addie Higel, however, was not dead. With medical care, she survived and moved back to Venice with her sons, living there until her death in 1928 at 88 years of age. One can only speculate about why she returned to a place from which she earlier fled. Was it the relationship with the murderous Frank Higel that made her flee originally, and not the conditions in Venice? If only she would have told her tale.

Harry Higel's Career as a Businessman and Real Estate Developer

Before his suicidal death, to facilitate the success of his children, Frank Higel had given each of his sons ten acres of his land in Venice.

Harry Higel, who undoubtedly benefited by witnessing his father's entrepreneurism, recognized greater opportunities as well as a better lifestyle twenty miles north of Venice. Consequently, he sold his ten acres and moved with his older brother, Frank Jr., to what would eventually become the city of Sarasota.

Sarasota has always had a welcoming attitude toward settlers and visitors and tourists alike, and certainly this was the case when Harry Higel arrived. Inspired by his father's entrepreneurism and energy, Harry L. Higel began to develop his career in real estate and related businesses. By 1890 he was well established in Sarasota and, in retrospect, was certainly in the right place at the right time, with many ideas about establishing his career. A prominent acquisition early on was Harry's Higel's purchase of the essential, well-located Sarasota dock, which is now Marina Jack's Pier and Restaurant. Its original appearance, with planks of wood for disembarking to the mainland, is shown on page 54. Despite its crude construction, which would be improved by Higel, the dock was vital; in fact, it was the lifeblood of the early community because it provided access for boats arriving from Tampa with essential goods for the settlers. From that strategically important start, Harry established his reputation and career, particularly his unique and well integrated combination of business interests and civic contributions. After the initial dredging to create the northern part of the Intracoastal Waterway, he became the first agent for the thrice-weekly *Mistletoe* steamer service from Tampa, taking advantage of his dock. Then he began operating his own steamer known as the *Vandalia*. Always at the leading edge, Harry Higel was also Sarasota's first retailer of kerosene and gasoline.

Harry Higel subsequently initiated a career as a real estate developer, taking advantage of an invaluable Philadelphia connection—his father's relationship with Hamilton Disston. Higel'ssuccess in Sarasota land acquisitions and sales is evidenced by his gift in 1892 of choice property at Main and Pineapple Streets, later known as "Five Points," for construction of the Methodist Church. This land was part of Hamilton Disston's extensive properties that he bought at a bargain price, but the price had risen to $14 per acre by the time Higel bought it. He later helped start the local telephone service and constructed a building to house the combination of the post office and telephone exchange.

In 1896, Harry Higel married Gertrude Edmondson, whose grandparents were among the original nonnative settlers of the area. Taking advantage of the Florida Homestead Act of 1862, Thomas Edmondson and Louise Whitaker, daughter of William and Mary Jane, had homesteaded 160 acres in the northwestern region of Clam Island—present-day Siesta Key, which was also known by then as Little Sarasota Key.

Edmondson probably introduced Harry Higel to the barrier island.

Political Career of Harry Higel and Seminal Impact on Sarasota

Harry Higel's political career, which intertwined with his business interests, began formally in 1902 when he was elected to the first town council as the Town of Sarasota became incorporated. Being such a prominent businessman and land developer, it seems likely that he was instrumental in creating the town's motto, "May Sarasota Prosper." In addition, Higel supported efforts to attract tourists with advertisements in northern newspapers, a strategy originally suggested by *Sarasota Times* founder C. V. S. Wilson. An ad in the *Chicago Tribune* during 1910 caught the eye of Bertha Honoré Palmer, which led to a visit by the "society queen" that would have an incredible impact on Sarasota as described by Frank Cassell in his book, *Suncoast Empire*.

Figure 7.6 Methodist Church built in 1892 at Main Street and Pineapple Avenue (now "Five Points") on land donated by Harry Higel. Note the white sandy "streets," bucket of water for horses, and small home of the Browning family to the right of and behind the church. (Courtesy of Sarasota County Historical Resources with thanks to Larry Kelleher).

Harry Higel was elected the town's mayor in 1911, served until 1914 and again in 1916-17, and was also a seven-term councilman. Among his politically linked civic contributions, Higel helped revive the Sarasota Yacht Club, which reopened as the Sarasota Yacht and Automobile Club in January 1913—an innovation as one of the first clubs to combine the yacht and automobile. Reflecting his vision of the automobile's future during the same year that the Ford Model T started rolling off the first assembly line, Higel advocated for better roads between Sarasota, Bee Ridge, and Fruitville, and the additional twenty miles to Venice that facilitated his visits to his mother.

His three terms as mayor were a crucial period, because on January 1, 1914, Sarasota was incorporated as a city. His long service as mayor provides ample evidence of how popular he was with residents. It was stated in the *Sarasota Times* on January 6, 1921, that "there was no limit that he would not go to for a friend." In the same article, Higel was praised for being "especially fond of children and never passed a child unnoticed." Among the 2,149 residents of Sarasota in 1920, he was considered a "standout, one of a handful of progressives who were pushing the community toward its destiny, men who saw in the virginal beauty and temperate climate of the area the surefire ingredients of a resort second to none… He was a dynamo, and he was liked and respected… Higel was as synonymous with Sarasota as the sun and sand." Thus, in his political career, Harry Higel was admired for his professional successes, vision, energy, and personal attributes. Consequently, as a civic leader, he became one of Sarasota's most prominent citizens with a personality that endeared him to most residents. He and Gertrude had three children—a son, Gordon, who served as Sarasota postmaster for thirty years, and two daughters, Louise and Genevieve. Louise left extensive records in the Sarasota County Historical Resources Center.

Early Development of Siesta Key: Entrepreneurship at Its Finest

For many years, Clam Island (now Siesta Key) was considered a tropical paradise with fantastic fishing, but it had few settlers. When its first decade of development began in 1907, culminating in construction of what was known as the Higel Bridge in May 1917, this pristine barrier island had become commonly known as Little Sarasota Key. Other than a few pioneer families, the 1910 census revealed only thirty-one adults; however, there were many transient fishermen on the island. On the other hand, thousands of sand fleas and mosquitoes carrying deadly viruses such as yellow fever, along with a variety of poisonous snakes, inhabited the dense jungle-like vegetation. Yet this beautiful barrier island with excellent fishing attracted local Sarasota residents and visitors alike, including ambitious, visionary entrepreneurs like Harry Higel.

Joining two other investors, Lewis Roberts and E. M. Arbogast, to establish the Siesta Land Company, Harry Higel (arguably the most energetic member of the triumvirate) embarked on developing the Siesta subdivision on Little Sarasota Key. As described in Chapter 5, the trio of leaders platted their land for development of streets and lots for both residential and/or commercial properties (see Figure 5.4, page 41). They called their project "Siesta on the Gulf." Not content with limiting their vision, Higel advocated for having Little Sarasota Key renamed Siesta Key to establish an identity separate from Sarasota and suggest a destination for rest and relaxation. In retrospect, this was tourism marketing genius at its finest, as Higel described the island as a "haven of rest where the waves of the water lap on the long white clean beaches, where gulf breezes blow, purifying and refreshing; where you can bathe, fish, gather oyster clams, scallops and crabs right at your door; where you can lose yourself in the raptor [*sic*] of thought and inspiration of soul, and feel that God really exists in this lovely land of opportunity, freedom and life."

Unfortunately, the timing of the Siesta Land Company was upset by an economic recession that discouraged prospective buyers. Rather than abandoning their goal, the trio developed a more ambitious plan, complete with canals and shoreline improvements. Between 1907 and 1913, dredgers were busy on Siesta Key extending Hansen Bayou through to Sarasota Bay and creating Bay Island. A new and better north entrance to Bayou Louise was also dredged out. Additional land was acquired and the plat was revised in 1913 to feature many more, but narrower, lots. A Chicago-based real estate firm, E. A. Cummings and Company, was engaged and a second development was planned—Ocean Beach Subdivision. As the *Sarasota Times* reported on October 9, 1913, "feverish activity" was underway and "of greatest interest to the young folks is the erection of a large pavilion with a dancing floor in the center, surrounded by a course for roller skating." This was the beginning of the entertainment industry on Siesta Key.

Pinnacle of Harry Higel's Career

Harry Higel advertised the original lots in Siesta Village, finished the dredging work on three canals to provide more boat access to the gulf for the properties he sold, and advocated for both hard surface streets on the island and a bridge connecting the key to the mainland. The Siesta Land Company spent $40,000 on improvements, establishing artesian wells, laying miles of sidewalks, dredging out canals, filling in low places, and building docks and bungalows. Siesta Key's improvements by 1915 were described as

follows: "People living on Siesta can enjoy the island lifestyle while taking advantage of Sarasota... Siesta on the Gulf is the desirable location in Florida for either a winter or summer home. It is located two and one half miles across the beautiful Sarasota Bay from the growing and prosperous city of Sarasota. It takes only 20 minutes to run from Sarasota to Siesta on a ferry. This is a beautiful water trip to make you see the surrounding keys..."

Perhaps the greatest triumphs of Harry Lee Higel on Siesta Key were two accomplishments from 1914 to 1917, which were also harbingers of his eventual tragedies: First, he constructed the magnificent Higelhurst Hotel along Big Sarasota Pass, the important tidal inlet and entrance to Sarasota's harbor. Second, Mayor Higel ensured construction of the first automobile bridge providing essential, direct access between Sarasota and Siesta Key. As with many political/governmental leaders, Harry Higel served his own interests as well as those of his constituency by his innovative civic projects. Streets and bridges, as well as the Siesta post office (see Figure 5.5, page 42) that opened in the summer of 1915, contributed to the popularity and reputation for leadership of Sarasota Mayor Higel. On March 16, 1915, the Sarasota Bay District voted for a $250,000 bond to construct 30-40 miles of hard surface roads and a bridge connecting the mainland with Siesta. As the first north bridge was anxiously awaited, Siesta Key seemed poised for a boom in tourism and settlement.

The Higelhurst Hotel

Named to recognize Harry Higel's German ancestry, "The Higelhurst" was arguably the most magnificent lodging facility on Florida's gulf coast. It was constructed to compete with the Bay Island Hotel, begun in 1912 and its grandeur would compete effectively. By 1914, when the Higelhurst Hotel was planned, hotels with luxurious amenities were beginning to attract wealthy northern tourists

HiGELHURST - HOTEL, SIESTA, FLA. *Heidt Photo*

Burned March. 30, 1917

Figure 7.7 The Higelhurst Hotel as shown from Big Sarasota Pass soon after its construction during 1914 (Courtesy of Sarasota County Historical Resources with thanks to Larry Kelleher).

who stayed for extended periods along the gulf coast of Florida. On September 17, 1914, the *Sarasota Times* reported, "Plans have been drawn by a local architect and the hotel is assured. The hotel will have 20 bedrooms and a large dining room large enough to accommodate 100 people." The estimated cost was $10,000–$15,000. Plans were also developed for several guest bungalows to be built close to the hotel, including streets and sidewalks along which the bungalows would be accessed directly. The construction project proceeded quickly, and the Higelhurst was built in under six months by six carpenters. It opened its doors on March 9, 1915, with more than two hundred people attending the grand opening reception. All of these guests traveled to and from Siesta Key on ferryboats. The *Sarasota Times* reported, "There was plenty for people to do. Dancing was provided, card tables were set up and refreshments were served. The last boat did not leave the Key until nearly midnight and a good time was reported by all."

The Higelhurst was attractive for numerous reasons. It provided hot and cold running water in each room, large baths, gas and electric lights, and telephones within the rooms. And, it was less than fifty yards of pleasant strolling to the gulf—i.e., Sarasota Big Pass. In retrospect, the hotel rooms were a bargain, with daily rates set at $2.50 and higher. And, the nearby fishing was still as superb as it had been for Amerindians, Spanish explorers, and Cubans.

With the Higelhurst Hotel operating as a prime tourist attraction during 1915 and 1916, Harry Higel's career as a real estate developer reached its peak. He and Gertrude Higel must have thoroughly enjoyed their grand opening evening of festivies and becoming the owners and hosts of a truly magnificent lodging facility on their beloved Siesta Key. After all, the Higelhurst adorned the Sarasota overlook of the 160 acres Gertrude's parents had homesteaded in 1881. Its location on Big Pass, looking out to the Gulf of Mexico on the left and Sarasota

Figure 7.8 The Higelhurst Hotel, and the successful result of a typical day of fishing off the shore of Siesta Key (Courtesy of Sarasota County Historical Resources with thanks to Larry Kelleher)

on the right, made the Higelhurst ideally situated, and it was an elegant structure to display at the entrance from the gulf to the growing city of Sarasota. Thus, the operation of the Higelhurst appeared to be a certain success. Harry Higel could look forward to the bridge completion and the sales of more lots by the Siesta Land Company.

The Higel Bridge: Key to Tourism on Siesta Key

The lack of direct access to Siesta Key for automobiles clearly limited its development. Although ferryboats were functional, the era of the automobile had arrived. Undoubtedly, the crucial element in the development of tourism on Siesta Key was a bridge connecting directly with Sarasota and beyond. The visionary Mayor Higel, by advancing his progressive civic agenda while serving his self-interests, ensured that the bridge was planned, funded, and constructed as expeditiously as possible.

It was an extraordinary achievement. The bridge was constructed from the mainland at a narrow and historically important location where Amerindians and Spanish explorers had settled and where the over-water distance is minimal (only about one thousand feet). Thus, Siesta Key's emerging hospitality industry was poised to blossom. The Bay Island Hotel, built in 1912, and other new resorts could attract customers not only for short- and long-term lodging, but also to enjoy delicious meals of fresh fish. In recognition and appreciation of Harry Higel's leadership, a stone marker was placed on the Siesta Key end of the bridge and stood for many years.

A Series of Tragedies Culminating in the Murder of Harry Lee Higel

At the peak of Harry Higel's success as a developer, a series of tragedies struck. Just thirty-three days before the bridge opening,

Figure 7.9 The original bridge from the city of Sarasota to Siesta Key showing the location of the dedication marker to Harry Higel (Courtesy of Sarasota County Historical Resources with thanks to Larry Kelleher)

the Higelhurst caught fire and "flames lit up the skies," as reported by the *Sarasota Times*. Because of its wooden structure and the lack of a fire department, the hotel was a tinderbox and burned to the ground in a matter of hours. Mayor Higel was across the bay in Sarasota when notified. Higel's son Gordon gave this first-hand account of the fire's impact on his father, the day after it occurred: "There in the distance was a dream that he had accomplished and here all of the sudden it's gone. And I can see him now. I looked up at him and tears were just coming down his cheeks. I was nine years old." Although in retrospect arson cannot be excluded, speculation centered on the usual cause of such disasters. The *Sarasota Times* described the event as follows: "How the fire started cannot be learned, but presumably from a fire in the kitchen range. The caretaker, Mrs. Mueller, left the hotel Thursday afternoon and came to Sarasota where she spent the night with friends. It was while she was away that the fire took place."

Ironically, Harry Higel had just signed a contract to add a three-story extension on the rear of the Higelhurst. Not only did these plans fail to materialize, but despite vigorous efforts, the Higels were unable to create another hotel, though he had immediately announced ambitious plans to rebuild. The replacement hotel was described as an edifice "three stories in height and will be constructed entirely of concrete blocks with an asbestos roof to ensure that it will be nearly fireproof." Unfortunately, however, Higel had little insurance, and more tragedies were to strike before another construction project could be initiated. Also, his leadership as mayor of Sarasota was finished after 1917. He had served three terms quite successfully. One must wonder if the abrupt, tragic loss of the Higelhurst drained energy from the previously "indefatigable" developer. Or perhaps he felt sufficient gratification with the Higel Bridge, many miles of superb roads on the key, and numerous properties to sell, potentially providing the capital for Higelhurst II.

Figure 7.10 Harry L. Higel Bridge dedication marker, which has now disappeared (Courtesy of Sarasota County Historical Resources with thanks to Larry Kelleher)

Concurrently, Higel encountered another problem that (according to many) was to prove fatal. Rube Allyn, a longtime resident of Sarasota, emerged as his antagonist. Rube had founded and managed an early newspaper called the *Sarasota Sun* that was unable to compete with the *Sarasota Times*, and his publishing operation collapsed in 1914. It was widely known that Allyn resented and probably hated Mayor Higel. It was also obvious throughout the community that Rube was frequently drunk and generally hot-tempered. The entire Rube Allyn family lived as squatters on one of Harry and Gertrude Higel's Siesta Key properties near the Higel bathhouses adjacent to the Higelhurst Hotel. This practice was not uncommon at the time. Land boundaries were indistinct and property values were not well established. Higel descendants have described how the Allyn children would run around naked and disturb guests. Higel found it necessary to talk with Rube Allyn about these behaviors and at least request, if not demand, change. Although we don't know what words were spoken, one can only imagine Rube's response, given his hot temper. Higel was a soft-spoken, kind man who likely did not threaten the Allyn family, but Allyn may have sensed the risk of eviction.

In any event, in the early morning hours of January 6, 1921, Bert Luzier and his son, Merle, found Harry Higel's unconscious body on Beach Road along the gulf shore as they were driving over to collect shells on the beaches of Siesta Key. The injured man was nearly dead, and the injuries were described in detail: "He was bludgeoned so horribly that he was unrecognizable, his face was a bloody pulp… His head was split open on the right side just above the eye, leaving a two-inch gap in his skull, and the left side was badly crushed, with several bad wounds on the back of his head. He was lying face-down in blood."

Bert and Merle Luzier brought the victim to the local physician, Dr. Joseph Halton. He promptly examined the severely injured man, saw a gold ring engraved with the initials "HH," and determined that his patient was none other than his friend, the former mayor, Harry Higel. Unfortunately, the medical facilities and capabilities in Sarasota were so limited that Dr. Halton felt unable to care for such severe injuries, and thus ordered the patient to be taken to Bradenton. From that stressful twelve-mile drive over poor roads, the goal was to move the critically injured victim by train from Bradenton to a hospital in Tampa. During the trip to Bradenton, Harry Higel died. He was buried in Rosemary Cemetery. The *Sarasota Times* described the burial procession as "one of the largest ever known in Sarasota."

A police investigation ensued. Because Sarasota was part of Manatee County, only a deputy sheriff examined the site of the murder, using bloodhounds and interrogating a few residents. Because only about thirty adults were known to be living on the key and half were women incapable of such a vicious bludgeoning attack, the investigation should have been straightforward. It was known that Higel generally strolled along the beach or one of "his" streets on Siesta Key every evening. His severely injured body was found on Beach Road in the northwest region of the island that he loved so well. Two suspects were identified according to subsequent comments about the police reports of 1921, which have been since discarded. The first was an African-American laborer who may have had conflicts with Harry Higel while digging shells nearby. The wounds on the victim resembled blows from a shovel or perhaps from an ax. On the other hand, he was not known to be on the key that evening. Thus, the police investigation centered on Rube Allyn because of the combination of potential motive and erratic, abusive

behavior. Allyn had quarreled openly with Higel since an election feud in 1915. Suspicion had been raised in 1917 that Rube set fire to the Higelhurst Hotel. Someone reported to the police seeing Allyn in the palmetto shrubs near the murder scene that evening and, in addition, a footprint found in the sand next to Harry's body appeared to match one of Allyn's shoes.

The *Sarasota Times* reported that Allyn was arrested: "It is known that Mr. Allyn arrived in the city last night and that he was carried out to the Siesta Bridge in an auto. Parties taking him to the bridge state that he complained of being in a depressed mood, the depression being so acute, he stated, that he decided to give up his work for a few days and come home." According to Higel descendants, while under arrest and in the crude Sarasota jail, Allyn confessed to the murder but later "took it back." Even though irate citizens had focused their attention on the jailed Rube Allyn as the murderer, law enforcement authorities were not convinced. Sarasota residents demanded justice for their beloved former mayor, who was by then regarded by many as the founder of their city. Soon after the arrest, an angry crowd assembled and someone found a rope nearby at the dock and fashioned a hangman's noose. The deputy sheriff in Sarasota, who reported to the Manatee police and was familiar with the larger, more secure jail there, recognized early the risk of a lynching and quickly moved the prisoner to Bradenton for security and a trial.

After sixty-one days in the Manatee County jail while on trial, Rube Allyn was acquitted of the murder due to the lack of convincing evidence. The investigation did not uncover the murder weapon, or anything beyond circumstantial evidence. Will the axe, shovel, or whatever took the life of Mayor Higel, possibly buried near the current Siesta Key Village, yet surface in an excavation? Subsequently, Allyn and his family left Sarasota and moved to Ruskin, a small town north of Tampa. Justice was never achieved in the Higel murder. Unfortunately, the police records of 1921 are no longer stored by either the city or the county police departments, precluding any attempts to reinvestigate the murder. Although the principle of "innocent until proven guilty" must apply, Rube Allyn is considered to this day as the likely murderer of the founder of Siesta Key tourism.

The brutal murder of Harry Higel brought grief beyond belief to the Higel family. They stayed on Siesta Key, but the atmosphere was forever changed. Later in 1921, the second child of Frank Jr. and his wife, Vilas, was born and named Harry Higel, in remembrance of Sarasota's mayor. Like his grandfather, Harry Higel joined the Navy and served with distinction in World War II. Later, he became a mechanical engineer and contractor/developer, building homes in North Carolina and Florida. As of this writing, Harry Higel is 96 years old and is full of memories, which he shared during interviews for this book. Another descendant, Laura Campbell-Burns, who is the great-great granddaughter of Frank Higel Sr., provided us with the historical details to make this chapter complete, and also shared that the family records show that Rube Allyn owed money to Harry and the debt was coming due.

Figure 7.11 Sarasota's original jail where Rube Allyn was likely incarcerated in January 1921 (Courtesy of Sarasota County Historical Resources with thanks to Larry Kelleher)

More Tragedies: The Post-Mortem Neglect of a Hero and Martyr

Adding insult to the fatal injuries, there have been two more recent injustices affecting the legacy of Harry Higel. First, after the north bridge was rebuilt as a more substantial structure in 1927, the Higel marker disappeared, as did the name "Higel Bridge." Many recent efforts to locate the marker have failed. In addition, no effort has been made to rename the bridge, so it goes simply as the "north bridge." This is in stark contrast to the Stickney Bridge, which connects the southern end of Siesta Key with the mainland. Yet the historic nature and significance of the original bridge in stimulating and supporting tourism cannot be overemphasized. In fact, it apparently was the first over-water connection with a gulf barrier island and assured access and the ultimate success of tourism. The second insult was an effort initiated in the 1980s to change the name of Higel Avenue, an important road connecting Harry and Gertrude Higel's original property to Siesta Key's main thoroughfare, Midnight Pass Road. Without intervention from Harry Higel's descendants, there might be no recognition whatsoever of this early civic leader and founder of Siesta Key tourism. Eleanor Higel Scott, the daughter of Frank Jr. and Vilas, wrote a letter to the editor of the *Sarasota Herald-Tribune* to argue successfully for retaining the name of Higel Avenue.

Authors' Conclusions

Harry Lee Higel, founder of Siesta Key tourism and a heroic leader of Sarasota, led an extraordinary and inspirational life with unmatched entrepreneurism in the early Sarasota community. Just like his father, he was energetic to the point of being obsessed. It is fascinating to recognize that "like father, like son," both lives were full of triumphs and tragedies. Moreover, it is clear that the Higel family has had seminal impact on three popular, very successful gulf coast communities that attract millions of annual tourists: Siesta Key, Sarasota, and Venice. Some people feel that the poor handling of the Harry Higel murder by Manatee County was a key factor in the separation that created Sarasota County. Sarasota citizens were increasingly dissatisfied by the quality of the law enforcement services and the poor quality of the schools and roads in the area. Six months after Harry Higel's death, and three months after Rube Allyn was set free in Bradenton, a referendum passed and Sarasota County was born on July 1, 1921. Consequently, it is reasonable to conclude that Harry Higel played a key role in the creation of the town and later city of Sarasota as a council member and three-term mayor, and that he then stimulated, albeit posthumously, the formation of Sarasota County. Although the impact of Harry Higel was huge, it is sad that he has largely been forgotten by residents of Sarasota and Siesta Key as a leader of their communities. His legacy deserves more recognition.

CHAPTER 8

Bridges Over Troubled Waters

Your time has come to shine… All your dreams are on their way…
See how they shine… Like a bridge over troubled water… I will ease your mind.

—Paul Simon, 1970

Harry L. Higel had decided as mayor of Sarasota that the time had come for Siesta Key to shine on May 3, 1917, when the first north bridge was dedicated and began to accommodate motor vehicle traffic from the Sarasota mainland. All his dreams were on their way. The Higel Bridge was one of the first bridges for two-way automobile traffic from the mainland to a gulf barrier island—decades ahead of others. By way of comparison , the original Goodland Bridge linking the mainland to Marco Island was built in 1938 but that barrier island was not fully developed until the Jolley Bridge was constructed in 1969. Similarly, the ABC bridges of Sanibel Island's Causeway were

Figure 8.1 The North Bridge, also known as the "Sarasota Beach Bridge," during the 1930s (Courtesy of Sarasota County Historical Resources with thanks to Larry Kelleher)

delayed until 1963. In Sarasota County, however, six bridges were built or rebuilt between 1917 and 1929.

In retrospect, it seems incredible that on the eve of the Florida's first statewide land bust and the Great Depression, there would be so many visionary, ambitious leaders advancing their agenda and persuading government officials and taxpayers to support their pet projects. On the other hand, they were figuratively and literally in same boat together. The civic leaders realized that to fulfill the motto "May Sarasota Prosper," connections for automobiles to the barrier islands were needed, instead of the ferryboats being used, while the developers recognized that profiting from real estate sales required bridges for the public to access their building sites. Perhaps neither faction accepted the reality of the impending bust and the "troubled waters" ahead of them.

Bridge Building Boom

As listed below, Sarasota County built six bridges across Sarasota Bay in a twelve-year period. Added to them is the bridge finished in 1922 connecting Anna Maria Island with Bradenton. Thus, a "great circle" was created from the barrier islands to the mainland.

Early Sarasota County Bridge-Building

1917: Higel Bridge – a flat, steel-and-wood structure from the Sarasota mainland (Siesta Drive) to Siesta Key

1923: Blackburn Bridge – a steel swivel or "swing" bridge turned manually with an enormous Allen wrench and still in use to connect the mainland with Casey Key (also called "Treasure Island" at the time)

1926: Ringling Causeway – a flat, filled-wooden-plank roadway bridging Sarasota

Figure 8.2 The beautiful Bay Island Hotel during the 1920s. (Courtesy of Sarasota County Historical Resources with thanks to Larry Kelleher)

Bay and a complex of man-made, dredge-and-fill islands replacing the Coral Isles and known collectively as "Ringling Isles" (now Lido, St. Armands, Otter, and Bird "Keys")

1927: North Bridge II – a concrete bridge replacing the original Higel Bridge

1927: Stickney Bridge – essentially a duplicate of the Blackburn Bridge connecting the Stickney Road extension of Clark Road with South Siesta Key

1929: New Pass Bridge – a long (874 feet), flat concrete bridge with sidewalks that connected the Ringling Isles such as Lido with Longboat Key, featuring sidewalks that were mainly used by fisherman

The Higel Bridge Launches Tourism on Siesta Key

When the first north bridge was built, it was accompanied by extensive dredging organized by the Siesta Land Company to serve Siesta Developments. Bayous and canals were created and named for the children of the Higel and Roberts families

(e.g., Bayou Louise, Nettie, and Hansen). A good network of roads and streets were likewise named for family members or other developers. These names continue today as reminders of the Edmondson, Higel, and Roberts pioneers. Similarly, streets were named later for leaders who followed soon thereafter, such as J. H. Faubel—hence Faubel Street at the continuation of Siesta Drive as Higel Avenue. Mr. Faubel is street-worthy because of his prominent and very effective role as the first manager and later owner of Siesta Key's most enduring resort, the Bay Island Hotel. If nothing else, the Higel Bridge ensured the success of the Bay Island Hotel.

The Bay Island Hotel: Key to Early Tourism

In 1906, E. M. Arbogast visited Sarasota from Marlington, West Virginia, and ferried over to Little Sarasota Key to explore opportunities for real estate development projects. He likely crossed Sarasota Bay on Big Daddy Roberts' boat, stayed at

Figure 8.3 The landscaping of the Bay Island Hotel was lavish and one of its most important attractions. (Courtesy of Sarasota County Historical Resources with thanks to Larry Kelleher)

the Roberts Hotel, and enjoyed Ocean's fabulous meals. He also must have toured the northeast head of the island with Lewis Roberts and Harry Higel. There, he became interested in strategically located properties along the north shore of Big Sarasota Pass. From a tourist standpoint, he saw the attractive possibilities of this particular part of the key, so he purchased a number of acres. These were later surveyed and platted into lots (see Figure 5.4, page 41).

Next, Arbogast planned for a beautiful hotel that would cater to tourists. A total $25,000 was spent to construct and furnish the building and to landscape the surrounding ten acres. To welcome the guests, automobile transport service was provided on the Sarasota side of the bay to meet the hotels' customers arriving on trains and take them to the city pier. A ferry line would then bring the guests in a scenic twenty-minute ride to the hotel. After they were settled, launches and fishing boats were provided at the hotel at all times for use by the guests. The fishing was fantastic and convenient because of the Bay Island Hotel Yacht Basin (see Figure 5.1, page 37).

Figure 8.4 The Bay Island became the "Gateway to Siesta Key" after it was man-made by dredging Bayou Hansen from Little Sarasota Bay to Big Pass. (Courtesy of Sarasota County Historical Resources with thanks to Larry Kelleher)

The hotel grounds were landscaped with shrubbery to blend in with the natural beauty of moss-grown oaks and stately palms on the island. Under Harry Higel's leadership, a 35-foot canal was cut across the key, creating Bay Island— the "gateway" to Siesta Key. Arbogast also built several cottages to be used in connection with the hotel. The December 14, 1911, issue of the *Sarasota Times* gave a description of the new hotel. "The hotel is three stories and has 65 rooms. It has a basement underneath, with cement floors, has a large bathroom for the gentlemen's use, and storage room for baggage. The first floor holds the offices and the dining room. Private bathrooms are provided on the second floor and every room provides views of the Bay and Gulf." The water for the hotel was supplied by a 400-foot-deep artesian well. Two large 30-horsepower engines provided power for operating the electric light plant, water works, and laundry. A 5,000-gallon tank supplied water for the laundry. An acetylene gas plant was installed so that every room in the hotel had gas lights, which were later transformed into electric fixtures.

Opening on January 25, 1912, with rates beginning at $2.50 a day, the Bay Island Hotel was known as "the most delightfully situated residential hotel in Sarasota." In the tradition of the Roberts Hotel, the menu featured Florida cuisine and consisted of Sarasota Bay oysters, stone crabs, clams, fish, and fruits and vegetables. It had a great start for the first five years, and its business expanded when the bridge to Siesta Key opened in 1917, providing a link to the mainland.

Despite the "troubled waters" of the Florida land bust, Great Depression, and subsequent calamities, the Bay Island Hotel thrived for forty years. Why was this hotel so successful from 1912 to 1952 when many others were failing? Credit must first be given to J. H. Faubel's management. He came from Pittsburgh, Pennsylvania, and had a great feel for the early hospitality business and the importance of repeat customers. Faubel also took advantage of great timing: getting established before the Higel Bridge opened, accelerating business thereafter, and profiting from the Roaring '20s with a nearby gambling casino and "speakeasy." The hotel's marketing of a "home-hotel" was also superb. The Bay Island Hotel's attractive brochure touted its many virtues and amenities, emphasizing that "None of the pleasant home comfort has been sacrificed for the more modernistic decorations while at the same time every modern facility has been preserved." Every room has "homey comfort so that the full rays of the warm winter sun can enter."

The Ringling Causeway Leads to a "Ghost Hotel"

The most ambitious land/water development plan requiring bridges linked to dredge-and-fill efforts was led by John Ringling in partnership with Owen Burns. Their ambition was far beyond a local vision. John Ringling was an affluent world traveler always looking for new circus acts. Much has been written about this larger-than-life businessman/"Circus King" and needs no repetition here. He arrived to winter in Sarasota with his first wife, Mable, during 1909, the year before Bertha Palmer's pivotal visit. In summary, after amassing a fortune in circus entertainment, Florida land speculation, railroads, ranches, and the growing oil industry, John decided to transform Sarasota County's northern barrier islands and island fragments into a paradise. The master plan included a luxury Ritz Carlton Hotel on Longboat Key that would rival Flagler's three hotels in St. Augustine. The 1883 U.S. Coast and Geodetic Survey shows that most of the land was fragmented immediately south of Longboat Key—that is, between Longboat Key and Siesta Key (see Figure 18.4, page 190). Being a big thinker who was familiar with European coastal developments that stood the test of time, Ringling decided to aggregate the isles by Herculean dredge-and-fill efforts, create new "keys," and connect them to the Sarasota mainland with "his" causeway. Thus, Bird Key, Lido Key, and St. Armands Circle can be considered creations of Burns and Ringling rather than being Mother Nature's products from sea and land interactions.

The vision of John Ringling was designed to draw the world's attention. It was to have been the crown jewel of Sarasota's Roaring '20s real estate development. Visionary developers like John Ringling and his business associate, Owen Burns (vice president and secretary of Ringling Estates), dreamed of transforming Sarasota into the Riviera of the United States. With wide boulevards, pink sidewalks, palm trees, and a hotel on south Longboat Key, the lovely isles would draw the world's rich and famous to visit and build fabulous Mediterranean Revival homes. St. Armands was planned to offer upscale shops and restaurants, just as it does today. Four dredges were put into service with four hundred men working on the Ritz Carlton Hotel project and another four hundred working on streets, sidewalks, wells, palm trees, the golf course, the Ringling Bridge, and infrastructure improvement. Bunkhouses were built that could house five hundred of the workers, with a nearby dining hall that offered board for $7.50 a week. The payroll was a staggering sum of $10,000 a week for the project. The local economy was the great beneficiary.

The Burns and Ringling plan on the keys completely transformed the area with

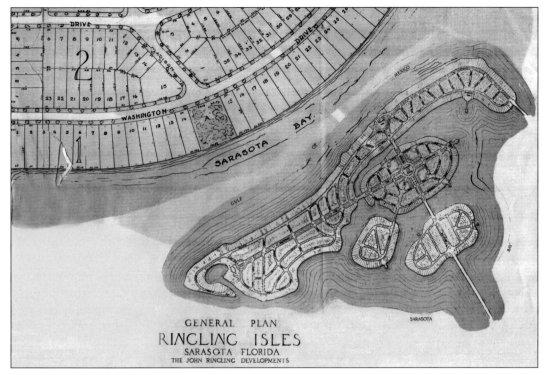

Figure 8.5 The Ringling Isles created by the dredge-and-fill operations of Owen Burns during the 1920s. By aggregating several spits of sand that John Ringling wanted for development projects and a connection to Longboat Key, Burns constructed St. Armands and Lido Keys

the aggregations that artificially created the "Ringling Isles" through extensive dredge-and-fill operations. As an article in *A Historical Geography of Southwest Florida Waterways* observed, these keys did not even exist a century ago. These observations are particularly relevant today as Lido Key attempts to salvage its beach. Knowledge of history helps one understand why Lido Key beaches lack resiliency.

The massive project appeared to be moving ahead successfully during the many months of the initial land and Gulf engineering efforts. The *Sarasota Herald* published comprehensive accounts of the progress and what it would mean for Sarasota. One headline stated, "Millions And Magic Transforming Keys Into Paradise." Concurrently, the Chamber of Commerce was promising "Sarasota's Growth Cannot Be Stopped," as money

from investors flowed in. While Burns was building the Ringling Bridge to the artificial keys, he wrote to Ringling, "The work on the causeway is proceeding well. I drove out about 700 feet in the Lincoln car yesterday, and I want to say to that it is a beautiful job." Advertisements assured that "when Owen Burns tells John Ringling his bridge is completed, prices will soar." Soon thereafter, John and Mable Ringling drove across the bridge to Ringling Isles in his Rolls Royce. The *Herald's* headline was, "Causeway Is Proof of John Ringling's Courage."

All of this proved too good to be true—at least in the short term. The vagaries of Florida weather and its impact on business spelled doom for the Ringling/Burns venture. Soon after the bathing pavilion opened, the "Great Hurricane of 1926" tore through Miami and crushed Florida's already struggling

Figure 8.6 The original Stickney Bridge in approximately 1930. It was a one-lane steel swivel or "swing" bridge turned manually to allow boat traffic through upon request. (Courtesy of Sarasota County Historical Resources with thanks to Larry Kelleher)

real estate market. Construction came to a virtual standstill, both on the Ringling Isles and the mainland. With the Great Depression and World War II following, the first Ritz Carlton became a "ghost hotel" until it was demolished in 1964. The Ringling Causeway became a fishing bridge on which the sidewalks were more important than the driving lanes. A fisherman could catch one hundred fish in a half day there. Nevertheless, the Ringling vision was realized after tourism boomed four decades later. No longer do "troubled waters" prevail over and beyond the Ringling Causeway.

The Stickney Bridge Stimulates Development of South Siesta Key

During 1927 the Higel Bridge was replaced by a better structure and another bridge opened near the southern tip of the Siesta Key as a one-lane swivel bridge. This facilitated access for the growing population south of the city of Sarasota. It also contributed to attracting not only tourists, but local residents as well. It became known as the "Stickney Bridge" because it recognized and still does a beloved character known as "Uncle Ben Stickney." Although some refer to the bridge now as the "South Bridge," it deserves to be known as the "Stickney Bridge," just as the "North Bridge" should be named the "Higel Bridge."

Reviewing the life and importance of Benjamin Stickney on Siesta Key helps understand why the bridge and the south access road to the key were named for him. In fact, during the early twentieth century, before bridges connected the keys to the mainland, a favorite place to have a picnic was at "Uncle Ben Stickney's." His homestead gained a reputation for hospitality far beyond Sarasota's borders, attracting residents and tourists that led to construction of Siesta Key's second bridge.

Benjamin Stickney was born in St. Louis in 1842 and eventually followed family tradition, working in the early hospitality industry. During 1894 he was the proprietor of Sarasota's famous DeSoto Hotel on Main Street—the area's first luxury hotel. After retiring, Stickney built his homestead on Little Sarasota Key under large spreading live oaks draped in Spanish moss like the ones that are prominent today in some Siesta Key neighborhoods. When Stickney died in February 1912, the *Sarasota Times* mourned the community's loss on the front page. The Baptist Church held the funeral service because it was the only church large enough to hold all the attendees. The *Sarasota Times'* tribute to "Uncle Ben" concluded, "… the murmuring waves along his shore breathe a requiem for the passing away of one who was loved and honored."

A variety of press reports over the years comment on the warmth and breadth of Stickney's hospitality. In the tradition of Greek

Figure 8.7 The Stickney Bridge after it was expanded to two lanes during the Beach Cottage Era. Note Mr. CB's north of Old Stickney Road and a trailer park where the Anchorage Condominiums are now located at 6415 Midnight Pass Road. (Courtesy of Sarasota County Historical Resources with thanks to Larry Kelleher)

hospitality, he welcomed many travelers stranded on the key during bad weather. Sitting in front of a blazing fire, the visitors would listen to Uncle Ben's stories as he prepared the evening meal. Although sometimes called the "Hermit of the Key," Stickney was a lovable character, everyone's friend, a nature lover, and the host of many picnics. Typical picnics, as reported in the *Sarasota Times*, included shell-gathering, walks along the deserted gulf shore, and exploration of the largely uninhabited key. Then, a meal would be served from large baskets. The food would be spread out on tables built by Stickney. These picnics and parties in a place of beauty and charm were accessible only by boat.

Modern Bridges Serve Automobiles and Boats, But Troubled Waters Remain

The one-lane swivel or swing bridge providing access to south Siesta Key was functional until more automobiles starting coming from either direction. It thus became obvious that two lanes were needed, so an expansion occurred after World War II. Two decades later, both the Higel and Stickney bridges were replaced by modern drawbridges. Clearly, the replacement bridges have served Siesta Key well. Although motorists can become frustrated when the center section is raised to allow boats to pass, this feature has been considered essential to accommodate the sailboats traversing the Intracoastal Waterway. On the other hand, during the long spring break period, which now extends from mid-February to mid-April, the backup of automobile and truck traffic has become more than annoying. Most Siesta Key visitors and residents consider the situation intolerable. Perhaps reducing the drawbridge openings will help. At the same time, however, the number of vehicles is increasing and the number of associated injuries has also been intolerable. Thus, the "troubled waters" have reappeared and will need attention.

A Third Siesta Key Bridge in the Future?

Few people realize that a third bridge to Siesta Key has been planned in the past and may need to be considered in the future. Although the North Bridge suffices for most of the year, it is bringing a volume of traffic that overwhelms Siesta Drive and Higel Avenue. As described in Chapter 19, there have been numerous automobile accidents at the curve just before Faubel Street, including fatalities.

Yet the issues involving the North Bridge pale in comparison to the Stickney Bridge. During the winter/spring season, the traffic is bumper-to-bumper for much of the day and accidents are not uncommon. Worse still, the vehicular density is heavy enough at times that traffic is backed up from Midnight Pass Road to Tamiami Trail and even beyond. When this happens, cars coming from the east cannot even cross Tamiami Trail, nor can north- and south-bound traffic turn towards the Stickney Bridge.

Consequently, if Benderson's "Siesta Promenade" (a massive mixed-use project with condominiums, hotel rooms, and commercial space) is approved and built at the Tamiami/Stickney intersection, then Stickney Bridge usage will undoubtedly reach the critical stage (which many feel has already arrived). Irrespective of these potential developments, it is likely that a third bridge may have to be reconsidered. As reported in the *Pelican Press* as long ago as September 13, 1973, the third bridge would need to be constructed about one mile north of the Stickney Bridge in the mid-key area. More specifically, the location preferred for a 1981-85 project would have brought the bridge over to Siesta Key from the southern end of the Phillippi Estate Park to the bayside at approximately the area across the street from the Gulf and Bay Club (just south of Riegel's Landing). This location would provide both advantages and disadvantages. Nevertheless, it seems virtually certain that a third bridge will come under review in the foreseeable future. Whether or not it is built will depend on the outcome of planning efforts and resolution of the current "troubled waters."

CHAPTER 9

An "Interlude" Sets the Stage for Siesta Key Development

It's almost as if Siesta Key went to sleep after 1930 and then woke up in the 1950s.
—Jeff LaHurd

The mid-1920s to the late 1950s seemed relatively stagnant on Siesta Key, but it was an important period that we call the "Interlude." These three decades set the stage for the key's subsequent development as a tourist destination. The period began with what may be considered the "Fishing Shack Era," when a population of about one

Figure 9.1 Fishing shack at least 70 years old on Midnight Pass Road on the bay side of south Siesta Key (Photograph taken by Larry Krambeer and provided thanks to Paula Krambeer)

Figure 9.2 Aerial view of the north end of Crescent Beach during the 1930s showing the closely spaced groins, some of which are partially submerged. Note the sediment reaching Siesta Key from the north via Big Sarasota Pass. Only one of these groins remains, although there were three in 2010. (Courtesy of Sarasota County Historical Resources with thanks to Larry Kelleher)

hundred hardy residents lived primarily in wood-framed fishing shacks. These simple homes fit in well with the status and mood of the country during the Great Depression. By 1945 only three hundred people were listed as permanent residents on Siesta Key, most of whom were hard-working fishermen. The 1942 U.S. Coast and Geodetic Survey, shown on color page 5, reveals that there were 74 houses and/or garages on Bay Island, 125 from Hansen Bayou to the Mira Mar section of Siesta/Crescent Beach, 122 on or near what would become the public beach, 32 in the mid-key area (between Stickney and the fork at Beach Road-Midnight Pass), and 93 located south of Stickney Road.

A variety of types of lodging options developed as Siesta Key transitioned from a predominance of fishing shacks to the "Beach Cottage Era." Beaches were used and abused

(see Figure 5.7, page 43) by the generally small population of beachgoers. The notion of becoming "America's Best Beach" could not have been on anyone's mind as numerous storms assaulted Siesta/Crescent Beach and necessitated installation of several groins. Here are the developments on the key from the Roaring '20s into the 1950s.

Sequence of Important Developments during the "Interlude"

1. The Out-of-Door School established for avant-garde learning

2. Entertainment thrives despite Prohibition and Great Depression

3. Modern luxurious resorts develop early in the evolution of Florida tourism

4. Baseball stars come to Sarasota and Siesta Key thanks to John Ringling

5. Artists and writers arrive and attract others, including many celebrities

6. Amenities and services develop to support an island-only lifestyle

7. Dredging projects create unique neighborhoods such as Palm Island

8. Residential clubs attract elite visitors (Gulf & Bay Club and Sanderling Club)

9. Air conditioning arrives as a game changer

The Out-of-Door School

Perhaps the most avant-garde institution in Siesta Key history, and which became internationally famous, is the Out-of-Door School (ODS), which was renamed the Out-of-Door Academy in 1977. Occupying a twenty-acre site on Siesta Key's drumstick head alongside Big Sarasota Pass, the school's learning and recreational activities were held in the sun and fresh air, including swimming, sailing, horseback riding, and other sports. When rainy days arrived, small wooden cabins were used for classrooms. These cabins, with screens and shutters to keep out the dense, swarming insects, doubled as dormitories for boarding students. ODS was established by Fanneal Harrison in 1924 with the assistance of Catherine Gavin. Both women had already dedicated their lives to the welfare of children. At a period characterized by rigid, rigorous, segregated schools, their plan was to offer a "place where physical, mental and spiritual development of the child may be normal and joyous." Or, as a poem by one of its students stated, "Going to school under blue skies, makes a child healthy, happy and wise."

During World War I in Europe, where many children were homeless, hungry, and suffering from illnesses, Ms. Harrison discovered the Decroly method of teaching

Figure 9.3 Out-of-Door School classes outside one of the original cabins (Courtesy of Sarasota County Historical Resources with thanks to Larry Kelleher)

Figure 9.4 Young children "skin swimming" at the beach used by the Out-of-Door School (Courtesy of Sarasota County Historical Resources with thanks to Larry Kelleher)

and the importance of each child's primary focus on biosocial development—that is, the integration of biological elements (e.g., genetic traits), psychological status (e.g., personality), and social factors (e.g., cultural, behavioral, and socioeconomic aspects). Developed by Dr. Ovide Decroly, a Belgian physician, psychologist, and educator, the method proposed "helping children to find out what they themselves want to know." Harrison and Gavin opened the school with ten students in three open-air buildings situated on three acres of the very quiet Siesta Key, where the nudity of children on the beaches was not an issue. Recollections of some early students explain why the ODS experience was memorable; for instance, students learning French developed a conversational competence around a "French table" in the dining hall. Children cared for a variety of animals on campus, including chickens,

goats, ducks, peacocks, parrots, snakes, and a monkey. Students were also expected to help create and maintain their personal learning environment. Carpentry classes for girls and boys produced easels, chairs, tables and a stage for the frequent pageants. Distinguished visitors such as Thomas Edison visited the school regularly during those early years. On a visit to Thomas Edison's laboratory in Ft. Myers, the students took a cake to celebrate Edison's birthday with him. Exposure to geniuses like Mr. Edison must have inspired many students.

During the 1930s, the shortage of funds led to occasional rumors that the school would close. When Harrison retired in 1939, new leaders took over and maintained the same philosophy. The school survived its financial crisis, outlived various changes in ownership, and thrives today as the Out-of-Door Academy, a non-profit organization.

Figure 9.5 Thomas A. Edison teaching and inspiring Out-of-Door School students. (Courtesy of Sarasota County Historical Resources with thanks to Larry Kelleher)

Entertainment Thrives Despite Prohibition and Depression

With the North Bridge providing most of the access to Siesta Key from the 1920s to the 1940s, entertainment for Sarasotans and visitors developed primarily within the drumstick head of the island. Cars drove directly to Siesta/Crescent Beach and parked on the sand. Prior to the bathhouse development, changing into a swimsuit was done primarily in cars. A day on the beach could be followed by a night of drinking, dancing, and gambling. The Volstead Act, which established Prohibition from 1920 to 1933, did not threaten drinking on Siesta Key because Sarasota County police rarely patrolled there. If they did come over the North Bridge in a police car, a surveillance system involving the bridge operator provided alerts to the proprietors. Consequently, there was rarely any risk to using docking sites along Big Sarasota Pass for booze deliveries, to stills used in

moonshine manufacturing, or to speakeasy bars. Brothels operating along Higel Avenue were also tolerated.

Siesta Key's original master of hospitality, Captain Lewis Roberts, developed one of the most popular entertainment sites at the intersection of Beach Road and the important street he named for his wife, Ocean Boulevard (see page 40). The beach casino drew crowds ten times Siesta Key's population. Always a business-minded innovator, Big Daddy Roberts originally used the site as a yacht club, and during the "Spanish craze" he renovated with Spanish-style stucco in 1922 and produced something resembling the Mission Revival theme. Nothing resembling missionary activity, however, went on in the Roberts Casino, with its large dance floor, bar, patio, and docking facilities for boats. Reports indicate that as many as three thousand patrons at a time found their favorite entertainments there during the late '20s boom period. Big Daddy's "Big Casino" continued beyond his death in 1935 and was not demolished until 1957.

A competitor soon appeared on Siesta Key. In 1925 Andrew McAnsh, a Scottish immigrant, built the Mira Mar "Little Casino" on the gulf front. It was a beautiful Spanish-style building with an elegant interior. McAnsh also applied the name Mira Mar Beach to distinguish the section of Crescent Beach where his club was located. The name, which means "view of the sea," was a favorite of his and was brought over from the mainland where McAnsh had already constructed the Mira Mar Apartments, Mira Mar Hotel, and Mira Mar Auditorium. His "Little Casino" was very popular and remained so for many decades, but it was demolished in 1982.

Modern Luxurious Resorts Develop and Connect with Nature

Another innovative development in 1937 that set the tone for modern tourism on Siesta Key was a practically perfect resort on the north shore—the famous Whispering Sands. Its waterfront location, beautiful landscaping, and extensive use of native materials demonstrated its deep connection to the outdoors. Strategically located on forty-five acres in a neighborhood now known as Sandy Hook, the vision for its development came from an avant-garde architect named Mary Rockwell Hook, who learned her skills while attending the École des Beaux-Arts in Paris. In her autobiography she wrote, "Whispering Sands tried hard to be a little tropical paradise. Its wide beach of fine white sand was a joy to walk or drive on. The entrance road followed the bayou through the palm trees. One entered through a citrus garden and the front door opened into a tropical courtyard." She envisioned the site as a haven for painters, writers, and other creative people.

Reflecting her ambition to achieve more architectural impact, Mary Hook sold the acreage on Siesta Key occupied by the Whispering Sands Inn in 1945 and focused on the development of Sandy Hook, immediately to the south. Sandy Hook became the development where exciting, modern architectural design was

Figure 9.6 Mira Mar Casino with car driving by during the 1930s. Note the wooden seawall and numerous tire tracks showing that Crescent Beach was being used regularly for vehicular traffic. (Courtesy of Sarasota County Historical Resources with thanks to Larry Kelleher)

first accomplished on the key. The first two homes were designed by Hook in the early 1950s and the third by Paul Rudolph, whose career later brought him international acclaim as he inspired other architects. Similar to many of the early upscale accommodations on the key, the post-World War II homes at Sandy Hook were designed to blend with and embellish their surroundings, applying a distinctly modern feel. Many architects of the Sarasota School of Architecture, including Ralph Twitchell, Victor Lundy, Tim Seibert, Jim Holliday, Mark Hampton, Bill Rupp, and Frank Folsom Smith, have been recognized for their important contributions to developing Sandy Hook—still a place today where innovative architectural design complements the magnificent natural setting.

Baseball Comes to Sarasota and Siesta Key

Readers may wonder why the arrival of Major League Baseball (MLB) teams could be regarded as an innovative phenomenon during the "Interlude" on Siesta Key. The novelty was that their national celebrities, the MLB stars, became prominent personalities while mingling with the local population of residents and tourists. This was very much in contrast to the affluent celebrities, such as the "Chicago crowd" that followed Bertha Palmer, who were not inclined to mix and mingle with the common folk, nor were they as popular and appreciated as MLB players. Baseball was not just the national pastime, it was an obsession, and many adults and children were baseball fanatics. From May 15 to July 17, 1941, for instance, the majority of Americans followed daily the feats of Joe Dimaggio as the "Yankee Clipper" hit safely in fifty-six straight games. During this interval, many office workers would take a very long lunch hour break and listen to a radio broadcast of Yankee baseball in a public setting; even some factories would broadcast

the games until "Joltin' Joe" got his first hit. Later that season, Ted Williams attracted almost equal attention as he strived to bat over .400—the last hitter to accomplish that rare distinction. Except for the World War II years, the nation's attention for seven months each year was riveted on baseball.

The six to eight weeks that MLB teams devote to spring training became especially important for the entire state of Florida when the popularity of the sport soared, thanks to Babe Ruth who, during his peak years was the most famous person in the United States. In February 1924 the New York Giants owner/manager John McGraw was persuaded by John Ringling to bring baseball—his team—to Sarasota. For Ringling, the publicity enhanced the value of the developing Ringling Isles and Causeway, or so he thought. McGraw, no doubt under the influence of Ringling, went into the real estate business, but generated more lawsuits than money as the bust supervened. Consequently, he took the Giants elsewhere in 1927.

Despite losing the New York Giants, the thrill of baseball games and mingling with the big league celebrities was already deeply rooted in the community. Just as in the modern era, baseball stars practiced in the mornings, played nine-inning games in the early to mid-afternoons, and then were free to party. And throughout the "Interlude," party they did on Siesta Key at the gambling casinos and at the many other attractions. The Boston Red Sox came in 1933, with stars like Ted Williams, who became an avid sport fisherman and ambassador for Florida fishing. During the "Interlude" many of the Red Sox stars stayed on Siesta Key, and the mix and mingle behavior of baseball players continued after 1958 when the Red Sox left for Ft. Myers because a succession of other teams made Sarasota their training site. Most recently with the Baltimore Orioles training at Ed Smith Stadium, their star third baseman, Manny Machado, could be seen almost daily socializing on Crescent Beach or around the Coquille townhouses where he stayed.

Artists, Writers, and Other Celebrities Arrive

Visiting or residing celebrities established an eclectic culture on Siesta Key. The nation's famous First Lady, Eleanor Roosevelt, was attracted to the key in November 1938 because her uncle, David Gray, lived at 3719 White Lane. After she arrived, however, the Out-of-Door School captured her attention. She respected innovations, loved children, and the students loved her. After World War II, Siesta Key progressed into an eclectic phase, with avant-garde people distinguishing themselves and establishing a new culture by their work and play. It has been estimated that during the 1950s, as many as seventy-five such celebrities lived or worked on Siesta Key, some deserving special attention.

Syd Solomon came to Sarasota in 1946 after distinguished service in the Army. The renowned abstract expressionist artist ultimately built his home/studio on Siesta Key. Syd's striking creations exemplify his fascination with the intersections of land, sea, and sky environments (more on him in Chapter 16). The great portrait artist Jerry Farnsworth established his School of Art in 1950 on Siesta Key's Higel Avenue, attracting fifty talented pupils. Another artist-innovator residing on Siesta Key during the period was Thornton Utz, who became famous for his unique magazine covers, including forty-five for the *Saturday Evening Post*. He cleverly portrayed the post-World War II American style, depicting suburban families living their everyday lives, rivaling Norman Rockwell. Last but not least, Gil Elvgren, who was considered the best pin-up artist the world has ever known, moved to Siesta Key in 1956, where he worked in a small studio above his garage at 7501 Midnight Pass Road and produced nationally acclaimed oil-on-canvas paintings.

Two superstar writers who lived on Siesta Key during the "Interlude," MacKinlay Kantor and John MacDonald, earned reputations for novels that became popular movies. After his career was well established, Kantor moved to Siesta Key and lived at 4105 Shell Road. Prior to arriving on the key, he published the majority of his thirty novels, his favorite topic being the Civil War. *Andersonville* won the 1956 Pulitzer Prize and was inspired by his experience in World War II as a correspondent who entered the Buchenwald concentration camps in April 1945 with the liberating troops. Several of his novels were made into movies, including a commissioned novel for Samuel Goldwyn Mayer published as *Glory for Me*. MGM Studios adapted the story into a movie that won seven Academy Awards under the title *The Best Years of our Lives*.

John MacDonald, who lived and worked on Point Crisp Road for twenty years, was the most prolific writer on Siesta Key if not the United States from the 1950s through the 1970s. In contrast to MacKinlay Kantor, MacDonald established his career after he moved to the still-pristine tropical island in 1951. Composing on his IBM typewriter and typing up to fourteen hours a day, seven days each week, he published seventy-five novels and over five hundred short stories—a prodigious output for a solo writer/typist. MacDonald summed up his passion for writing fiction as follows: "My purpose is to entertain myself first and the other people secondly." His writing was in fact the joy of his life as well as the basis of his worldwide recognition. In 1955, 1964, 1972, and 1980 he won, respectively, the Ben Franklin Award for the best American short story, the *Grand Prix de Litterature Policière* for the French edition of *A Key to the Suite,* the

Figure 9.7 John D. MacDonald taking a break from typing a novel on his IBM typewriter

Mystery Writers of America's Grand Master Award and the American Book Award for his mystery *The Green Ripper.*

The *New York Times Book Review* in 1985 stated that "Mr. MacDonald's books are always about boats, and hot sun, and the putative glamour of resort life, as much as they are about the persistence of evil and the near-randomness of honesty"—themes obviously inspired by his Siesta Key lifestyle. At the twilight of his career during the late 1970s, MacDonald observed the radical changes, including high-rise condominiums, affecting Siesta Key's landscape. This led to his 1977 *New York Times* bestseller *Condominium,* written from his stunning new home designed by Tim Seibert along Big Sarasota Pass. The dramatic novel featured a fictional Siesta Key and its destruction by hurricane

forces. It is a must-read novel for Siesta Key residents.

Amenities and Essential Services Develop

When only a few hundred people lived on Siesta Key during the 1940s, the kinds of stores and support services now taken for granted were nonexistent. There were no physicians, clinics, hospitals, or pharmacies available, and the ambulance services were inadequate. Food shopping was difficult except for fish, with early residents remembering fondly the Fish Market with its smoker. It was well located near the Higel-Roberts intersection and supplied healthy, delicious fish. Finding equivalent fresh fruits and vegetables regularly on the key was nearly impossible, but gardens were common.

To address the need for a reliable food supply, George Connelly opened Crescent Beach Grocery and Sundries in 1952. Connelly had a limited supply of meats, canned goods, breads, and produce, but the number of customers was small then also. Connelly needed to attract more customers, so he changed the named to the Beach Shop and broadened his merchandise to provide one-stop shopping. After the "Interlude," when ownership changed hands, the store was renamed Crescent Market, and in 2003 it became the Crescent Beach Grocery as George's daughter, Nancy, and her husband, Bill Singleton, renovated the old store and opened a modern grocery, now approaching its seventieth year of continuous operation. Neither Nancy Connelly nor Bill Singleton had careers that directed them to enter the grocery business. She holds a Ph.D. in cultural anthropology and he had a graduate degree in archaeology. After Nancy Connelly's tenure as a museum director and then the executive director of a national organization that has a museum, and Bill Singleton had served in various positions as a university director of technology services, they left those jobs and bought back the market. Soon thereafter, their partnership restored the grocery store to become a great asset again on the key. Now, it is particularly well known not only for groceries and exotic and gourmet foods, but also for providing good value, personal service, and a warm, friendly environment.

The lack of health care on Siesta Key from the pioneer era to the Interlude was a glaring deficiency, especially as the resident population aged with arrival of so many retirees. John Davidson solved that problem.

New Tabby Smoker for Mullet - Siesta Fish Market, 1917

Figure 9.8 The Siesta Key Fish Market's mullet smoker in 1917. Mullet was the most important commercial fish caught by nets from Sarasota Bay and was originally preserved by salting and then icing, but smoked mullet were tastier and a favorite with the early settlers of Siesta Key. The economic importance of mullet was such that when Sarasota incorporated as a town in 1902, its seal consisted of a mullet with a rising sun over palmettos with shells at the base. (Courtesy of Sarasota County Historical Resources with thanks to Larry Kelleher)

Figure 9.9 George Connelly selling food, cigarettes, and beach items such as sunglasses during the 1950s at the Beach Shop. (Courtesy of Nancy Connelly)

In 1955, as a newly graduated Illinois pharmacist, Davidson came to Florida on vacation and fell in love with the Sarasota County area. He became a sales representative for a drug distributor in 1956 and was assigned to Sarasota. Davidson pursued his dream, looking for a site for his own store, and opened Siesta Key's first drugstore in 1958 at Ocean and Canal. He vividly remembers sweeping the sidewalk in front of his business every morning and closing every evening at 9 P.M. Davidson not only recognized the key's need for a drugstore but also the importance of attracting a physician, so he recruited the vacationing Dr. Freeman Epps to move his practice from Atlanta to Sarasota County. Davidson and Epps had mutually beneficial business relationships that also benefitted

their mutual patients. Later, this partnership would build the shopping center that is so prominent in the Siesta Key Village today and features Davidson Drugs at center stage.

One other amenity/service that the island surely needed was garbage and trash removal. From the beginning of Amerindian habitation until well into the Interlude, garbage and trash were dumped at selected sites. The many prehistoric shell middens—at least eleven—on Siesta Key, give testimony to this practice. For most of Siesta Key's history, the "town dump" was at 5394 Midnight Pass Road. Residents and visitors would drive, walk, or bike there with bags of their garbage and throw them on the pile. Residents we interviewed describe a horrible, often unbearable stench around the dump,

Figure 9.10 Nancy Connelly and her husband, Bill Singleton, working at Crescent Beach Grocery, which they renovated and upgraded to become a great asset for Siesta Key

and there must have been thousands of flies also. This was another problem that had to be solved to prepare for the tourism boom. Fortunately, near the end of the Interlude, a waste management program began to serve Siesta Key and keeps very busy to this day. Interestingly, a Catholic church, St. Michael the Archangel, with a parish hall and large parking lots, was constructed on the dumpsite in 1958. Its successful development as a busy parish has helped everyone forget about the previous eyesore and stench.

Dredging Projects Create Unique Neighborhoods

An aerial photograph of Siesta Key after 1951 reveals an unnatural feature not present prior to the Interlude. In fact, the landscape was changed radically by the U.S. Army Corps of Engineers to create a ten-mile-long waterway system. Extensive dredge-and-fill activities led to the "Grand Canal" and a distinctive, heart-shaped extension encircling what became known as Palm Island, as shown on page 91. This neighborhood has a mixture of retirees, families, and part-time residents living in about 150 houses. It is not a deed-restricted community but does include the

Palm Island Neighborhood Association, formed in 1951. According to the comments of residents, Frank Archibald, the original planner of the community, made the heart shape of the waterway for his wife—the shape earning Palm Island the nickname, "the heart of Siesta Key."

Creation of the ten-mile-long waterway with Palm Island carved out was a dream come true for developers and the Sarasota County construction industry, but a nightmare for naturalists and ecologists. Controlled dredging and protected environments resulting from the 1972 Clean Water Act effectively stopped indiscriminate dredging from further damaging the Sarasota Bay and barrier island habitats. By then, however, almost all of the salty marsh and about one-third of the mangroves had been destroyed.

Residential Clubs Expand Siesta Key's Development with Elite Snowbirds

Given the stresses of everyday life and the growing, diverse population near the end of the Interlude, private clubs became attractive to developers and affluent property owners. Some aspects resembled

Figure 9.11 The heart-shaped Palm Island soon after it was created by dredge-and-fill operations in the early 1950s. Note the multiple beach-dune ridges, the result of sediment accumulations over many decades. See also Figure 1.2, page 3. (Courtesy of Sarasota County Historical Resources with thanks to Larry Kelleher)

the organization and financing of country clubs that were very popular in the East and Midwest, with exclusivity a key element in the original versions. Two distinctly different clubs that have complex histories were created on Siesta Key during the late 1940s and were the forerunners of the "Condominium Era."

The "Sanderling Story," described in 1992 in that club's fortieth anniversary booklet, summarizes a fascinating tale of how a visionary developer can preserve and even enhance a natural Florida tropical island environment. It began in 1946 when the area south of Point of Rocks was largely uninhabited land, and a far-sighted developer, Elbridge S. Boyd, formed Siesta Properties Inc., where his deep appreciation of nature could be applied to the project. It was divided into four units or components. The first unit comprised beachfront lots

of up to two acres with at least 150 feet of beach frontage, priced generally at less than $10,000 each. Units number two and three were designated waterway lots on Heron Lagoon that sold for $8,000. Number four was on the east side of Midnight Pass Road and included a boat basin dredged from marshy land. Early residents recall that oysters, blue crabs, mussels, and an occasional alligator inhabited the lagoon, along with large tarpon—the survivors of fish trapped by the storms of the 1920s. Between 1946 and 1958, a total of sixty-seven houses were built—generally beach cottages for the winter season. As the number of property owners increased, the need for a homeowners association became apparent. In the early 1950s, the Siesta Club became the governing body of the homeowners. Soon, an inequity became apparent that needed resolution to encourage continued growth.

Siesta Club members who owned houses on the gulf enjoyed a private beach that sloped gently to the water from their backyards, but property owners on the waterways and boat basins lacked swimming accommodations. A small number of the residents had purchased cabanas at Turtle Beach Cabana Club—another Boyd development that served an exclusive group who refused to expand their membership. Consequently, the only alternative for the waterway and boat basin occupants was to start another, completely separate cabana club on Siesta Properties land acquired from Mr. Boyd. The result was Sanderling Beach Inc., established in 1952 with its own directors and officers. To improve the Sanderling property, Paul Rudolf was commissioned to design original buildings, which won the grand prize at a Brussels World Fair competition and helped launched his career and international acclaim.

Although the Siesta Club and Sanderling Beach Inc. were equally important, the name Sanderling began to overshadow the Siesta Club. In 1974 a special meeting of both organizations was called and a successful merger resulted in the creation of the Sanderling Club. Over the subsequent five decades, the spirit of has Sanderling prevailed as large homes and mansions have been built to replace the original beach cottages. Fortunately, both the Rudolph-style cabanas and clubhouse still exist in original form and are used as the centerpiece of the Sanderling Club in a preserved tropical paradise.

Another type of private club that evolved adjacent to the public beach was the Gulf and Bay Club. Developed on land that was much different than that of the Sanderling Club, it was originally occupied in the 1940s by newspaper heiress Eleanor "Cissy" Patterson. She was an ambitious journalist and newspaper editor who became prominent as a publisher and newspaper owner when she bought the *Washington Herald* and the evening *Washington Times* from William Randolph Hearst in 1937. A hands-on editor who insisted on the best of everything in her merged newspaper, Patterson encouraged society reporting, added a women's page, and hired many women as reporters. After achieving great success in Washington, D.C., and notoriety throughout the East, Patterson turned her attention to wintering in the Sarasota area. To invest wisely while ensuring privacy, she bought the thirty-five acres that were to become the Gulf and Bay Club and built a luxurious home on the beach, with rooms for her guests. During the cold winters of the 1940s, and nearly until her death in 1948, she enjoyed living in her gulf "beach house" in which each room was lavishly furnished after a different movie set. For instance, the *Gone With the Wind* room featured the chandelier from the dashing Ashley Wilkes' Twelve Oaks Plantation.

Paul T. Babson, founder of Standard & Poor's Corporation, and his brilliant wife, Edith, purchased Cissy Patterson's property to winter and retire on Siesta Key. They worked as a team and developed the Gulf and Bay Club as an exclusive resort for their pleasure and for their friends and relatives. It was a nonprofit organization that collected revenue from the visitors staying there—generally for short vacations. The Babsons and their guests enjoyed lawn bowling, walks along the beach, shuffleboard, tennis, and playing golf on the bayside at a small par-three course operated by the Gulf and Bay Club. Swimming was similarly delightful. There was also a romantic outdoor dance floor with lighted palm trees at each corner. Many areas were kept natural as tropical, almost wild jungles. The Babsons were assisted in their efforts by managers Edward and Louise St. Phillips. They were recruited from the Brook and Bridle Inn of Wolfeboro, New Hampshire, which Ed managed and where the Babsons spent their summers, including dining there

Figure 9.12 Cissy Patterson's beach home during the 1940s at 5730 Midnight Pass Road on the site where the Gulf and Bay Club was developed by Paul and Edith Babson

every evening. Ed and Louise and their family eventually moved to Florida, and Ed was said to be the last manager of the Bay Island Hotel when it closed in 1952. Next, Ed served a more active role as the manager of the Gulf and Bay Club, and Louise was in charge of the gardens.

When Paul T. Babson died in February 1972 while wintering on Siesta Key, his creation was well established and being enjoyed by all the Gulf and Bay Club residents and guests. His son, Donald, took over the leadership as Siesta Key's "Condominium Era" was getting underway. He decided to sell the property to a developer who had plans drawn up for a complex of condominiums. The first building, labeled "A," was constructed in 1979. During the late 1970s, an area in front of the pool became a popular beach bar, with a Tiki-hut style that eventually became popular elsewhere on the key. Unfortunately, the Tiki beach bar could not be continued beyond

1989 because of Sarasota County prohibitions on commercial activities on beaches and in recreational parks.

Air Conditioning—Florida's Most Valuable Innovation

During the Interlude, no technological development or other innovation was more significant than the advent and availability of air conditioning in the 1950s. Although the invention of air conditioning is often overlooked, it undoubtedly boosted tourism and population growth. Many historians have attributed the great increases in Florida's population, almost a tenfold rise since World War II, primarily to air conditioning. Recently, the value of AC was demonstrated dramatically and tragically during the aftermath of Hurricane Irma when one-quarter of the population lacked electrical power and heat stroke deaths occurred.

Figure 9.13 Sheet music published in 1949 advertising Sarasota as "The Air Conditioned City" and encouraging automobile, train, airplane, and bus travel (Published by the P.M. Publishing Company, Kansas City, MO)

The first successful research on air conditioning was done in Apalachicola, Florida, during 1842 by John Gorrie, M.D., who used compressor technology to create ice and cool air for his hospitalized patients. Dr. Gorrie was granted a U.S. patent in 1851 and hoped to eventually use his ice-making machine to regulate the temperature of buildings. He is recognized as the "father of air conditioning" on his statue in the U.S. Capitol building.

Engineer Willis Carrier invented the first commercially successful air conditioner in 1902. Carrier's invention controlled both temperature and humidity by "pumping air at a set velocity over coils refrigerated at a set temperature…" Numerous versions based on Carrier's initial design appeared nationwide, but air conditioning was mostly restricted to industrial environments such as cotton mills, cigar factories, pepper mills, breweries, and bakeries. Subsequent improvements in technology brought air conditioning to the home. Carrier himself developed the major advance that decreased the size of AC units while improving their efficiency. With the Carrier Air Conditioning Company of America leading the way, air conditioning was soon used in public buildings such as movie theaters, banks, and department stores, as well as in homes, where window units worked well. By the late 1950s air conditioned hotels and motels had become commonplace. Tourist destinations such as Sarasota quickly took advantage of this game-changing invention as Sarasota became "the Air Conditioned City."

CHAPTER 10

Transition from Fish Shacks to Beach Cottages to Condominiums

Change is the only constant.
—Albert Einstein

As Siesta Key's Interlude was coming to a close, the stage was set for tourism to blossom on this still largely unblemished barrier island as well as throughout Florida. The tourist boom that started during a transition as the Fishing Shack Era progressed to the Beach Cottage Era. Next, to accommodate more residents and visitors while generating more revenue, during the 1970s and beyond the beach cottage resorts that had ample acreage on the gulf shore were either replaced with condominiums or expanded by adding high-rise condominium buildings. The transition periods we discern can be viewed as a progression of overlapping changes as Siesta Key went through one transformation to the next. And the transitions have continued beyond the Condominium Era.

The Tourism Boom Promotes Beach Development

Florida's statewide tourism boom started in the mid-1950s and accelerated during the 1970s with the opening of Walt Disney World in Orlando. The state's population growth mirrored that trend as businesses grew and retirees began arriving in greater numbers. Consequently, Florida's population increased from 2.8 million residents in 1950 to 9.8 million in 1980. This more than threefold rise in three decades has never been seen elsewhere, and the phenomenal growth rate continued as Florida had reached 18.8 million residents by 2010. Clever ways of marketing Florida's attractions have clearly paid dividends. The legislature's role has also been significant. Adopting the nickname "the Sunshine State" and maintaining its income-tax-free status has encouraged tourists to visit and later to become Florida residents.

The mood and affluence of Americans help explain the Sunshine State's growing tourism industry and population. After the deprivations of World War II and the anxiety associated with the Korean conflict and the initial phase of the Cold War, Americans were ready for a break. The combination of peace and prosperity encouraged Americans to seek more pleasure on all fronts. Even if the economy wasn't booming for everyone, there were plenty of good paying jobs in most sectors. The population of children was growing dramatically. Baby Boomers entered the 1950s and 1960s with high expectations. Just as significant was the relative ease of travelling long distances. Passenger train travel was still desirable, and other alternatives were taking over. Airlines such as TWA, Pan Am, and Eastern were bringing tourists quickly and comfortably to the Sunshine State.

Yet the major change in long-distance travel was the advent of the car culture featuring big, powerful, gas-guzzling automobiles with amenities like radio and air conditioning. Their low miles-per-gallon performance was of no consequence then because the price of a gallon gasoline was low: 18¢ in 1950, 25¢ in 1960, and 36¢ in 1970. In addition to pumping gas, the gas-station attendant cleaned the windshield and checked the oil. After gasoline rationing during World War II, drivers were eager to buy all they needed for traveling long distances. The combination of the Eisenhower Interstate Highway System and growth in the motel industry had an even greater impact. By the early 1960s, Interstate 75 had been completed from the Canadian border, through Michigan's Upper Peninsula, the Midwest, and Georgia, to its original terminus at Tampa. Soon thereafter political pressure extended it generally along the Tamiami Trail route to Miami, a total of 1,786 miles. Somewhat similarly, the 1,920 miles of Interstate 95 were patched together along the east coast. Both interstate highways have been a blessing for Florida tourism as well as for snowbirds.

Motels Establish a New Model

Cheap, abundant gasoline and interstate highways were important in facilitating long-distance automobile travel to Florida's beaches, and so was development of the motel industry. Not only did motels support Florida tourism, they also stimulated development of tourist destinations along the way. Motel chains evolved a very effective business model that is still used today, and many of its features were eventually adopted by Siesta Key beach cottage and condominium owners/managers.

The Milestone Inn, opened in 1925 in San Luis Obispo, California, is regarded as the world's first lodging facility designed especially for automobile travelers—a "motor hotel" or "motel." Its name was changed first to the Milestone Mo-Tel and ultimately to the Motel Inn. Situated along the highway and with convenient parking, the motel concept was much more attractive than the auto camps and rustic cabins generally available to American motorists at the time. A major breakthrough in the motel industry came in 1951 when residential developer Kemmons Wilson and his family returned to Memphis, Tennessee, after a road-trip vacation to Washington, D.C. Wilson was upset by the filthy, unsafe motels he and his family encountered on the trip. Moreover, most motels lacked an on-site restaurant, thus requiring an additional drive by tired travelers to buy dinner. The annoyed and entrepreneurial Kemmons Wilson decided to build his own motel on the main highway (U.S. 70) from Memphis to Nashville. He cleverly adopted the name of Bing Crosby's hit 1942 musical film *Holiday Inn*. Wilson also planned that every Holiday Inn would have TV, air conditioning, a restaurant, and a swimming pool. In addition, all of them would be required to meet a long list of standards to ensure that all guests would have the same pleasant experience at every Holiday Inn.

The Memphis Holiday Inn launched Wilson's innovative motel chain and established a trend that the growing hospitality industry embraced. The original Holiday Inn set a perfect standard and featured its immediately recognizable sign (called the "Great Sign") that, like McDonald's golden arches, established a new, eye-catching advertising method along the highways. Lastly, to secure repeat guests, Holiday Inn developed an IBM-designed national room reservations system in 1965, allowing a traveler to book ahead or reserve a room for the next stay before checking out. Within a few years, Holiday Inns were proliferating as franchised operations. By 1968 when it reached the 1,000-location mark, Holiday Inn was averaging a new hotel opening every week—incredible success that was obviously addressing a pent-up demand. Other chains such as Best Western and Quality Courts (later the Quality Inn chain) followed suit. Still others, like Howard Johnson's and Ramada Inn, were forced to upgrade. Soon, there were plenty of good lodging options to choose from along America's highways.

Thus, automobile travel after the mid-1950s had become an integral and pleasurable part of vacationing. Tourists had taken Dinah Shore's advice when she sang the theme song of the sponsor of her 1950s TV show: "See the USA in your Chevrolet... America is asking you to call." If a 1953 Chevy Bel Air purchased for $1,741 was not your preference, there were plenty of other cars to choose from made by GM, Ford, and Chrysler. For some, the stay at a high-quality motel was so enjoyable that

the family would remain for a couple of extra nights and do some sightseeing in the local area. Thus, tourism on a national level was also boosted by the trend to "See the USA" along the way to a vacation destination. New experiences in motels could be memorable, like a family's first exposure to television, or later to color TV.

Siesta Key's Motel-like Beach Cottages Launch Tourism

The lessons learned from the motel industry did not escape notice by innkeepers along the gulf coast. During the 1950s resort communities previously dominated by hotels within cities began to expand their offerings of delightful experiences in convenient, inexpensive motel-like facilities on the beaches. By the late 1940s Siesta Key had a few beach cottage resorts. Siesta Lodge and Shedrick Cottages were hosting about twenty families near Point of Rocks.

SIESTA LODGE   –   SIESTA KEY   –   SARASOTA, FLA.

Figure 10.1 The Siesta Lodge at the corner of Old Stickney Road and Midnight Pass Road was one of the early Cottage Era motels and eventually became the site of Captain Curt's Crab and Oyster Bar as described in Chapter 15

Figure 10.2 Shedrick Cottages in the 1940s on Crescent Beach near Point of Rocks. Note the jungle-like terrain on either side of the six buildings and the cars on the beach. (Courtesy of Sarasota County Historical Resources with thanks to Larry Kelleher)

Crescent Beach was just as attractive at that time as it is now but practically deserted except for a few cars and fisherman. South of Stickney, Mid-Night Pass Beach Cottages were also available, but they were essentially a group of fishing shacks. By the mid-1950s, however, much more elaborate beach cottages could be rented, such as Gulf Shore Cottages. They were typically wood frame buildings using readily available, inexpensive materials—generally cypress wood milled nearby. The cottages tended to have large window fans in the 1950s, but many became air-conditioned during the next decade. Front porches, ideally facing the gulf shore, were common and promoted socializing. A swimming pool was also possible, but not likely. After all, these lodging facilities were on the beach where the gulf breezes were blowing in to cool the cottages. In some cases, there might be a small diner. The number of restaurants was limited, so visiting tourists liked to barbeque or fry the fish they caught that day. In addition, throughout the gulf shore beaches crabs could be readily caught after sunset. The senior author vividly remembers many evening adventures when a flashlight, broom, and burlap bag were all one needed to gather up a family meal of twenty crabs in about an hour. Catching them was fun, but dumping them into a tall pot of boiling water where corn on the cob had just been cooked was even more exciting.

MID-NIGHT PASS BEACH COTTAGES,

Figure 10.3 Mid-Night Pass beach cottages in the 1940s (Courtesy of Sarasota County Historical Resources with thanks to Larry Kelleher)

Just like motels, beach cottages were typically single-story structures with rooms opening directly onto a parking lot, making it easy to unload suitcases or groceries from a vehicle. A second story, if present, would generally include a long porch-like balcony served by multiple stairwells. If on the beach, the two-story version usually faced the gulf. Developers often economized by building long rows of connected units rather than separate cottages. They were typically constructed in an I-, L-, or U-shaped design that included guest bedrooms with kitchens and often a small living room. In such cases,

Figure 10.4 Gulf Shore Cottages in the 1950s. Note the undeveloped roads. (Courtesy of Sarasota County Historical Resources with thanks to Larry Kelleher)

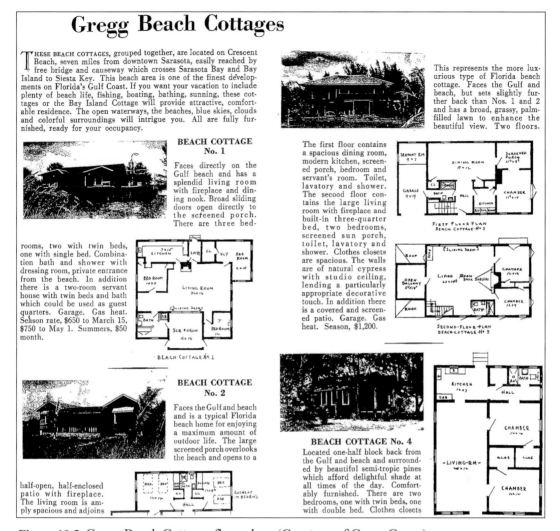

Gregg Beach Cottages

THESE BEACH COTTAGES, grouped together, are located on Crescent Beach, seven miles from downtown Sarasota, easily reached by free bridge and causeway which crosses Sarasota Bay and Bay Island to Siesta Key. This beach area is one of the finest developments on Florida's Gulf Coast. If you want your vacation to include plenty of beach life, fishing, boating, bathing, sunning, these cottages or the Bay Island Cottage will provide attractive, comfortable residence. The open waterways, the beaches, blue skies, clouds and colorful surroundings will intrigue you. All are fully furnished, ready for your occupancy.

This represents the more luxurious type of Florida beach cottage. Faces the Gulf and beach, but sets slightly further back than Nos. 1 and 2 and has a broad, grassy, palm-filled lawn to enhance the beautiful view. Two floors.

BEACH COTTAGE No. 1

Faces directly on the Gulf beach and has a splendid living room with fireplace and dining nook. Broad sliding doors open directly to the screened porch. There are three bedrooms, two with twin beds, one with single bed. Combination bath and shower with dressing room, private entrance from the beach. In addition there is a two-room servant house with twin beds and bath which could be used as guest quarters. Garage. Gas heat. Season rate, $650 to March 15, $750 to May 1. Summers, $50 month.

The first floor contains a spacious dining room, modern kitchen, screened porch, bedroom and servant's room. Toilet, lavatory and shower. The second floor contains the large living room with fireplace and built-in three-quarter bed, two bedrooms, screened sun porch, toilet, lavatory and shower. Clothes closets are spacious. The walls are of natural cypress with studio ceiling, lending a particularly appropriate decorative touch. In addition there is a covered and screened patio. Garage. Gas heat. Season, $1,200.

BEACH COTTAGE No. 2

Faces the Gulf and beach and is a typical Florida beach home for enjoying a maximum amount of outdoor life. The large screened porch overlooks the beach and opens to a half-open, half-enclosed patio with fireplace. The living room is amply spacious and adjoins

BEACH COTTAGE No. 4

Located one-half block back from the Gulf and beach and surrounded by beautiful semi-tropic pines which afford delightful shade at all times of the day. Comfortably furnished. There are two bedrooms, one with twin beds, one with double bed. Clothes closets

Figure 10.5 Gregg Beach Cottages floor plans (Courtesy of Cyrus Gregg)

the lodging units shared a foundation, roof, and utility systems, which reduced not only construction expenses but also operating costs. Attached garages for guests' cars were expensive, so parking spots were provided in front of each unit or, less commonly, carports. These 1950s-era structures can be seen today at Jamaica Royale and many other resorts. Lastly, each resort with multiple beach cottages had a distinctive sign—not the "Great Sign" of Holiday Inn but something tasteful that identified the facility.

Many early beach cottages thrived on Siesta Key in the booming 1950s and into the 1960s. Their names highlighted the warm gulf waters and the pristine, sparsely populated beach. Examples include Sarasea Circle, Crescent Beach Cottages ("all equipped with the most modern housekeeping facilities"), Gulf Shore Cottages (with "four duplex efficiency units and ten one-bedroom units"), Point O' Rocks Vacation Apartments (see Figure 2.3, page 11), where "each unit has a six by six glass Jalousie picture window, affording a full view of the Gulf…" and also "modern tile baths, tub and shower, complete kitchens, hot water heat… and an individual car port at the rear." The name of the Crescent

Beach Cottages was changed to Crescent View Cottages as the managers, Ruth and Elmer Ball, expanded the occupancy from 1956 to 1966. Ruth Ball said they "were always busy in season" and everyone enjoyed the safe "lazy, slow lifestyle of the key." She added, "It was so safe, we never locked anything, not even the cottages… We never had to hunt for keys because they were always open."

The Gregg Cottages, where Boston Red Sox players liked to stay during spring training, were typical of upscale lodging facilities of the time. They usually had screened porches for cooling, and some included associated servant's quarters, as with cottage number 1. Note also the affordable prices. The season rate from November through April was only $750; monthly rates were $50–$100. By the next decade, as the demand increased, the prices doubled, but the number of beachfront cottages limited the population of visiting tourists. A parcel of land of approximately twelve acres with the eight Gregg cottages only accommodated about thirty people during the season. When they were demolished and replaced by the Coquille townhouse-design condominium complex, more than one hundred residents could be accommodated, while the adjacent Peppertree Bay complex easily housed over one thousand people. Eventually, as the demand increased further, it was clear that all such valuable land could become more lucrative if the potential number of guests was increased *and* if a new model of investment ownership was introduced. From the late 1960s to early 1970s, therefore, the Beach Cottage Era was transitioning to the Condominium Era. In less than a decade, a complete transformation of Siesta Key along Crescent Beach occurred as the skyline from 6200 to 5700 Midnight Pass Road became full of high-rise buildings.

Vintage postcards shown on color pages 7 and 8 depict the dramatic transformation that occurred within two decades. One can only imagine the shock of long-term residents like John MacDonald as these high-rise buildings arose from the sand. Beach views along Midnight Pass Road were disappearing forever. And a new model of facilitated joint ownership took over and transformed Siesta Key through another transition.

From Cottages to Condominiums: "The Year of Construction"

Despite the nationwide turbulence of the 1960s with hippie culture and drugs almost everywhere—or perhaps partly because of it—Florida's tourism not only continued its boom but also began to accelerate. The single biggest event boosting visits to the Sunshine State occurred on the October 1, 1971, when Walt Disney World opened. Thereafter, Mickey Mouse and his friends were as attractive as the beaches. The combination of Orlando attractions and beaches accounted for 113 million visitors and $109 billion for Florida in 2016. Being strategically located in central Florida, the magnificent Magic Kingdom thrived, as did all attractions that followed, including Epcot, which opened in 1982. Visitors flying in to Florida and renting a car for a 10-day, 2-weekend stay have had a statewide impact. Tourists often spend a few days at Walt Disney World or another theme park like SeaWorld and then stay for close to a week at a beach destination. With only a two-hour drive from Siesta Key, a trip to an Orlando destination is quite convenient.

During the 1970s Florida transitioned to another real estate boom period we refer to as the Condominium Era. As mentioned previously, it became apparent that land along Siesta/Crescent Beach was too valuable for scattered beach cottages or rows of connected villas. Moreover, local developers welcomed the concept of condominium ownership, while prospective investors/buyers relished the opportunity for relatively easy purchases with a promise of profits. The condominium model, a modern type of shared real estate ownership, was much better for ownership than the club organization, and it took off like wildfire throughout Florida in the late 1960s and 1970s, especially in the southern coastal regions. This trend developed for a variety of reasons. The original impetus came as long ago as 1958, when an imaginative coalition of developers, lawyers, and legislators in Puerto Rico passed the first condominium law. Florida government leaders and the construction industry quickly appreciated the advantages of shared ownership and promoted development. So did the federal government. The Housing Act of 1961 allowed the Federal Housing Authority to insure mortgages on condominiums, which led to a huge increase in the funds available for condo projects. Few pieces of federal legislation have had such an immediate impact. In 1963, the Florida Condominium Act created enabling legislation, and by 1969 every state had a similar law. Not surprisingly, the nation's condo craze was spurred on by South Florida.

By importing Puerto Rico's creation, Florida suddenly was positioned to address some theretofore unsolvable problems. During the 1960s Florida was experiencing economic growth combined with high unemployment and rising inflation. The Sunshine State led the nation in population growth and had the potential to expand the construction industry. The number of middle-class and more affluent retirees was growing nationwide, and a high proportion wanted to settle in Florida and avoid state income taxes. Concurrently, the tourist boom had become a year-long phenomenon, thanks to air conditioning and two-income families. It has been estimated that for at least a decade the demand for housing throughout Florida exceeded the available supply by tenfold. This situation was a dream come

true for developers and bankers. Marketing proceeded widely and aggressively. Entire condominiums and condo complexes were sold out overnight before they were built with only a promise of construction and no time line.

The resulting chaos generated serious problems throughout Florida and certainly on Siesta Key. Eager, gullible buyers were given unrealistic dates for when their "dream homes" would be ready for occupancy. The inability to synchronize with retirement dates and the sale of the "old home" was a blow to many retirees. The developers' common use of bait-and-switch tactics was not just unethical—it was illegal, though generally not prosecuted. Buyers frequently had to settle for paint, carpeting, and fixtures of lower quality than they saw in the tastefully decorated model units.

Unfortunately, buyers had very limited recourse because Florida law at that time did not require disclosures about the details of contracts and leases, including escalation clauses, or about the construction materials used. This deficiency led to the most egregious abuses in the condo industry, with a range of construction deficiencies affecting everything from the foundation to the roofing, with inferior plumbing and wiring in between. While condo purchasers with their fixed incomes suffered for the sake of being in paradise, many developers and lenders continued to focus on their profits and loan profitability, respectively, rather than the needs and competence of the buyers. Not surprisingly, greedy developers and lending institutions did not want municipal inspections, so many found ways to avoid having their completed projects examined for compliance with building codes. A clever mechanism was devised— the notorious Certificate of Occupancy. When this certificate was issued, condo buyers naturally assumed that they had the stamp of approval and that their "dream home" met all the local code requirements as determined by municipal building inspectors. This was not always true, however, because of incomplete inspections and deceptions. One only needs to read John MacDonald's 1977 novel *Condominium* to learn more about what can happen and its consequences on a barrier island like Siesta Key—the fictional Fiddler's Key in MacDonald's bestseller. Eventually, after many legal actions, Florida amended the Condominium Act in 1971, but the state had to rewrite it in 1991 after twenty-eight years of deficiencies.

With this perspective in mind, it is fascinating to examine the evolution of the condo craze on Siesta Key. Some unfortunate scenarios occurred there, although they pale in comparison to the nightmares that occurred and continue in Dade County, where construction defects, fraud, escalation clauses, and other abuses have led to public protests and litigation. In some cases existing beach cottages were simply converted to condominiums, as was the case with Island House. The more common strategy was to build a larger facility on sparsely occupied land. Noteworthy high-rise condo building projects of the mid- to late 1960s included Jamaica Royale's twin towers and the Horizons West high-rise building on the beach side of its impressive villas. The rationale was clear for these two developments. Both had available land in front, toward the gulf shore. Both preferred more residents than the limited number that could be accommodated in their ground-level units. However, despite their well-conceived plans and schedules, both were challenged to complete their ambitious projects. Horizons West needed to acquire more land to the north; fortunately, however, the Gregg family had an abundance of land and were willing to sell. This allowed Horizons West to have a construction

project that proceeded in phases, finishing the brick villas first and then building a steel-framed, eleven-floor tower with nine floors of attractive multi-bedroom units with balconies. The tower has held up well, and in recent years has been renovated unit-by-unit. Jamaica Royale wound up with two towers, but not without its own construction difficulties. The six-story Tower I was built in the mid-1960s, with ground-level parking that would also serve its 112 villas. However, financial difficulties ensued during the construction of Tower II. In fact, the *Pelican Press* reported on October 25, 1973, that Jamaica Royale was a "high-rise failure" as the tower was unfinished. Its completion was delayed until 1976. Also of great concern to early occupants we interviewed was that the gulf at high tide brought water within 50 feet of their seawall; one interviewee commented that it was not certain in the early years if Tower I would be "swallowed by the Gulf of Mexico." In 2017, our measurements revealed 475 feet of beach from the Jamaica Royale seawall to the gulf, but this may be jeopardized in the future, as described in Chapters 19 and 20.

Other condo construction projects moved along swiftly. Peppertree Bay acquired sixteen acres of gulf-to-bay land from the Palmer estate, cleared out the native tropical plants and built a combination of beachfront villas and high-rise buildings that opened in 1974 with a huge capacity of 362 units. Others followed, generally ranging from about 50 to 150 units. The condo craze then proceeded throughout the 1970s and beyond. The *Pelican Press* dubbed 1978 "The Year of Construction," and that trend continued after 1978. The Gulf and Bay Club built its first high-rise building in 1979 and added five more in the ensuing years.

Using both the gulf and bay sides, developers proceeded with large and smaller projects all along Midnight Pass Road

Figure 10.6 Palmer beach cottage moved from Peppertree Bay property to 6100 Midnight Pass Road for Hugh and Cay Gregg

between Stickney and Beach Roads, and wherever else land could be acquired. These construction projects completely transformed Siesta Key as shown on color page 7. Some were "mid-rise" (five to ten stories) construction projects, but the typical size was eleven floors. At present there are more than seventy condominiums operating along the gulf beach or on the bayside, mainly along a one-mile stretch north of the Stickney Bridge. Almost all the mid-key beach cottages have been replaced except for one noteworthy exception, an original Palmer house, which is described in Chapter 13.

The condo craze also generated many new businesses, such as condominium security services, while expanding the workload of others, such as landscaping and pool maintenance companies. With the variations in construction quality, it should come as

no surprise that the plumbers, electricians, carpenters, and painters have benefitted financially. This will undoubtedly continue as a condo renovation period is evident in the twenty-first century. When storms like the 2016 tornado and Hurricane Irma in 2017, there's always plenty of repair work to be done.

Cultural Transitions Underway on Siesta Key

Not only has the Condominium Era changed the skyline and beachside occupancy of Siesta Key, it has also altered the culture. No longer does "everybody know everybody." In fact, some people come to the key to get away from it all and don't want to know anybody. This situation was exacerbated by a change in condominium rules regarding lease duration. Instead of the previous two- or three-month minimum requirements for seasonal stays on the key, many condominiums switched to offering short-stay opportunities of one week or even one weekend. This has become the twenty-first century pattern.

Consequently, the Condominium Era began with a predominance of residents and now supports a largely short-stay visitor population who "live by the moment." This may be more lucrative for the condo owner/investor group and local businesses, but it has ruined the peaceful, eclectic nature of the key and its ability to attract artists, writers, and musicians. Siesta Key is no longer what Harry Higel advertised as a "haven for rest."

Continuation of the Condominium Era with a New Emphasis

Condominium construction continued at reduced rate throughout the 1980s and well into 1990s. A few more have appeared since 2000. Most of the projects have been tasteful and attractive. Huge projects like Peppertree Bay and Crystal Sands were, in retrospect, built too close to Siesta/Crescent Beach and are eyesores. Eventually, as land became scarce and construction height maximums were imposed, construction projects were limited to the mid-rise category. When high-rise construction was curtailed, developers turned their attention to smaller projects that became known as luxury condominiums. By building fewer but more expensive units, they addressed a new market and kept revenue flowing to both the construction industry and lending institutions. Summer Cove and Seagrove, built from 2004 through 2006, are good examples. When the Great Recession began in 2008, prices fell and construction essentially halted. But developers cannot be stopped for long. The 2017-18 project, *Oceane*, provides an example of a contemporary luxury condo project. It features an exclusive private gated community of six elegant, uniquely designed, 4,500-square-foot residences located directly on the water at 4740 Ocean Boulevard and within walking distance

Figure 10.7 The front of the "Ask Gary House" facing east

Figure 10.8 The beachside of the "Ask Gary House" facing west.

to Siesta Key Village. Each unit has two master bedroom suites, a media room, a private elevator, a large living area, and expansive views of Big Pass along 374 feet of the waterfront. The price is about $4 million each. These living quarters are a quantum leap from the fishing shacks and beach cottages that launched Siesta Key's transition to tourism.

In addition to luxury condominiums, more and more luxury homes are being constructed on Siesta Key. These are generally in gated communities like the Sanderling Club. They are refreshingly different from the Spanish Mediterranean style that dominated Sarasota County mansions for several decades. Now that Casa del Cielo has been demolished, one mansion stands out along Siesta/Crescent Beach—namely the "Ask Gary House," just north of Point of Rocks. Featured in the MTV series entitled *Siesta Key*, this 30,000-square-foot, seven-bedroom, seven-bathroom mansion was constructed over eight years by Gary and Beth Kompothecras as an adaptation of the Vanderbilt's Marble House in Newport, Rhode Island. Built in 1892, it was the mansion that lead to the Beaux Arts craze, named for the École des Beaux-Arts in Paris, where architect Mary Rockwell Hook and artist Syd Solomon studied. Many of the elements of the Gilded Age style can be seen in the east façade of the Kompothecras house, which is perfectly symmetrical. Its landscaping highlights its balance and brings the eye toward the grand entrance, an elaborate portico that is accessed by the open arms of a curved driveways. The side of the house that faces the beach is even more impressive and is often featured on the MTV series in scenes that show off its views and swimming pool. Lastly, the interior of the house is just as impressive and has spectacular features

Figure 10.9 The Stagecoach Hotel (Chattanooga, TN) chandelier in the "Ask Gary House"

reminiscent of the Cissy Patterson house. For instance, Gary and Beth Kompothecras installed the staircase from the movie *Titanic* and a 1950s chandelier from the famous Stagecoach Hotel in Chattanooga, Tennessee. This unique house, which the senior author enjoyed touring in April 2017, thanks to Gary, can be viewed on walks along Siesta/Crescent Beach to Point of Rocks or via virtual tours on MTV.

CHAPTER 11

Spring Break Begins with the Amish and Mennonite Tourists

When you come down here, you can pitch religion a little bit and let loose... You'll never find another place in the world that's like this one.
—Amanda and Alva Yoder, *New York Times*, April 15, 2012

From December to April, one of the most impressive sights on Siesta/Crescent Beach is the daily appearance of Amish snowbirds in their distinctive garb. They begin arriving at about 9:15 A.M. on SCAT (Sarasota County Area Transit) bus 33, which operates only from November to April, but not on Sundays—Sarasota's busiest bus during those six months. The bus originates from Cattleman Station and picks up the Amish and Mennonite visitors in Pinecraft at the corner of Hines and Clarinda Streets, next to the unique Amish church at 1325 Hines Avenue. Many riders arrive at the bus stop on bicycles that they park and then line up—unless their bike needs some work done on it down the street at Lapp's 25-year-old bicycle shop. The 8-mile ride provides a pleasant 34-minute journey. The excitement builds as the bus crosses the North Bridge and rolls toward the beach. Happy conversations prevail, and most of these discussions are in Pennsylvania Dutch, the German dialect used by the Amish for centuries. Return trips to Hines and Clarinda are available until 8:15 P.M. to allow sunset viewings.

Most noteworthy perhaps is the fact that excursions by Amish and Mennonites to Siesta/

Crescent Beach have been underway annually for about nine decades. Incredible as it seems, these Anabaptist people initiated annual winter/spring break trips to Sarasota and Siesta Key during the 1930s. To appreciate why they came and how the way of life of these annual tourists fits well in Sarasota County and particularly on Siesta Key, one needs to understand their origin, beliefs, and culture, as well as the distinctive Amish attire. We were privileged to learn about these snowbirds through a combination of interviews, especially with J. B. Miller, by literally rubbing shoulders with some Amish visitors, and by studying Noah Gingerich's book, *The History of Pinecraft, 1925-1960*. We also read recent issues of *The Budget*, a weekly newspaper "serving the Amish-Mennonite Communities Throughout the Americas."

Origin and Practices of Florida's Anabaptists

The Mennonite people are Christians who trace their origin to 1525 in Zürich, Switzerland, when the Anabaptist concept of "an-other" baptism originated. Thus, an Anabaptist is "one who baptizes again." Members of the

Figure 11.1 SCAT bus stop 33 in front of the Amish church at 1325 Hines Avenue where Amish passengers are picked up or dropped off during November through April

Mennonite Church are those who originally experience a "believer's baptism" even if they were baptized as infants. In 1536 their religion expanded as a result of the efforts of Father Menno Simons, who followed in the footsteps of Martin Luther to challenge the teachings of the Roman Catholic faith as well as the authority of the Pope. But the power and ubiquity of the Catholics led to severe local persecutions and eventually widespread migrations in German-speaking European territories and then abroad. Their diaspora continues to the present as these peace-loving people have disseminated to over fifty countries. They came to Florida during the Great Depression and played an important role in the economy when they settled a few miles east of the Sarasota Bay to establish farms and other businesses, as well as becoming an early group of tourists enjoying Siesta/Crescent Beach.

Figure 11.2 Bikes parked near the Amish church and people queued up for a ride to Siesta Beach

Wherever they live, the Mennonites form distinct ethno-religious groups following the New Testament of the Bible but generally not being outwardly recognizable—that is, their clothing may be contemporary and their employment patterns and use of technology modern.

The Amish, in contrast, wear distinctive garments that make them prominent on Siesta/Crescent Beach, and they also display

Figure 11.3 Lapp's bicycle shop where bikes of all types have been available for rent or purchase for more than twenty-five years and where expert repairs are accomplished by Jake Lapp for residents and visitors

a unique lifestyle. These Anabaptists trace their origin to Jakob Ammann who led a schism in 1693 in German-speaking Switzerland that also resulted in persecutions and migrations. Amman was a tailor familiar with the sumptuary laws regulating attire and is ultimately responsible for the unique garments of the Amish. Wherever they go, the Amish are always recognizable by a combination of unique clothing, large families, and their orderly behaviors. All of the women wear single color dresses of cotton or other fabrics that are often pastel but never white, while the men use suspenders and, if married, maintain a plain beard. On Siesta/Crescent Beach they have been the most noticeable strollers for many decades.

Amish behaviors are always governed by a set of rules known as the *Ordnung* (German for order)—a critical feature of Amish communities that governs day-to-day living practices. Church members who do not conform and will not repent are excommunicated. Alternatively, Amish Church members may be shunned to limit social contacts. The *Ordnung* also includes positive expectations for lifestyle, recommending certain behaviors and technologies. These include style and cut of clothing; hairstyle; marriage between baptized members only; and even carriage design. They place the highest priority on family and believe that large families are a blessing from God. Amish couples have an average of seven children and ensure that all family members socialize with relatives and neighbors. In fact, wherever Amish live, they enjoy a rich social life, which can be appreciated on Siesta/Crescent Beach as groups of young Amish people congregate. The *Ordnung* applies both locally and while traveling, so all the expectations and restrictions must be followed to uphold their unique community while they vacation on winter/spring breaks. Yet less surveillance

occurs during excursions to Siesta/Crescent Beach and one- to two-week stays in Sarasota County, especially on the keys. Thus, although labor-saving and entertaining modern devices are prohibited by the *Ordnung,* some restrictions are relaxed when they stay in Florida lodging facilities.

Anabaptists' Migrations Bring Them to Sarasota County

The continued and often brutal persecutions of Anabaptists in Europe became intolerable during the early eighteenth century, especially for the easily recognizable Amish. But the religious tolerance of America was well known in Europe. Pennsylvania was especially famous for religious tolerance and therefore attracted Anabaptists. The first Amish to arrive settled in Berks County, but they soon found better, safer land in Lancaster County, where they have forever been known as "Pennsylvania Dutch." Their way of life has thrived while their talents and work ethic have brought affluence to many of them through niche businesses such as high-quality furniture manufacturing. Although their wealth generally does not show outwardly, when an Amish man removes his thick wallet to pay for a meal or ride bus #33, its abundant cash is striking.

The second migration to America evolved into a third diaspora as Amish dissemination extended to other regions where a combination of good farmland and tolerant communities could be found. Currently, among about 300,000 Amish people in North America, the largest populations live in Ohio (about 55,000), Pennsylvania (about 51,000), and Indiana (about 38,000). These states collectively account for the largest group of Sarasota residents and Siesta/Crescent Beach visitors. Interestingly, however, the Amish now live in thirty-one states, so when they come to

Sarasota County there is more interstate mingling than one would anticipate. As longtime resident Katie Troyer said, "All of these groups can mingle down here in a way they wouldn't at home."

The reason Amish and Mennonites came to Florida originally is similar to all their migrations—they were seeking good farmland and tolerant communities. Soon they were also seeking rest, relaxation, and pleasure, especially on beaches like those of Siesta Key, during their winter/spring breaks. The first to arrive and stay were groups of Amish and Mennonites who came in 1926 soon after much of Florida had been devastated by the Great Miami Hurricane. There they found plenty of farmland at $600 per acre by purchasing Palmer properties during a period of a depressed Florida economy and land bust. Although much of the cheaper land was marsh and muck along Phillippi Creek, these enterprising, skilled farmers drained the marshland. They bought land in Fruitville and soon grew celery, lettuce, and radishes—produce that fits in well with a short growing season. They concentrated on celery for three decades while other Anabaptists visited for both relaxation from the hard labor up north and for the fabulous estuary fishing. During the 1930s and beyond, the entire community thrived despite the Great Depression.

Development of Pinecraft—The World's Only Anabaptist Village

The Anabaptists settled into a new community of Sarasota County that was named Pinecraft. The name Pinecraft has been attributed to the platting document of February 1926 signed by Earl and Mary Craft and the many pine trees on or near the property. The site of their village was determined by several factors. Proximity to the celery fields was perhaps the most important consideration, and the availability

of land in the Sarasota National Tourist Camp provided the opportunity. It was a group of 466 campsites providing about 40 by 40 feet of land for each family. By 1932 Pinecraft was created as the only truly Amish village in the world. Approximately five hundred lots were platted east of Phillippi Creek between Bay Vista Avenue (later Bahia Vista) and what was originally called Second Avenue South.

An important milestone in Pinecraft history occurred in 1946. Satisfying the need for an Anabaptist Church in Sarasota County, a large bakery building at 3340 Bahia Vista Street was purchased for $7,500 and converted to the Tourist Mennonite Church. Initially, this landmark building was used by both Mennonites and Amish in separate services. After 1956, however, the Amish developed their own church nearby at 1325 Hines Street where during the spring break season up to one thousand people gather every Sunday. Over the years, the Tourist Mennonite Church has been a crucial site for many activities, including a school, because of its prime location and large parking lot, which serves as a gathering place and the terminus for buses from the North.

How They Come for Winter/ Spring Breaks: A Long Bus Ride

By 1960, when the Florida tourist boom was just becoming well established, about 5,000 Anabaptists were already visiting annually. Now there are closer to 10,000 Amish and Mennonite tourists per year. They no longer can be accommodated in Pinecraft, so the "overflow" visitors stay on Siesta Key or in other communities close to the gulf beaches. They come as early as November but more likely arrive by busloads from mid-December through March. One of the questions most frequently asked while observing Amish

Figure 11.4 The Tourist Mennonite Church built in 1946 and now a center of Amish and Mennonite gatherings as the Pioneer Trails buses arrive and depart from the church's parking lot behind the building

strolling on Siesta/Crescent Beach is, "How do so many of these horse-and-buggy people get to Florida?" In the early years, Mennonites would often drive and often bring Amish along. Other Midwestern Amish might hire a driver for the trip. Yet the largest number would come by passenger trains. Train travel was popular and pleasant from the 1930s into the 1960s, but eventually railway mergers and reduced service eliminated that mode of transportation. Then, the Amish typically had to arrange bus transportation that could involve multiple transfers when riding bus lines like Greyhound. This changed in 1984 when as a great service to Amish and Mennonite people Dave and Irene Swartzentruberm started an important transportation program, the Pioneer Trails bus line, from Millersburg, Ohio.

Since the inception of the Sarasota trips, these buses have brought thousands of Amish and Mennonites annually. March is the heaviest month for these travelers. As many as a thousand per week arrive during peak periods. Dave Swartzentruberm estimates that the passengers are 75 percent Amish and 25 percent Mennonites. During the 2016-17 season, Pioneer Trails buses transported about 6,400 people—3,400 of whom traveled from the Midwest to Sarasota and then back. In addition to the Ohio residents, Pioneer Trails shuttles many Amish from Indiana and fewer from Michigan to the southbound origination point in Cincinnati, where a caravan assembles for the eighteen-hour ride to Sarasota. Up to six Pioneer Trails buses can arrive around noon at the Tourist Mennonite Church parking lot on Tuesdays, Thursdays, and Saturdays. The parking lot is always full of excitement then, especially on Thursdays, when one of the buses brings *The Budget*, the nationwide weekly newspaper of the Anabaptist communities. In addition to the Swartzentruberm-served passengers, there are other bus services from the Midwest

THE BUDGET ™

Serving The Amish-Mennonite Communities Throughout The Americas

4 Sections · 52 Pages	National Edition	Single Copy
Volume 127 · Issue No. 52		$1.50
Sugarcreek, Ohio 44681	**Wednesday, April 26, 2017**	

Index

It's wedding season! The little couple mentioned by Tobie C. Yoders in the Hillsboro, Wisconsin, letter have been paying attention. They seem to have the "or for worse" down pretty good. Page 4.

He didn't let being in a precarious position affect his appetite! Must be crawdads are tasty. Sam and Lydia Chupp of Pearlsburg, Virginia, snag this one. Page 20.

"He who laughs last, laughs best." What do you say, Mom? Crab Orchard, Kentucky, scribes John and Miriam Troyer were up early enough to catch this. Page 28.

Most people try to keep other people from finding out about the skeletons in their closet, but Orla and Barb Troyer from Carbondale, Illinois, are going public with theirs. Page 13.

Things were a bit tense and exciting until the arrest was made. Wilma Yoder of Readstown, Wisconsin, reports it was way too close for comfort. Page 3.

Ben had a hair-raising experience when what to his wondering eyes should appear... Yikes! Mrs. Susan Raber of Nashville, Michigan, provides the details. Page 38.

Mrs. Jonas Kurtz of Punxsutawney, Pennsylvania, writes of the bad accident concerning grandson David Troyer. Page 40.

FOXWORTH, MS

April 19—David Strites and 2 girls drove their daughter Victoria's car to Romulus, N.Y., where she is teaching school. They rented a car to come home in. The rest of their children stayed with John Strites.

Nelson Groffs were in Punta Gorda, Fla., on a brush cutting job. Wilmer Swiegarts were living in their trailer, taking care of the school boys and other chores.

Eldon and Regina and baby Derek of Daviess County, Ind., came to visit her family, Anthony Swiegarts, for last weekend.

Daniel Strites were in Tenn. for a seminar by Deeper Life Ministries. The children were at grandpa Richard Roger's.

Lyndon Barkholders were in Pensacola, Fla., for church work. having counsel meeting and Communion.

Our Easter weekend meetings are over. The speaker was James Yoder of Mt. Joy Church in Daviess County, Ind. His wife and family were along. A fellowship meal was enjoyed on Son.

I (Martha) was in the hospital from Good Friday to Tues. for a severe kidney infection.

My husband, Paul, was admitted to the hospital on Thurs. We hope to go home by Mon.

Lyndon Burkholder, John Strite, and Jerald Wittmer flew to Pa. for Pilgrim bishop and ministers' meetings, and also conference. They all plan to be back before Sun.

Klaas Reimer is flying to Great Lakes, Mich., where he will be having their weekend meetings. Audrey and the boys are home taking care of the 2 broiler houses they own.

Zachary Strite left for Daviess County where he is helping Eldon Martin with his spring planting. He's enjoying driving these 200 plus h.p. International tractors as they plant hundreds of acres.

Mrs. Paul Strite

WATERFORD, IRELAND

April 23—A heavy cloud cover has been hiding the sun for most of the past week. Temperatures are quite comfortable and there has been very little rain. So the weather has actually been quite pleasant, except for those who feel the only nice day is a sunny day!

Sharon Smucker is enjoying the visit of 3 friends, Karen and Rhoda Beiler and Regina Jantzi. All 3 are presently serving with Master's International Ministries in Ukraine.

Diane Beachy returned today from her visit with home folks in Ohio. Staff and customers in Jaybees will be glad to have her cheerful presence there again!

Two first time visitors joined us for our worship services this morning. They are from Kilkenny, about an hour's drive north of us.

Natalia Jones has gone to Bulgaria again for an extended period of time. Her health problems continue to plague her, and she feels much better in the drier climate of Bulgaria than in the more damp and cool climate here in Ireland.

Jeanette Gregory Smith has been suffering with headache and backache for the past week. Their son Richard arrived from England last evening, bringing with him Jeanette's mother for a week's visit.

As was planned, my wife had her second surgery for breast cancer this past Thurs. The doctor was well pleased with the surgery. They removed some more tissue and lymph nodes, which they will be testing to see how far the cancer has spread. They said we should have the results of these tests in 2 week's time. These results will help to determine further treatment plans.

Barbara was in the hospital for one night and was ready to come home by Fri. evening. She is obviously weak from the trauma of having surgery, but has virtually no pain, so that is a great blessing.

The boys' camp had 4 different groups of youth coming for a one day camp experience during the week. Group size for the one day sessions can be anywhere from 10 to 15 youth. While the time frame is more limited with a one day experience, doing these one day sessions enables us to reach many more young people with at least a touch of the love of God for that day. With the promise of Jesus that even a cup of cold water given in His name will not go unrewarded, our prayer is that at least a few of the seeds of truth sown in the hearts of these youth will grow and bring forth fruit to eternal life.

Martin, the lad from Germany who was here for more than a month and participated in two 10 day sessions, returned home on Fri. It was interesting to hear his comment to his mother as they met in the airport. He told her, "They sell me every day that I need Jesus." We are thankful that this message came through to him, and we pray that he will heed that call before it is too late.

Dan Yoder

LOOGOOTEE, IN
Mt. Joy

April 22—We are having a cool weekend after a warm week.

Last Sun. evening Marvin Graber was taken to the hospital, being dehydrated after not being able to keep anything in his stomach. There was a blockage somewhere that caused his kidneys to start shutting down. He was transferred from Jasper hospital to Evansville where he had some more dialysis treatments and seems to be responding well, and hopes to come home soon.

Mark Graber, 52, passed away on Tues. after being diagnosed with cancer 4 months ago. He leaves behind his wife Ellen, 3 married sons and 6 grandchildren. He attended the Pleasant View Mennonite Church. He was a nephew to Mary Ann Graber and Esther Yoder.

David and Mag Graber, Mo., Marcus and Tanya Mast and 2 sons, Dela., lodged at Mary Ann Graber's. Frieda Mast and son Dustin were guests at Jerry Yoder's. These all were here for the funeral.

Wednesday evening we dismissed church because of our counsel meeting service Fri. evening. We will have Communion in the morning, with Bro. Glenn Kilmer giving bishop oversight.

We are planning a fellowship dinner tomorrow, and we want to bid Katrina Graber farewell. She is planning to go to Ireland for 2 years. She doesn't leave the state till the middle of May, but plans to leave here May 4 to spend time with family in Miss. and fly from there to Ireland.

April 23—Our visitors in church this morning were Marvin and Martha Mast, Va. They were here for the funeral and are staying at Mary Ann Graber's. Also Jana Rose Yoder came for the first time.

Our kindergarten teacher, Marissa Graber (Ivan), had a checkup at her doctor's in body on Thurs. and found out her lower left lung wasn't clear. She is in the hospital at this point for treatment and we pray she will be able to attend our school program and picnic the first weekend in May. Glenda Carpenter (Lester) is taking her place in the classroom.

Sheila Wittmer, Pa., arrived to help her aunt, Cheryl Yoder, with household duties. It sounds as though she is doing a good job, as she claims the recognition of washing the most dishes of the 5 adults in the household for the last 9 days. The one who gives you a hard time, is often the one who appreciates your help the most. Sheila!

Well, I guess I'll have to quit since I can't seem to think of anything else, but I don't like the feeling I have that I'm missing something important.

Joy Yoder

CHETOPA, KS
6021 Trego

April 19—Beautiful weather! Pleasant sunny days with nice showers between. Strawberries are ripening, and wheat is heading.

South district church was at Edward Kramers' and is to be at Matthew Waglers' next.

It's a boy! Duane was born to Emery and Marie Hershberger on April 7, weighing 9 pounds 4 ounces. He joins 2 brothers and 6 sisters. Grandparents are Mrs. Annie (Toby) Hershberger, Bloomfield, and Alvin Kurtzes, Albia, Iowa. The little guy has caused some concern with the cough he is having, but I think it's going some better now.

The Abe Kurtz family of Mt. Vernon were making calls in the community on Sat. and had lunch at Matthew Kurtzes'.

Perry Summrys, Ervins, Elvins and Raymond M. Yoders and girls spent Sat. at the zoo in Tulsa, Okla. The Floyd Summry family of Mt. Vernon had planned to join them there, but it didn't work out after all, to their disappointment.

Matthew Herschberger has gone along to Kansas City with his sister Rosanna of Mt. Vernon for another surgery this week.

Teacher Leah took the upper graders to visit Memory Lane School on Mon. afternoon. Teacher Frieda then brought the lower graders here to our house to sing, which was very special, and much enjoyed.

The lower graders also had "pet day" that day, each bringing a pet along, quite a variety, ponies, puppies, kittens, bunny, ladybugs and a younger sister, who also came along to help sing!

I was able to go to church again on Sun. after missing several times. My knees and back are feeling a lot better, thankfully. My cane is resting in the closet, hopefully for a long time!

Paul Kemp is dealing with shoulder/neck/arm problems. X-rays indicate his having had a whiplash sometime and they feel it was quite awhile ago, where he had a deal with an unruly horse/colt. Chiropractor treatments are beginning to loosen it up, but the doctor feels it will take awhile yet.

Pete and Lydia Yoder

MONTICELLO, KY
Pleasant Ridge

April 16—Was this the most lovely week of spring? It was a gorgeous, blossom filled week with new life and green growth all around us.

We were thankful to be together for the sacred Communion emblems today, with fellowship dinner afterwards. With different flu ailments around it was good that almost everyone could be there. Teachers Norman Yoder and Mary Lou Yoder were home for this. Co-teacher Marilyn Kauffman had come with Mary Lou.

Sylvia Yoder enjoyed prime time in a cabin nestled in Pa. mountain hills with her 6 daughters, also visiting family close by.

On Sun., the 9th, Neals were at the funeral of Edward Hochstetler, Danville, Ohio.

Loyal's MS has been showing up again which affects his balance and walking. He brought a helper along today, a shiny new walker. Plans are for Loyal and Irene to go out to S.Dak. this week for his treatments at Ortmans'.

The schoolchildren did well in presenting their program on Thurs.

evening. It was focused on the life, crucifixion and resurrection of our Saviour. Thanks also to the teachers for the hours of organizing and practicing that are a big part of this inspiring arrangement.

Summers were to the funeral of Lehman Martin in Altamont, Tenn. and Johns, Sherman and Michaels had been to the viewing. I'm sure Michaels are glad they had the privilege of visiting Lehman recently.

While Eddies were at an Ind. wedding, Charles, Jeffrey and Twila Nissley visited at Roberts'. Eddies want to be at Roberts' by Sun. evening, going on home to N.C. on Mon.

Rosalyn was with Glenda and Katrina at St. Jude's Target House for most of a week. Benjs Kayla had a cold she did not go along, but did go down with Thomas for this weekend. On Good Friday Arlene and Eugene were down and shared dinner with Thomases and Rosalyn, coming back with Rosalyn that afternoon. I'm forgetting that Paul was also along and instrumental in Rosalyn's ride to Memphis.

Ray Millers enjoyed visits of her cousins recently. Matthew and Lydia Klemmer and 3 children, Newbern, Ala., stopped in Sun. evening, the 9th. They made a short visit at school on Mon. forenoon before traveling on. Later John and Lana Speicher of Lobelville, Tenn. stopped in for a few hours.

On the 12th Floyd Yoder admitted his brother Marvin's farm sale at Clayton, Ill.

Katie's sister Barbara (Raymond Schrock) had stroke symptoms Wed. evening. Tests have not pinpointed the cause yet. Neals were in Tenn. to be with Raymonds Fri. and Sat.

A special card, an invitation to the wedding of Kendall Gingerich and Sharon Stoltzfus in Advance, Mo. We are honored, even if we may not be able to attend! Kendall was one of the young men that was in our home over the 2016 Bible School year.

Mrs. Stanley Schlabach

VIROQUA, WI
Chaseburg West

April 19—Forecast is for rain today. So far it's holding off. Farmers were sowing oats and plowing, hauling manure and all that goes with farm life.

Our church was at Emery U. Millers', Communion. All the ministers from the other district were there. This was on April 9. Church next to be at our house. The North Communion was at Ben W. Millers' for Urie Masts on Good Friday. Bishop Noah Swartzes and 3 more ministers were there from Taylor. I don't have the names for the 3. The East was at John E. Weavers', Communion, on April 16. Milk price at low of $10.70 for 3.5 milk.

The County Today, a farm newspaper, had some news on milk. Canada shut the U.S. off dairy products and 2 big milk companies were sending products to them. Now they are sending out letters to the farmers as of May 1 they can no more take their milk. They are looking to ship to other companies but all is full. So we will see what happens.

A boy born to Sammy N. Millers named Mosie. Grands are Dan M. Millers and Neil I. Millers. This was on the 16th.

Tomorrow is the wedding at Eli Masts' for their Emma and Levi J. Miller (Joes).

Emery A. Weaver

DEATHS

Rosetta Burkholder, 66, Bellefontaine, Ohio

Samuel David Hostetler, 81, Berryville, Arkansas

Lovina J. Schrock, 92, Blair, Wisconsin

Mary N. Schwartz, 77, Geneva, Indiana

Breanna D. Troyer, 3, Wooster, Ohio

Eli D. Yoder, 81, Deer Lodge, Tennessee

Full Obituaries—Page 5

Figure 11.5 *The Budget* newspaper, "serving the Amish-Mennonite communities throughout the Americas" since 1890

and Pennsylvania that bring Anabaptists to Sarasota County. After their winter/spring break, the Anabaptist snowbirds board the buses at the Mennonite Tourist Church parking lot and return home by mid-April for the northern farming season and to receive communion—a semiannual ritual. Perhaps just as important a reason to leave by then is that the crucially important *Ordnung* is reviewed and potentially modified during the two weeks before communion.

Enjoyment of the Beaches and Pinecraft Festivities

As Amanda Yoder said, "When you come down here, you can... let loose." The Amish and Mennonite families do "let loose" and enjoy themselves in Pinecraft and on the beach. When the roads were paved in 1949–1950, the mobility of the Amish was greatly enhanced as they began using their characteristic three-wheel bicycles. These very practical and safe bikes have baskets on the handlebars

and some are electrically powered. There are hundreds in use around Pinecraft and even provide transportation for some to Siesta/Crescent Beach. Communication among Amish tourists utilizes every means but modern technology. There is an active word-of-mouth network, a type of non-electronic Craigslist at the old post office, and most importantly, the Anabaptists' version of Facebook—*The Budget*. This extraordinary newspaper has been published in Sugarcreek, Ohio, since 1890 and has remained true to its motto of "Serving the Amish-Mennonite communities throughout the Americas." The news section of the newspaper is actually the minor component because the Facebook-like letters dominate, with more than five hundred in each issue. Consequently, for their entire history, Anabaptist snowbirds have provided unique firsthand accounts of life in Sarasota and on Siesta/Crescent Beach with their vivid descriptions published in *The Budget*. Stories of their fishing

Figure 11.6 An electrically powered bicycle facilitates cruising and shopping in Pinecraft

Figure 11.7 The Amish version of Craigslist at 1240 Yoder Avenue in the old post office building. It displays classifieds ads, information on jobs, and local community events, as well as personal greetings

successes during 1940s through the 1970s are especially entertaining.

Many letters in *The Budget* describe meals, including the seafood feasts served after fishing Sarasota Bay. Amish meals are always communal, and food plays an important role in Amish society. The value placed on community meals with a wide variety of delicious foods partially explains their commitment to operating large restaurants, bakeries, and produce markets. Numerous such establishments along Bahia Vista Street have been an economic force in Sarasota County, and eventually Amish and Mennonites have expanded to the keys.

Back to the Beach

From the beginning, the Amish and Mennonite visitors loved Siesta/Crescent Beach. They came not only for pleasure: Some worked at the Out-of-Door School; others worked as fishermen, especially when the Intracoastal Waterway was a typical estuary teeming with fish. The beach has always had a great attraction for young Amish and Mennonites, allowing them to socialize with each other away from the scrutiny of their elders. Many a romance has been sparked on the white sand of Siesta/Crescent Beach. Later, it can become the perfect setting for a honeymoon. Just like everyone else, Amish and Mennonite beachcombers search the gulf shores for sand dollars and shells, build sandcastles with children, fish, sunbathe, or just sit and relax in the ocean breeze. Some Amish also go swimming. Although it would be rare to see Amish women in bikinis, some men are known to wear swimming trunks. For the more adventurous among them, Amish couples may even take to the skies, literally, on a parasailing trip.

Unquestionably, the most distinctive and eye-catching feature of the Amish on

Figure 11.8 Amish people relaxing on Siesta/Crescent Beach wearing plain clothes contrasting with the extra cheeky swimwear nearby

Siesta/Crescent Beach is their distinctive clothing. Although many Siesta Key visitors might consider the variety of swimsuits that can be seen on the beach as more colorful, it can be argued that a cluster of Amish dresses is the most distinctive and attractive attire on the beach.

The Value of Amish and Mennonites to the Sarasota Community

We should all be grateful that the Mennonite and Amish families selected Sarasota County during the 1930s and beyond as their "home away from home." They found excellent agricultural potential and capitalized on it for their good and the good of their adopted region

of Florida. As they discovered Siesta/Crescent Beach early on during their annual winter/spring breaks, they set an example that others followed a few decades later. It is a tribute to the area that they were welcomed and that they have been supported consistently over the years. Imagine how important the Mennonite and Amish presence must have been throughout the Great Depression and during World War II. They have brought diversity, peace, and prosperity. In fact, they embody the city motto: "May Sarasota Prosper." Many permanent Amish and Mennonite residents are skilled in crafts that serve Sarasota County and beyond: carpenters, painters, furniture dealers, and more. Clearly, Mennonites and Amish have done well by doing good in Sarasota County for nine decades.

CHAPTER 12

Becoming America's Best Beach

Siesta Beach boasts that it has the finest, whitest sand in the world, which attracts sand collectors and beach lovers from all over. The clear, clean waters along this gently sloping beach-face make for ideal swimming.

—Stephen Leatherman ("Dr. Beach"), May 25, 2017

The variable names applied to Siesta Key's internationally acclaimed beach has undoubtedly caused some confusion. The fact is, however, that Siesta Public Beach is contiguous with Crescent Beach and both have been recognized by awards, which leads us to use the term Siesta/Crescent Beach throughout this book and to assert that the entire three-mile strand can currently be considered "America's Best Beach." Other than a higher density of beachgoers, the boundaries of Siesta Public Beach can only be distinguished by the lifeguard stations, two unlabeled marking poles about 400 feet from the water's edge, and the pavilion-associated facilities adjacent to the parking lot. In other words, during quiet times of the morning and evening one can stroll along, as many do, from the last remaining groin—which is referred to on maps as an "old pier"—to Point of Rocks

Figure 12.1 The last remaining groin on Siesta/Crescent Beach known also as the "old pier" on maps

and hardly be able to recognize where Siesta and Crescent Beaches intersect.

The Beginning as "Sarasota's Beach"

It was neither by accident nor by original design that Siesta/Crescent Beach became so large. Prior to the acquisition of public land for the beach, Siesta Key residents, other Sarasota residents, and visitors enjoyed the same beach during the first half of the twentieth century. A real estate brochure from 1924 entitled "SIESTA—Sarasota's Loveliest Gem," advertised "an unprecedented sale" of seventy home sites on the key and described "Sarasota Beach, dream resort of the west coast" as follows: "Picture a firm, hard, white sand highway, stretching away and away into the distance; fringed on one side with palms, palmetto, pines, coconut palms, with here and there glimpses of orange groves... Without exaggeration it may be said that Sarasota Beach is the finest, the smoothest, the firmest and the safest beach on all the West Coast of Florida."

Visitors to "Sarasota's Beach" in the 1920s to the 1940s would generally drive their cars over the Higel Bridge, travel west by southwest along what was then called Siesta Road to Crescent Beach Road, then park their oil-leaking vehicles on the glistening white sand. Some of the cars got stuck in the sand and had to be pushed or towed off the beach. Although scenes like that on page 43 may seem surprising, parking cars on beaches was a way of life all along the gulf coast. Beachgoers changed into swimsuits in their cars because it was considered immodest in the post-Victorian period and well into the Roaring '20s to drive to the beach wearing bathing clothes. Thus, the cars doubled as bathhouses. As a welcome addition, between 1919 and 1930, bathhouses with dressing rooms were constructed on Siesta/Crescent Beach. Even

so, the beach was often deserted, as shown on pages 84 and 99.

Development of a Widely Acclaimed Public Beach

As the post-World War II tourism boom began, it was obvious that Sarasota County had a treasure on the former Little Sarasota Key. In 1950 members of the recently formed Siesta Key Association and other residents urged the Sarasota Board of County Commissioners (BCC) to "protect the public interest" in beaches. In 1952 a special bond election was held to authorize the expenditure of $250,000 to acquire public beach sites in the county. Support for the bonds was overwhelmingly favorable, with 77 percent voting in favor of the bond issue. Encouraged by the empowering vote, the BCC appointed a Beach Committee to identify beach properties for acquisition, realizing much of the choice property was privately owned. The goal was to create a beach for the public that would be large enough for an increasing population of beachgoers—a feature that is recognized in the many awards to Siesta/Crescent Beach. Chapter 90 of the Sarasota County Municipal Code empowered the BCC to acquire land with the following statement in Article I:

> The Board of County Commissioners of Sarasota County, Florida, is hereby authorized to acquire recreational facilities by gift, purchase at public or private sale, with or without bids, base or eminent domain, and is authorized to own, operate and charge fees for the use of such facilities for the people of Sarasota County, and to acquire lands necessary therefore, by condemnation or otherwise, such recreational facilities to be for public playgrounds, bathing beaches, swimming pools, bathhouses, picnic shelters and such other properties...

Figure 12.2 Comparison of the original Siesta Public Beach with its appearance in 2017. Note the larger beach size in 2017, with increased depth and width. The 35 acres of land acquired in the second transaction with H.A. Gregg may be seen to the right of the Siebert Pavilion, i.e., to the southeast

In his book *Quintessential Sarasota,* Jeff LaHurd summarized the rationale and acquisitions as follows:

> After World War II, Siesta Key's population grew to the extent that the need for a public beach became evident. A bond election authorized $250,000 to purchase a suitable site. The Harry Gregg tract, with 1,100 feet of beach frontage, was the first choice. After condemnation proceedings (Gregg had earlier offered a 99-year lease), the parcel was bought for $80,000. Subsequent land purchases gave the county 40 acres of public beach with 2,400 feet of beach frontage.

Eventually, those "subsequent land purchases" expanded Siesta Beach to 63.7 acres, despite considerable public opposition to large expenditures. More than half of the land came from tracts owned originally by H. A. Gregg and purchased by Sarasota County, including a transaction of $1,827,000 in 1970. More information on the Gregg contributions is provided in Chapter 13.

The Seibert Pavilion

To enhance the appearance and functionality of the public beach, the County Commissioners next hired architect Edward J. (Tim) Seibert to design a new pavilion. The Siesta Key Beach Pavilion is a showcase for Seibert's impressive talents and accomplished his architectural goals with its impressive vertical and horizontal features, its broad roof overhangs, and the extraordinary relationships of indoor and outdoor spaces. Even when you are within the building, you *feel* like you are outdoors.

The structure was completed at a cost of about $55,000 and dedicated in the spring of 1960. As described in *Architectural Record* of August 1963, the building was recognized for its outstanding use of low-maintenance materials such as reinforced concrete and concrete block. An underground concrete wall was constructed to protect the facility against inevitable storms. Improvements such as better restrooms were made in the 1980s to upgrade the pavilion but did not alter its beautiful appearance. More renovations followed in 2015-16 as part of a $21.5 million overall enhancement project for Siesta Public Beach.

Awards and Recognitions for Siesta/Crescent Beach

Through the acquisitions and improvements described above, Siesta/Crescent Beach earned its international reputation as one of the most beautiful beaches anywhere in the world. At the Great International White Sand Beach Challenge held in 1987, it was recognized as having the "whitest and finest

Figure 12.3 View of the Seibert Pavilion from the beach in the 1960s

sand in the world," and many other honors ensued, including the Travel Channel's 2004 award for "the Best Sand Beach in America."

Various criteria have been used to rate and rank beaches, the most extensive of which is that of Professor Stephen Leatherman, Director of the Laboratory for Coastal Research at Florida International University. He visits and evaluates all the beaches that have the potential to achieve a competitive ranking in his evaluation system. Known as "Dr. Beach," Professor Leatherman applies his system annually to swimming beaches that can be used by the public. His comprehensive system includes fifty criteria, many of which are objective, such as the presence of lifeguards. All of his criteria are fully described on his website (http://drbeach.org/online/dr-beachs-50-criteria/). For example, under "beach condition," a measure of beach resiliency, the ratings from low to high are "erosional, stable, and depositional." Another factor is the presence of "wildlife (e.g.,

shore birds)," which is rated from "none" to "plentiful." Other factors are quantitative measures such as EPA water quality data, beach width at low tide, water temperature, and determination of rip current potential with a dye ball water tracer Leatherman developed in his research program.

When Dr. Beach announces his rankings each year during the Memorial Day weekend, his "Top 10" list attracts a national audience and is of great interest to resort communities that relish publicity. After Siesta Beach was ranked #1 in 2011, the Sarasota Convention & Visitors Bureau reported that the news accounted for more than 425 million downloads from its website. Similarly, when Dr. Beach announced on May 26, 2017, that Siesta Beach was again ranked #1, after a #2 ranking in 2016, the spike in national interest was extraordinary. According to Dr. Beach's announcement:

Siesta Beach boasts that it has the fin-est, whitest sand in the world, which attracts sand collectors and beach lovers from all over. The clear, clean waters along this gently sloping beach-face make for ideal swimming. The beach is hundreds of yards wide, attracting fitness fans and volleyball players. Siesta is a year-round beach that is very popular with snowbirds during the winter months. There are lifeguards along this crescent-shaped beach along with full amenities. Recent upgrades include expanded parking, while maintaining the beautiful natural environment, and a free trolley to transport beachgoers.

TripAdvisor uses another system for rating beaches based on the quantity and quality of reviews posted on its website. In 2017, Siesta/Crescent Beach was ranked #1 in the annual TripAdvisor Travelers' Choice Awards. It was also named the best on TripAdvisor's rankings in 2015. Moreover, Siesta/Crescent Beach ranked #5 in the TripAdvisor's world rankings and was the only beach in the United States to make the top 25. TripAdvisor published the following praise for Siesta/Crescent Beach: "Pristine beach that never seems to end…

Photographer's dream… A place in the sun that warrants returning again and again."

Improving Siesta Public Beach

Siesta/Crescent Beach has much more to offer than its "finest, whitest sand in the world" and "pristine" environment. Fortunately, Sarasota County has recognized the importance of making improvements to "Sarasota's Beach." The need for more and better parking and amenities was obvious. These issues and others were addressed by a major renovation project in 2015-16 that required $21.5 million of investments for the future. A key element in the vision of the planners was to make the beach more welcoming from the time beachgoers parked until they were actually walking on the beach—that is, to make the entire experience enjoyable and interesting.

The many months of renovation efforts expanded and renovated the parking lot (it now has 980 parking spots), improved pedestrian access to and from Beach Road, modernized and expanded the restrooms, upgraded and elevated the concession area, and restored the

Figure 12.4 The beach walkway leading to the Seibert Pavilion during a busy period in 2017

historic 1960 pavilion. The white and blue colors used in the renovation are attributable to good planning, welcoming beachgoers to the white sand and the blue gulf waters. The project also included extensive landscaping improvements. To add a sustainable and natural element to the design, the renovators planted about 1,300 palm and canopy trees, most of them native to the area, to replace old nonnative pines. There are also countless wide-open beach access points to and from the cool, white sand of Siesta/Crescent Beach. Signs at these access points proudly proclaim "Sarasota Florida SIESTA #1 in the USA." Another innovative addition is a portable walkway/mat that provides wheelchair accessibility and allows beachgoers to wheel large carts, strollers, and coolers close to the water's edge. It is located in the middle of the half-mile-wide public beach and leads from the pavilion to near the third lifeguard station—i.e., the green shack.

A new structure also updates the old Sea Turtle Pavilion, which now includes a ramp to make it accessible. Green space and picnic tables surround the pavilion and an accessible and much-needed second concession stand—the Siesta Sun Deck—was also added. Many more restrooms were added, even though there are still not enough sometimes. The food and bathrooms of the Sun Deck are appreciated, but its best feature is the spectacular views from 19 feet above the beach at any time of day and especially at sunset.

There are also more picnic pavilions that can be reserved and an excellent playground. The playground fits the beach perfectly, with a tower that looks like a very large sandcastle with a flag reminding children they are playing at "Siesta Beach #1." For older beachgoers there are many tennis courts. Also, because of its sand quality, Siesta/Crescent Beach is very popular for volleyball—either casual, pickup games or tournaments.

Finally, the Seibert-designed pavilion now combines the best of the old and the new.

Figure 12.5 View of Siesta Beach from the Siesta Sun Deck during 2017

Figure 12.6 Siesta Beach with two lifeguard "high chairs" in 1972. Note the relatively narrow depth of the public beach

Renovating the historical pavilion was a priority during the planning given that this half-century old structure is arguably as much a symbol of Siesta Public Beach as the lifeguard stations. The pavilion now has even better bathrooms that are well situated next to a larger shelter by the old concession stand. Adjacent to the pavilion is a new, sorely needed building that serves as a station for the Sarasota County Sheriff's Office and lifeguards. This aspect of the project also included new landscaping with coconut palm trees and other native vegetation, enhancing the beauty of the pavilion and welcoming visitors to the beach.

Evolution and Perfection of the Lifeguard Stations

Dating to the 1960s, the Siesta/Crescent Beach lifeguard stations were "tall chairs on top of telephone poles," as the head lifeguard informed us during an interview. There were only two lifeguards needed then, when there were fewer swimmers and less beach area

requiring surveillance. During the early 1980s, the lifeguard stations were changed to two grey shacks replacing the "high chairs," and distributed along the half-mile of beachfront. When these lifeguard stations were replaced around 1997, they were painted in the four primary colors and arranged in alphabetical order by color—i.e., blue, green, red, and yellow—from north to south. This decision was not driven by aesthetic considerations, as most people assume. Rather, it was to help children avoid getting lost on the beach. Parents are advised to tell their children "go to the _____ (color) house if you feel lost," the color being the lifeguard station closest to the family's site on the beach. The red lifeguard shack on the cover of this book stands out among the four. It is said to be the most photographed lifeguard station in the world. It is the newest on the beach, having been replaced with minor remodeling in March 2017.

The lifeguards of Siesta Beach are exemplary, and most are also trained as emergency medical technicians. At each

Figure 12.7 Drum Circle leaders convene for warming up before the Sunday evening session begins

station there is a chalkboard where the lifeguard reports the water temperature, weather forecast, and other helpful information such as "be sure to wear plenty of sunscreen today." The lifeguards and their colorful stations have been significant factors in Dr. Beach's evaluation of Siesta/Crescent Beach.

The Drum Circle Drums Every Sunday

Siesta Key's Drum Circle is nationally recognized as an innovative, entertaining, and enduring feature of the public beach. The harmonized beating of about thirty different kinds of drums creates a primordial rhythmic sound that is always entertaining and often spiritual. A free weekly tradition since 1996, the Drum Circle begins about one hour before sunset on Siesta Public Beach about 500 feet east of the shore and just southwest of the Seibert Pavilion. Interviews with Drum Circle leaders clarified how it began and has evolved on Siesta Key over the past twenty-plus years. It developed originally in late September

1996 to celebrate the autumn equinox following a creativity workshop sponsored by the Ringling School of Art and Design. Then it continued for a number of years with people from local churches and members of the Native Descended Nation, "who were very involved in the spiritual aspect of the drumming circle," according to David Gittens, the seminal organizer of the Drum Circle. Gittens continued, "The foundation of all this, twenty-two years ago, was Vietnam War veterans, peace activists, and spiritual people. We were bringing the message of peace and love and light... It was down by Beach Access 8 and we kept it there a long time. It was just supposed to be a full-moon drum circle, but people liked it so much we started doing it every Sunday."

The name Drum *Circle* applies better to the early years when the drummers gathered spontaneously. Another Drum Circle leader, Dr. Marguerite Barnett, who has been dancing in colorful costumes almost every Sunday for two decades, elaborated. "What we had in the old days was actually a circle of drummers—drummers sitting in a circle... It became a group of drummers

Allan F. Newsham

WOUNDED WARRIOR PROJECT®

THE GREATEST CASUALTY IS BEING FORGOTTEN.®

Figure 12.8 Beach drum circle of people where dancing in the center can be enjoyed by all ages

on one side playing to a circle of people… When we moved to the public beach, it went from a sacred atmosphere to a carnival atmosphere." Consequently, as crowds of observers—that is, an audience—joined the Drum Circle, it was transformed from a circle of drummers to a circle of people. It is an egalitarian group of drummers that includes regulars and sit-in drummers, some of whom are simply vacationing

Figure 12.9 Sarasota County Police on tall horses for patrol during the Drum Circle performance

nearby. One regular drummer says that a hierarchy of drummers would neither be appreciated nor tolerated. The crowds now begin to form about two hours before sunset, and the entire atmosphere changes from week to week. You never know what you're going to find there; for instance, bagpipe players have also shown up to play along with the drums. When the winds are optimal, the rhythmic drumbeating can be heard more than a half-mile down the beach. Undoubtedly, the Drum Circle of Siesta Key is unique.

Mounted police officers patrol the area during the Drum Circle to better monitor the sometimes large (and imbibing) crowd, and as many as four other law enforcement personnel may be observing the crowd from near the Seibert Pavilion or closer to the crowd. Their presence helps to maintain a pleasant, orderly event, but they will intervene if necessary.

An Abundance of Planned and Unplanned Activities

With a gulf coast setting as beautiful as Siesta/Crescent Beach, it is not surprising that a wide variety of planned and unplanned activities, as well as special events, occur on a regular basis. Planned activities include Easter sunrise religious services, weddings, and volleyball tournaments, all of which can be witnessed for free by beachgoers. In fact, one of the favorite experiences of beach strollers is to walk along and observe what is happening on a given day. Almost everything is wholesome and fun.

Chapter 90 of the Sarasota Municipal Code lists twenty "Prohibited Conditions, Activities or Uses" that apply to public beaches and provides guidance to the organizers of events. Most of the ordinances pertain to keeping the beach clean and

Figure 12.10 Drum Circle guest requiring removal by police for misbehavior

safe, and others limit vehicles. Many of the planned events occur in front of or adjacent to one of the access pathways. The beach in front and just south of Access #13 is especially attractive for the Easter services and weddings because of the spectacular views and convenient parking. This area faces Point of Rocks, where the view is spectacular. It is also in front of the "Ask Gary House" described in Chapter 10. Scenes of this beach area are shown often on MTV's *Siesta Key* series.

Commercial activities such as the sale of food or drink are strictly prohibited except at the Sarasota County concessions stands. Other ordinances pertain to noise and behavior. In addition, from the May 1 through October 31, nesting marine turtles are protected species along all the beaches of Sarasota County. During this time, no night lights are allowed on the beach, including flashlights, spotlights, and any kind of flash photography. It should be noted that in the list of twenty prohibitions there is no mention of swimwear, nor has there ever been in Sarasota County despite occasional complaints and requests to prohibit certain kinds of attire. Consequently, the ever-changing swimwear fads and fashions seen on Siesta/Crescent Beach have not been restricted as they been elsewhere—a topic covered in Chapter 17.

The beach accommodates exciting national volleyball tournaments as a result of

Figure 12.11 Phil meets Bucky on the beach—amateur sand sculpture of the University of Wisconsin mascot, Bucky Badger, with the senior author

the 2016-17 renovations. In April 2017 the Eighth Fiesta on Siesta Women's Collegiate Sand Volleyball tournament brought 325 female athletes and thousands of spectators. It is the nation's largest collegiate sand volleyball competition with thirty participating colleges from coast to coast. In the future a men's division will be added, but the sixteen volleyball courts erected on the public beach can accommodate even more competitions.

Family reunions are another kind of planned activity that is popular on Siesta/Crescent Beach. These may last the entire day, and generally do, as families want to stay for sunset and take advantage of the opportunity for memorable photographs. For large gatherings, a semicircle of beach chairs is typical—as wide as fifty feet. Everyone can find something interesting to enjoy in addition to just soaking up the sun and swimming, floating, or surfing in the warm gulf water. Because children find so many ways to play on the beach, the situation is ideal for parents and grandparents to mix and mingle, drink, eat, and have many memorable conversations.

Of all the year-round beach activities, the most common is undoubtedly digging in the cool, soft white sand. Children love to dig holes and build creative sandcastles. While watching the most talented among them, the authors often wonder if a future architect or engineer is developing skills for a professional career. The advanced version of digging up the sand is amateur sand-sculpturing. Many incredibly impressive animals made of sand can be spotted, as well as fascinating symbols and signs. Sand-sculpturing contests, amateur and professional, are another one of the many annual events on Siesta/Crescent Beach. Thanks to Siesta Key Community College (SKCC), the Amateur Sand Sculpture Contest began in 1972 and has grown larger and more interesting since then.

Perhaps the most popular game among the older beachgoers is bocce, as the game is called in Italy, or bocce ball, as it is generally labeled here. As many as ten competitions with standard bocce balls and a few modified versions with golf balls may be seen on a one-mile stroll from Siesta Public Beach to Point of Rocks. Beachgoers often play catch with a Frisbee, a football, or a baseball. There is never a dull moment while walking along "America's Best Beach."

CHAPTER 13

The Glory and Generosity of the Greggs

The most remarkable thing about the handicapped is that they are seeking but an ordinary future. It is up to us to help them in any way we can.

—Harry Alan Gregg

Among the unsung heroes responsible for the ascendency of Siesta Key and "America's Best Beach" are members of the Gregg family. Hailing from New Hampshire, where they are famous as longtime leaders and philanthropists, the Greggs played a major yet under-recognized role on Siesta Key for eight decades. It all started when Harry Alan ("H.A.") Gregg brought his family to Sarasota shortly after the real estate bust in the late 1920s. Born in 1883 to a hard-working New England family with a distinguished ancestry, H.A. was an eighth-generation descendant of a family that came to America in 1718 and settled permanently in New Hampshire. In our current political climate, when the value of immigrants is being challenged again, the Gregg family history is worth reviewing.

The Greggs originated from Scotland, where the clan's original New World settler, Captain James Gregg, was born in 1672. After first immigrating to Ireland in 1690, where he worked productively in the northern Irish Province of Ulster, he sailed to Boston and soon moved about forty miles northwest to a heavily forested area with other Scots-Irish colonists who had left their homes in Londonderry to begin a new life free of persecution. A few years later, their town was

chartered and became Londonderry, New Hampshire. There, James operated a gristmill with his son, John, who was born in Ireland in 1702. The Greggs became patriots during the conflicts between America and England, and the third generation fought in the Battle of Bunker Hill. By the fifth generation, the Greggs, led by Joseph, were operating a lumber mill and supply business that eventually generated the family fortune. This was expanded by Joseph's son, David, who acquired large acreage of wooded property in Michigan to support his lumbering businesses, and then moved to Nashua, New Hampshire. Next, David Almus (David Jr.), born in 1841, founded several "Gregg and Son" businesses. In addition to lumbering, the Greggs manufactured furniture, doors, and window dressings, as well as establishing a grain dealership and a wholesale grocery business. He also started a grain dealership and wholesale grocery business. This seventh-generation Gregg must have been a master at multitasking and entrepreneurism. He became president of the Indian Head National Bank when it opened in 1865 and a member of the New Hampshire legislature in 1874-75. His most successful business, Gregg & Son Millwork, was especially lucrative as the

523 South Gulf Stream Avenue

This spacious home is ideal for a large family or two families who wish to reside together, with plenty of room for all. It is located three blocks south of Main Street and overlooks Sarasota Bay and the Gulf, one of the finest home locations on all of Florida's scenic Gulf Coast. 100-foot bay frontage and private pier, 250-foot depth to Palm Avenue on the rear. A magnificent grove of oak trees, one tree having a spread of more than 100 feet, makes an ideal setting for this home. Completely furnished and ready for occupancy. The state of furnishings and decorations marks it immediately as a residence of distinction, character and perfect comforts. Accommodations for family and servants are complete. Season rental, $1,800. Sale price, $36,500.

535 South Gulf Stream Avenue

Truly one of Florida's finest waterfront homes, available for the first time as a rental home. The location is perfect, facing west over Sarasota Bay with a wonderful view of the islands less than a mile away. Magnificent oaks shade the grounds and landscaping is carefully calculated for striking semi-tropic effect. Every detail of this magnificent home, furnishings, decorations and arrangements, leaves nothing to be desired for comfort, luxury or beauty. There are four large bedrooms and the two glassed-in sleeping porches will provide plenty of lounging space in Florida's wonderful sunshine. This home, too, would be perfect for a large family or two congenial families who wished to enjoy the best of a Florida vacation. Steam heat. Servants' quarters. Garage. Season rental, $2,800. Sale price, including 650 South Palm Avenue, described in this folder, $52,500.

650 South Palm Avenue

Three blocks south of Main Street, shopping and theatre centers, in choice residential section. Located in the same oak grove as 523 and 535 South Gulf Stream Avenue. A highly desirable home. Walls are of natural cypress panels giving an unusual decorative effect. Three bedrooms, two baths. Electric heaters. Servant's room and bath. Garage. Season rental, $800.

Figure 13.1 Gregg's rental homes on Gulf Stream Avenue and South Palm Avenue advertised accurately as "luxurious" and among the many properties in the city of Sarasota and on Siesta Key that were purchased by H.A. Gregg (Images from a brochure provided by Cyrus Gregg that reflect the 1930s to 1950s period)

home construction boom after the Civil War enabled David to capitalize on the demand for high quality millwork.

David Almus Gregg was not just an extraordinary businessman, but also a very generous person, dedicated to his family and to helping less fortunate people in his community. He brought his son, Harry Alan ("H.A."), into the family businesses early and before long H.A. took over their operations. One can only imagine the business acumen that H.A. Gregg acquired from his brilliant, energetic father. He benefitted doubly by having a father who also instilled personal values and commitment to generosity and community development. These attributes would eventually benefit families in Sarasota County and even more so in New England.

New Hampshire winters and even much of the spring season can be brutally cold and snowy. After H.A. Gregg had inherited his father's businesses and ensured their productivity, he and his wife, Margaret Prentiss, decided to bring their family to Florida for the winters. Fortunately for Siesta Key, they chose Sarasota, and by 1930 the Greggs had bought houses on Gulfstream Avenue (#523 and #525) near Main Street. The houses were excellent examples of Sarasota's upscale homes at that time. The timing was ideal for Gregg to take advantage of inexpensive Florida real estate, but he was as opportunistic as a person can be and he had wealth to invest. H.A.'s habit of taking advantage of every opportunity that came his way, of course, was a trait he learned from his father.

While wintering in Sarasota, H.A. Gregg and his family would regularly drive across the "new" north bridge to Siesta Key, ostensibly to enjoy the beach and gulf. These excursions enabled Gregg to survey the landscape with his visionary outlook and identify potentially available properties. While the nation experienced the Great Depression in the 1930s, there were plenty of bargains on Florida's largely uninhabited gulf coast barrier islands. The ever-opportunistic Gregg, therefore, bought inexpensive, beautiful, strategically located land around what would eventually become the public beach. These large properties apparently totaled nearly 100 acres and had more than 2,000 feet of beach frontage. All of this uninhabited land was on the gulf side of Midnight Pass. To appreciate the size of Gregg's acquisitions, one needs to realize the present Siesta Key Public Beach

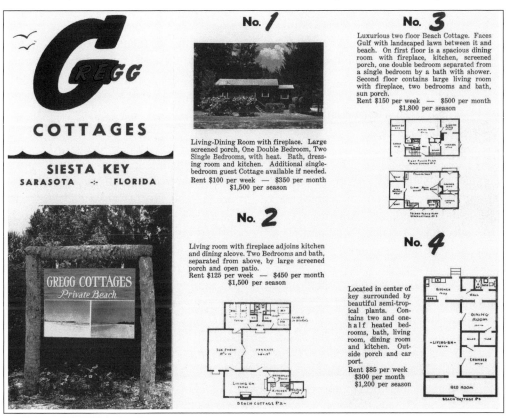

Figure 13.2 Gregg's Cottages on Siesta Key showing the floor plans and rental rates of four of the eight rental units at 6100 Midnight Pass Road

has 2,400 feet of frontage; nearly half of that was originally Gregg property.

In addition to the land next to the eventual public beach, Gregg bought a sixteen-acre tract about one-quarter mile south, adjacent to land owned by the descendants of Bertha Palmer. This second property included both gulf frontage and frontage on the bay side of Midnight Pass Road. Again, in retrospect Gregg seems to have been a visionary by investing mid-key and avoiding the partially developed but constraining and unattractive northern head of the Siesta Key "drumstick." Later, in the 1950s, Gregg Cottages would be built on the gulf side—attractive group of eight bungalows with one or two bedrooms typical of Siesta Key's Beach Cottage Era. These beach houses were intended for vacationers and notably for the Boston Red Sox ballplayers visiting in February and March for spring training. The bayside mid-key property ultimately became famous and an important part of the Gregg glory when the Summerhouse restaurant opened in 1979.

How H.A. Gregg Contributed Land for the Siesta Public Beach

The unique sequence of events by which the Gregg family's generosity contributed at least half the land for "America's Best Beach" reflects H. A. Gregg's commitment to the welfare of children and his talents as a businessman. When Sarasota County began to acquire gulf coast beach property, the challenge for the Sarasota Board of County Commissioners was how to secure enough land to meet the projected public needs. Expansion to at least forty acres with 2,000 feet or more of gulf frontage became the goal. This brought the unused part of the Gregg property into focus as Sarasota County targeted Gregg's land. A standard real estate purchase agreement might have sufficed. Instead, in a heavy-handed maneuver the county chose to assert an eminent domain "seizure," taking advantage of Florida's powerful laws that favor public purposes over individual property rights. The legal theory of eminent domain is straightforward: The government can seize private property for the public good in exchange for *full* compensation paid to the owner(s). The term "government" is applied liberally and includes federal, state, county, and municipal governments, as well as legislature-delegated public utilities such as Florida Power & Light. The takeover process is typically initiated by governmental condemning of the property and filing a lawsuit—the eminent domain action—against the owner. To be successful against Gregg, Sarasota County had to prove that 1) the Gregg property seizure was necessary—i.e., for an expanded public beach; 2) the taking of the property was indeed for a public purpose, which was obvious; and 3) it had prepared a good faith estimate of the real estate's value. The first of the three requirements was debatable in the mid-1950s, given the relatively low number of beachgoers at the time.

On the other hand, Sarasota County's vision and predictions about growing public use as tourism expanded certainly proved indisputable over time. In addition, Sarasota residents and visitors alike had been using Siesta/Crescent Beach as the premier public beach—Sarasota's Beach—for at least three decades, rather than Longboat, Lido, or Turtle Beach. With regard to the third requirement of the condemnation suit, the county offered H.A. a ridiculously low "full compensation" amount of $80,000. To his credit, and clearly reflecting the Gregg family tradition of generosity, commitment to family values, and love for children, H.A. Gregg chose not to contest the proposed compensation. As his descendants point out, he and his family were deeply committed to the public good and philanthropy.

Figure 13.3 Aerial view of Siesta Beach showing H.A. Gregg's land to the southeast that was sold to Sarasota County for $1,827,000 in November 1970 to approximately double the size of the public beach

Sarasota County Wanted More of H.A. Gregg's Land

When the Sarasota Board of County Commissioners came back to H.A. Gregg in 1964 and sought to acquire his remaining land just south of the public beach, the heavy-handed, government style was not welcome this time. No pun intended, but Gregg decided that it was time to "draw a line in the sand." Among his other concerns was the fact that the property was being actively used by the family. It consisted of a 35-acre tract of improved land with two desirable homes and a storage building. The location at the junction of Midnight Pass and Beach Roads was ideal with respect to eventual development and real estate valuation. And the immediate neighborhood was attractive. Specifically, the 35 acres were just northwest of the well-developed 38-acre Gulf and Bay

Club, with 780 feet of gulf frontage. It was described this way in the *Sarasota Herald Tribune* on July 2, 1964: "The property is about 715 feet in depth on the north side where it adjoins the present county beach. It has 1,731 feet frontage on Beach Road... The southerly line is longer than the north side... Beach frontage is figured at approximately 1,140 feet for the entire tract, according to the maps." But the county claimed that the beach "fluctuated from a depth of about 60 feet in 1952 to about 300 feet presently," i.e., during July 1964. The county, to rationalize a low-ball purchase price, relied on its tax assessor to assert beach erosion potential and apply the narrower depth of the 1950s when determining the price. The assessor stated that "one storm could greatly erode the built-up area." During March 2017, the authors measured the depth at the midpoint of the former Gregg property at 860 feet.

Gregg was cooperative with the expansion goal, but losing two family homes meant that the Greggs would eventually need to build another house on their more southern property one-quarter mile away at 6100 Midnight Pass Road. This expense and the rising value of beachfront property, and possibly also taking into account his earlier "gift," led Gregg to set an asking price of $880,000. The county's appraised value in 1964 was $335,110. Consequently, a deal could not be reached at that time. More negotiations would take place in 1970. In the intervening years, it became clear that the beach was not eroding and that property values were indeed rising. Consequently, Sarasota County and H.A. Gregg reached an agreement on November 9, 1970, in which the Greggs were paid $1,827,000 and given an easement. The county's second acquisition of Gregg land thus became the southern end of the public beach and the site for the tennis and volleyball courts. In addition, Sarasota County's fire station on Siesta Key was built on southeastern end of the parcel at 1170 Beach Road. The second acquisition of Gregg property accounts for the large size of the public beach and more than half its current acreage, as was confirmed by Walter Rothenbach, former Sarasota County Parks and Recreation director, who, despite public opposition, ensured that Siesta Key would one day be able to boast of having "America's Best Beach."

Creation of an Architectural Masterpiece: Casa de Cielo

A home for the entire Gregg family was built in 1980 close to the beach in front of Gregg's Cottages at 6100 Midnight Pass Road. An architectural gem, it served the

Figure 13.4 The Gregg family in 1959, four years after Hugh (back row, center, with Cay on his right) completed his term as governor of New Hampshire. Harry Alan is in the second row holding a child, with his wife, Harriett, on his right. Cyrus Gregg is on the far left sitting next to Harriett, and his younger brother, Judd, is in front of him sitting on the floor

Figure 13.5 The Greggs' unique beach home designed by Carl Abbott and named *Casa del Cielo,* as photographed from a drone showing the horizontal planes (terraces) and the piano-shaped roof

extended Gregg family quite well. H. A. Gregg's grandsons, Cy (who contributed much to this chapter), and Judd (who served five terms in the U.S. Congress, served two terms as governor of New Hampshire, and then three terms in the U.S. Senate) visited at least annually with their wives, children, and eventually their grandchildren. The house was designed in an innovative modern style and raised 15 feet above beach level with beautiful views of the gulf. The architect Carl Abbott, who is featured in the next chapter, had been conveniently living with his wife and two young sons in Gregg's Cottage Number 2 (page 133). He had also recently designed a magnificent restaurant just across the street on the Gregg's bayside property that became known as The Summerhouse, also described in the next chapter. The style of the Gregg home was original not only for Siesta Key but for the entire United States. It reflected the brilliance of Carl Abbott, whose concept of "In/Formed by the Land"

and modern style eventually led to numerous awards.

The house incorporated features of The Summerhouse and was named *Casa del Cielo* by H.A.'s second wife, Harriett. She was deeply engaged in its design and requested that Carl Abbott create "a beach house with a lightness and uplift... spaces that are exhilarating." Abbott's design, in his words, featured "a series of light, floating terraces supported on tall concrete columns." In his remarks when Casa del Cielo received the 1982 Florida Association of the American Institute of Architects' Award for Excellence, Paul Rudolph, former chairman of Yale's Department of Architecture, said, "This house's three horizontal planes, which do not in plan follow each other, but interpenetrate one with the other, is a valid idea…The forms of the house grow from the dominant view lines to the beach and Gulf of Mexico… One terrace thrusts to the west to the winter sunsets, the other terrace thrusts

Figure 13.6 The stunning interior of *Casa del Cielo,* designed by architect Carl Abbott, with its "exhilarating" staircase (Photograph: Steven Brooke)

to southwest end of the crescent-shaped beach." Truly, the house was an extension of the site—that is, it was "In/Formed by the Land." This is exactly what Harriett Gregg wanted. Consequently, the Gregg family referred to Casa del Cielo as "Harriett's home." Interestingly, this modern, uplifted building was located about fifty feet behind the historic 1940s Palmer house that embodied the Siesta Key beach cottage style. The contrast was striking and allowed those who saw both houses to appreciate the evolution of architecture from the Beach Cottage Era to modernism.

Continuation of H.A. Gregg's Philanthropy and Commitment to Children

In addition to displaying generosity with his glorious properties on Siesta Key, H.A. Gregg became interested in children's health care needs in New Hampshire during the 1930s. Previously, during the 1920s,

he had established the Nashua Fresh Air Camp for underprivileged children at Sunset Lake in Greenfield, New Hampshire. Next, Gregg helped establish the Daniel Webster Council of Boy Scouts and the Nashua Boys Band. Then, he became committed to helping handicapped children "seeking but an ordinary future." At the age of 53, he, along with Dr. Ezra Jones, founded the New Hampshire Society for Crippled Children. This followed Gregg's summer program in Nashua in which he arranged for host families to take poor children into their homes for the summer during the Great Depression. Next, H.A. Gregg organized a summer camp for children on the top of Crotched Mountain, one of New Hampshire's beautiful mountains. It was there in 1936 that he met Dr. Jones, an orthopoedic surgeon dedicated to rehabilitation. Both of them were deeply concerned about children with congenital deformities of their limbs and the victims of that dreaded summer disease, polio. Because the risk of polio was highest for city

Figure 13.7 The Palmer/Gregg beach cottage in front of *Casa del Cielo* with the Horizons West Tower in the background

dwellers, a summer camp in the clean air of a country mountain, together with the New Hampshire Crippled Children's Society, were very important achievements.

One day a local resident suggested that Gregg consider the property on top of Crotched Mountain for expanding his children's programs. Gregg was so thrilled with the idea that both he and Dr. Jones set a plan in motion to build a rehabilitation center and hospital on Crotched Mountain. To do this, during the 1940s and early 1950s, Gregg and Jones embarked on a fund-raising campaign throughout the northeast, raising over $1.5 million for construction costs and creation of a hospital and endowment. This was considered the most ambitious fund-raising effort in New Hampshire at that time. The Crotched Mountain Rehabilitation Center began serving patients in 1953 and was ready for the tragic national polio epidemic of the

1950s. H.A. Gregg's intensive charitable work on behalf of children with handicaps during the 1940s and 1950s, while running several businesses, occupied most of his time in New Hampshire. In addition, the Gregg family's annual journey to Florida and his real estate challenges on Siesta Key must have left H.A. Gregg with limited time for relaxation. He was 67 years old during the eminent domain action, and he was 81 while negotiating the second transaction for Siesta Public Beach. The Gregg family had also become busy with New Hampshire and national politics. H.A. Gregg himself had served as the Nashua Police Commissioner and later took on the responsibility of reorganizing the city charter and serving on the Nashua Common Council. The next prominent role in New Hampshire for the Gregg family was served by H.A. Gregg's third son, Hugh.

The Achievements of Hugh and Catherine Gregg

Born in 1917, Hugh Gregg became nationally recognized as the youngest governor in New Hampshire's history, serving from 1953 to 1955. Hugh and his wife, Catherine, known best as Cay, are jointly responsible for leading the efforts to preserve New Hampshire's distinction of holding the first presidential primary election. Their lives were intertwined with Siesta Key for seven decades. Hugh, in fact, was educated during his winter/spring stays at the Out-of-Door School (in addition to Phillips Exeter Academy). Like his father had before him, Hugh Gregg inherited the role of managing the family businesses. He graduated from Yale University in 1939 and Harvard Law School in 1942, after which he returned to Nashua and started a law practice. During World War II, he served in the U.S. Army Counterintelligence Corps (1942–1946). A Republican, he was elected in 1947 as a city alderman in Nashua, and was subsequently elected mayor in 1950, a term cut short because of military duty. He served again in Army Counterintelligence (1950-1952) during the Korean War.

As a prominent businessman involved with the family mill-working business, Hugh Gregg was instrumental in setting up the Nashua Foundation, one of the first large-scale non-profit "incubators" for start-up businesses in the country as they took over the Indian Head Mill buildings from Textron and helped the city recover from the loss of textile mills in the 1950s by recruiting new industry. Hugh was known for a sense of humor, reflected in a small hardback book he published titled *All I Learned About Politics, by Hugh Gregg*. All of its pages are blank.

Completing a Glorious Period on Siesta Key

In summary, the glory of the Greggs and their generosity in the development of Siesta Key has permanently benefitted the barrier island that was primitive but pristine when they first visited during the late 1920s. H.A. Gregg is as responsible as anyone for creation of "America's Best Beach," as well as providing land for the essential fire station. Hugh and Cay Gregg devoted their efforts to mid-key development. They recognized the value of their bayside property and the genius of architect Carl Abbott to create the Summerhouse and then later save it from demolition. The Gregg home, Casa del Cielo, was equally impressive but was lost to developers in 2017 after the Gregg family descendants sold their remaining property on the Siesta Key and left after nine decades. Its demolition was tragic. Still, its many innovations retain instructional value in the field of architecture.

CHAPTER 14

Convergence of Stars at
the Summerhouse

I wanted a building that wasn't there...with a rich night blue sky... to lift the ceiling.
—Carl Abbott, July 26, 2000

Sarasota County has a history of destroying historically significant buildings for the sake of "progress." There are many examples of important buildings that fell before a wrecking ball, including the Seaboard Coast Line train station and the El Vernona (Ringling Towers) Hotel. If they had been replaced by architectural gems, more tolerance would be appropriate, but aesthetically pleasing structures did not appear. On the barrier islands, the Lido Casino with its unique art deco style and memorable history also failed to survive despite a public outcry. As Jeff LaHurd wrote on May 8, 2011, in the *Sarasota Herald Tribune*, this "centerpiece" being demolished was "history wasted." On Siesta Key, the Mira Mar Casino could also have been renovated rather than destroyed. On the other hand, the historically minded leaders of the Out-of-Door School/Academy preserved their seminal buildings on Siesta Key, and another extraordinary building/landscaping complex has also survived and been enhanced: the Summerhouse Restaurant. Its story is a tale of how stunning architecture combined with delightful experiences and clever politics can preserve memories that have the power to prevail over a potentially destructive development project. We are grateful to Cy Gregg, Carl Abbott, and Paul Mattison for sharing the details with us to supplement documents provided by Larry Kelleher at the Sarasota Historical Resources Center.

Origin of the Summerhouse

The bayside, mid-key property that Harry Alan (H.A.) Gregg acquired around 1930 ultimately became an important part of the Gregg legacy on Siesta Key when a magnificently designed restaurant opened in 1979 as Gregg's Greenhouse Restaurant. The property was typical of an uninhabited gulf barrier island and remained in its natural state of dense tropical vegetation throughout the twentieth century. This nature-rich environment, however, provided added value that H.A. Gregg could not have imagined possible. Thanks to a brilliant architect, Carl Abbott, the jungle-like ambience became the inspiration and driving force for the award-winning design of Gregg's Greenhouse Restaurant, which later became the Summerhouse Restaurant. Eventually the Summerhouse became the "go-to" place on Siesta Key, if not all of Sarasota, as the next generation of Greggs inherited H.A. Gregg's properties.

The unique history of the Summerhouse, which was saved from the wrecking ball by historic designation, is compelling enough to deserve a full review in this chapter. It truly resulted from a convergence of stars— Governor Hugh Gregg and his wife, Catherine (Cay), plus Carl Abbott, whose career was rising as an innovative architect, and finally a young chef/restaurateur, Paul Mattison, who deserves the credit for the ultimate success of the Summerhouse and who has subsequently had incredible impact in Sarasota County.

The Summerhouse story begins with Hugh Gregg. Sometime after his father, H.A. Gregg, died in 1972, 65-year-old Hugh began spending more time on Siesta Key and eventually settled in at 6100 Midnight Pass Road with his wonderful wife— environmentalist, historic preservationist, and philanthropist, Catherine (Cay). During the transformation of Siesta Key from the Beach Cottage Era to the Condominium Era, faced with rising taxes and sensing the time was right for an upscale mid-key restaurant to serve the expanding population, Hugh and Catherine decided in the late 1970s to use their bayside property for a fine dining facility. This momentous decision led to the Summerhouse in 1979.

Architectural Options for the Restaurant Site

Governor Gregg's original concept was to construct a barn-like building at 6101 Midnight Pass Road that would resemble a New England barn. He, of course, would have been very familiar and comfortable with such a facility. Fortunately, he approached Carl Abbott, who was a busy architect establishing his illustrious career with the firm Zoller & Abbott. Abbott had lived across the street from jungle-like site and knew it well. He brought to the project a perfect combination of understanding nature-site-building relationships and the unique a vision of the architectural features

that would emphasize and integrate with the surrounding landscape. Although modernism is his signature, Abbott has always been very much influenced by the immediate environment surrounding his buildings. His special sensitivity to nature developed during his childhood. Born in a small town in coastal Georgia, Abbott became interested in nature, the landscape, and art. In an interview with the *Sarasota Herald Tribune* on January 16, 2011, he said, "As I learned more about landscaping, I learned about architecture. It was like, 'Oh, my, they are all interrelated. I can tie them all together...' I break buildings down into two stages. One is the concept. Is it a beautiful, valid concept that is functional and working and handsome? The second is, how well is this carried out? Not the quality of the contractor, but the quality of the architect."

Sarasota County in general, and Siesta Key in particular, have always respected innovative architects and have been proud of the original Sarasota School of Architecture. None have been more talented or respected in this regard than Carl Abbott. His architectural contributions and widespread recognition enabled him to have some impact as the drama unfolded to save the Summerhouse. Abbott is the youngest and last member of the original Sarasota School of Architecture, as well as a Fellow of the American Institute of Architects. He received a bachelor's degree from the University of Florida, then earned his master's degree at Yale under the renowned chairman of the Department of Architecture, Paul Rudolph. After Yale, Abbott worked in London with his Yale classmate Lord Norman Foster, one of the most innovative and internationally acclaimed architects in the world. Following a stint in New York City, Abbott moved to Sarasota in 1966 to develop his own practice. He is one of the most highly awarded architects in the Florida/Caribbean region. His regional recognitions include a host of AIA Florida awards, including the Medal of Honor for Design, the Architectural Firm Honor Award, and the greatest number of Test of Time Awards ever presented for "architectural designs of enduring significance." On the national level, Abbott was elected a Fellow of the American Institute of Architects. He also received *Millennium Magazine's* Millennium Award as "one of the outstanding architects of the twentieth century."

By the 1970s, Carl Abbott had perfected his "In/Formed by the Land" vision along the lines of Frank Lloyd Wright's unique architectural style. Consequently, for the Gregg restaurant project Abbott proposed a glass-enclosed structure to be built in the northwest corner of the three and one-half acre property with what many would call "window walls." He told Hugh Gregg that this was "one of the last pieces of jungle on the Key, and that a hidden glass building in the jungle would be more unusual, and more appropriate (*Sarasota Herald Tribune,* March 14, 2004). Later he said, "I wanted a building that wasn't there… one that celebrated the surrounding landscape." For the construction, Abbott selected the largest glass panels he could find in 1975. These 10-foot sheets of uninterrupted glass were actually removable. They were framed with durable western cedar that was bleached to a driftwood color. The foundation footprint and construction work *per se* preserved the magnificent surrounding foliage including old oak and palm trees. Cay Gregg, who played a major role in partnership with Carl Abbott and her husband, was deeply dedicated to preserving the fauna and flora that would surround the "greenhouse" restaurant. To enhance the site further, the project was completed with addition of eye-catching flowering foliage. These embellishments included bamboo and gold trees, and tall orchid trees. In his book *In/Formed by the Land*, Abbott describes the restaurant this way:

Located on an island populated with high-rise condominiums, the building is a glass pavilion in a tropical jungle, providing a needed oasis of green… consists of delicate glass walls…seats 300 … wings composed of 20-foot modules provide intimate seating… The wings provided an intimate fine dining experience that was previously missing on Siesta Key and rare in Sarasota. And the entry was magnificent with a prominent ficus tree and a thalo blue ceiling to simulate a rich night sky.

The "rich night sky" was breathtaking, according to some Summerhouse diners, and inspired the "convergence of stars" theme for this chapter. Carl Abbott's design broke up and spread out the dining area so that 200-plus guests could each have an intimate experience. Some have called it an "X-shaped building," but it really was the wings designed for intimate dining that give this impression. Perhaps the most stunning part of the Summerhouse was the balcony, which seemed to float above the trees. Some of the happiest happy hours in Sarasota County were spent there at a magnificent bar that is still in use. The fact that the happy hour originally extended from 5 to 8:30 P.M. made the bar Siesta Key's favorite elegant hangout. Imagine an "hour" that can last for three and a half hours of prolonged socializing at a captivating bar situated in a jungle-like setting.

The Restaurant Struggles and Is Sold

When the restaurant opened in 1976 as "the Greenhouse" (also know as "Andersen's Greenhouse" or "Gregg's Greenhouse"), the building was an immediate success. On the other hand, the food left something to be desired in the early years. Moreover, managing the operation and keeping the facilities clean was a greater challenge than anticipated. In fact, running a successful restaurant is not just an occupation but a way of life and often becomes a family preoccupation. This is true

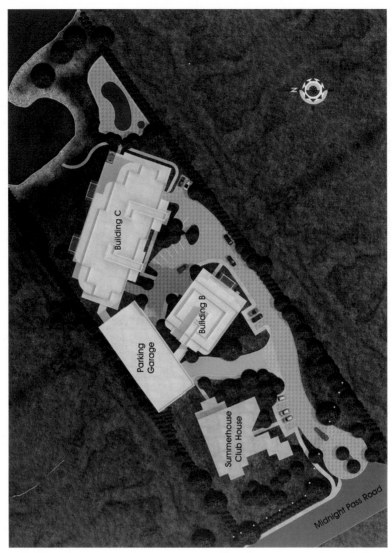

Figure 14.1 The footprints of the Summerhouse, showing the intimate dining wings, and the Summer Cove buildings

everywhere, but was even more true in Florida during the 1970s, where the population swings were immense—up to a tenfold increase in business during the tourist season. In an effort to deal with such challenges, Hugh Gregg had hired a restaurant management company that he assumed would allow him to keep up with his business and political activities in New Hampshire. Unfortunately, the restaurateur he brought on board lacked the experience and skills needed to offer consistently good food and service. In addition, although a crowd could be expected during the winter/spring season, the off-season slump led to significant operating losses. The bottom line was clear: a spectacular building is not enough for a restaurant to succeed. By 1981 failure was likely, but the Gregg family is so success-oriented that Hugh Gregg had other options on his mind, especially as he learned more about the demands of restaurant operations.

One day, George Perreault visited for lunch and was taken in by the atmosphere. Perreault was already a successful restaurateur in

Figure 14.2 Paul Mattison displays three of his culinary creations at the Summerhouse

Aspen, Colorado. He thought the building was so unique and charming that it should be matched with good food and an appealing menu. The original menu was limited, but the 5-8:30 P.M. "happy hour" remained magnetic, especially with "all drinks at half price," and continued to draw a crowd. Governor Gregg himself was dissatisfied with the management firm he had entrusted with establishing and maintaining a restaurant in keeping with the Gregg's reputation. Moreover, the demands of the Summerhouse on his entire family were daunting.

Fortunately for both Hugh Gregg and George Perreault, their paths crossed on a fateful day in 1981. According to Perreault, "I went to lunch with a client, and I made a remark that somebody ought to buy this place and make it a restaurant... The food was so bad." Hugh Gregg, instead of being offended (probably because he felt the same way) offered on the next day to sell the Summerhouse and its adjoining acreage

to Perreault for about $2 million. Perreault accepted and was immediately pleased with his acquisition and the opportunity to run "an upscale restaurant." As he said, "lo and behold, the opportunity fell into my lap." He hired a senior chef, Jim Weaver, from his Colorado restaurant, and the operation improved, although the struggles resumed in the mid- to late 1980s. Finally, the turnaround came in 1991 when Perreault lured another chef from Aspen.

Paul Mattison Transforms the Summerhouse

Enter Paul Mattison, arguably the all-time best chef/restaurateur of Sarasota County, who brought not only impressive cooking skills but also management ability, entrepreneurism, and a much broader vision to the Summerhouse. Mattison began his culinary career at age 15 at home in New York City where his Italian grandmother, Esther,

Figure 14.3 One of Paul Mattison's cooking classes, with his students enjoying wine while learning the master chef's techniques

taught him both cooking and gardening while instilling a commitment to fresh vegetables. He then worked in a local Greek restaurant and followed the owner's advice to obtain professional training at the Culinary Institute of America. Mattison moved to Aspen to refine his skills and become recognized by Zagat. When he moved to Sarasota and took over as executive chef at the Summerhouse in 1991, the restaurant finally had a star restaurateur who was equal to the magnificent edifice Carl Abbott had created. The business rebounded almost immediately as the restaurant broke even in 1992 and generated profits annually for the rest of its operations. Mattison pointed out during the twenty-fifth anniversary celebrations in 2000 that the main problem before he took over was inconsistency. "When I came on board, service was good but there was no direction in the kitchen... the food was really hit or miss." He added, "Consistency is important because if customers don't get what they expect, they won't be back."

Mattison also introduced what has become known as the "Mattison Concept." His visionary initiative—which George Perreault resisted initially because it changed his business model and had limited potential for profits—included cooking classes and off-site catering. The former, while not directly producing significant revenues, created relationships and new customers. Even though happy hour was shorter, the Summerhouse became a "go-to" place for several reasons: the combination of the indoor/outdoor tropical ambience, a piano and bar upstairs, and the wide-ranging menu with consistently excellent food. Former diners say "the food was fit for a king." Some diners we interviewed said Paul Mattison's signature dish, tournedos rossini, was the best meal they ever ate. Mattison's fourteen years of operating the Summerhouse were glorious and, considering its earlier struggles, added to the glory of the Gregg family's legacy. Hugh Gregg must have been thrilled to literally walk across the street from Casa del Cielo and enjoy every aspect of the Summerhouse. During Paul Mattison's's fourteen years at the Summerhouse, there probably was no better restaurant in Florida.

Rescuing the Summerhouse brought stardom to Paul Mattison, but that achievement was only the tip of the iceberg in his culinary/community career. He now owns and manages an extraordinary combination of culinary operations featuring three restaurants in Sarasota and a newer one in Bradenton. Each restaurant varies in ambience and menu, but all are known for offering Chef Paul's signature menu items, outstanding service, and quality ingredients, while supporting the community, regional farmers, and food suppliers. In 2001, Mattison, along with Jason Sango, strengthened the Mattison's concept, which now includes not only cooking classes but also Mattison's Catering Company and Mattison's Culinary Adventure Travel.

Chef Paul and his loyal, dedicated staff, some of whom came from the Summerhouse, are also committed to giving back to the community. His generosity is well known throughout Sarasota County as he gives culinary classes and demonstrations for charity organizations like the Boys and Girls Club, Girls Inc., Sarasota County, and Selby Gardens. He can be found at many local fundraising events and regularly conducting fascinating cooking demonstrations and wine-pairing dinners. Not surprisingly, Mattison has received several prestigious culinary awards, while his community-based efforts have also been nationally recognized.

All Good Things Must Come to an End

As 2004 dawned Paul Mattison was not only fully in charge of the Summerhouse, he was also busy establishing Mattison's City Grille and the Mattison Concept. George Perreault had two other businesses in Sarasota County and felt ready to cash in on the appreciated property he had bought two decades earlier from Hugh Gregg. Concurrently, among residents and visitors to the area, there was "a thirst for *luxury* living in Sarasota" and particularly on Siesta Key. Throughout the 1970s and 1980s

Figure 14.4 Convergence of stars when Governor Hugh Gregg, his wife, Cay, and Carl Abbott dined at the Summerhouse

the developers of the Condominium Era had concentrated on constructing a large number of units per building that were modest in scale and décor, but the affluent 1990s brought more and wealthier retirees to Florida along with a statewide population boom. They had the capital and desire for a more luxurious lifestyle, but there was very limited land still available on Siesta Key for large condominium projects. On the other hand, as Carl Abbott said, the former Gregg site at 6101 Midnight Pass Road had "been on the radar screen for developers for years." And why not? Siesta Key had nothing else to compare with the famous 3.42-acre site. Its location and natural, tropical landscape made it a developer's dream, but the Summerhouse restaurant footprint was an essential component for any development.

Also in 2004, George Perreault was 80 years old and "looking to simplify." Before long, an offer was literally on the table from Snavely Siesta Associates, based in Cleveland, Ohio. This visionary company made a timely offer and proposed construction of a three-building complex with forty-five luxury condominiums. It would be called Summer Cove. Snavely principals had a good understanding of Sarasota County issues along with a plan that would surely be appealing to affluent buyers. CEO Polly Snavely commented, "We call ourselves Sarasota locals because our family has had a home there for the past twenty-five years" and that Summer Cove was "going to have a casual Siesta Key feel to it, but still have a sophisticated, elegant touch… West Indies style."

It was announced in February 2004 that George Perreault had reached an agreement with Snavely to sell the restaurant building and all 3.42 acres for a development project that would include razing the Summerhouse. The project, however, would have to be approved by the Sarasota County Planning Commission, which required assessment of several site issues, such as impaired storm water drainage and

other "adverse impacts." This development review process evolved into much more prolonged, more public, and more complex process than Polly Snavely could possibly have anticipated.

Architecture and Memories Save the Summerhouse Building

The decision to sell the site, which was under contract in February 2004, would have meant the end of the Summerhouse, and its demolition was already planned. But Carl Abbott entered the picture again to play a major role. Ironically, a "Best of Carl Abbott" bus tour that focused on a few of his nearby creations had been scheduled for March 21, 2004. In an interview a week before, Abbott said, "I'm not ready yet to think it might actually be torn down… Perhaps the new owners would at least consider saving the building as a clubhouse for the condos." This insightful comment proved to be prophetic.

In Sarasota County, Abbott's award-winning projects include Harriet Gregg's Casa del Cielo, Lido Bayfront House, the Saint Thomas More Catholic Church complex near Gulf Gate, and of course the Summerhouse. His book *In/Formed by the Land*, which we highly recommend, describes all these structural works of art with their beautiful landscaping and the concepts that he developed to perfection. Buildings such as the Summerhouse are very difficult to photograph, as the authors learned, so we can only offer a few views of the current building. Even the photographs in Abbott's book don't do the building justice. By 2004, when the Summerhouse was in jeopardy, Abbott was internationally acclaimed and deserved to have his unique creation preserved. His association with the Sarasota School of Architecture proved to be the saving grace as ten months of public and private drama unfolded.

Many of these signs greet beachgoers along the walkways from the parking lot to the finest, whitest sand in the world.

Notice sand from Longboat and Lido Keys being transported from north to south where it accumulates on Siesta/Crescent Beach by natural marine processes described in Chapters 2, 12, 16, and 18. Note the heart-shaped Palm Island neighborhood and adjacent Grand Canal, and the dunes protecting "America's Best Beach." (*Beach Scene* magazine, courtesy of Adam McLean, Publisher).

700-650 MILLION YEARS AGO

Peninsular Florida was originally embedded within the African and South American continents as part of the supercontinent Gondwana, rather than being part of the future North America in Laurasia. Florida's rock basement, which is similar to the foundation of North Africa, was located at approximately the South Pole when its nearly 8,000 mile migration via plate motion began toward Laurasia.

350-250 MILLION YEARS AGO

A long series of continental collisions was occurring and led to new land mass aggregations, forming the Earth's last supercontinent, Pangea, while suturing the eventual Florida peninsula to ancestral North America that included the Panhandle region and creating the massive Appalachian Mountains range.

250-200 MILLION YEARS AGO

Peninsular Florida's land mass was located more than 1,000 miles inland with no ocean contact, but then break up of Pangea from 200 to 160 million years ago initiated creation of Florida's distinctive shape and the surrounding seas.

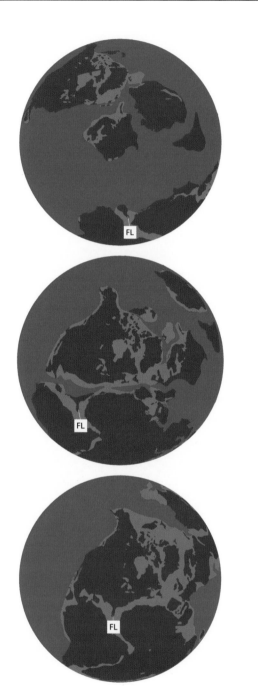

Geologic events from about 700 to 200 million years ago. (From a variety of sources).

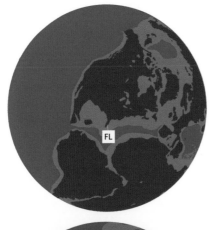

150-100 MILLION YEARS AGO

While Florida's Gondwanan-derived rock was separated from North America by the Georgia Seaway Channel over the Laurasia-Gondwana suture zone and covered with warm, shallow water, its surface was altered by formation of a 3-4 mile thick calcium carbonate (limestone) layer resulting in ultimately the ancestral Florida Platform.

100-40 MILLION YEARS AGO

Appalachian Mountain erosion through chemical and physical weathering continued and caused an enormous volume of quartz-rich sediment to be transported through the ancient Georgia Seaway to the Atlantic shore, filling that ancient rift, while Florida's collision with Cuba caused the southern margin to aggregate with Cuba creating the Straits of Florida.

6.5-1.6 MILLION YEARS AGO

Delivery of the Appalachia-derived, physically weathered and purified quartz sand was continuing from north to south and along the Gulf Coast by longshore transport processes which are still active today and account for the white sandy beaches predominantly composed of the same hard silicon dioxide mineral, but very little new sand has been delivered from regions north of Florida since then.

Geologic events from about 150 to 1.6 million years ago. (Illustrations created by Julia Farrell Patton from a variety of sources).

The "Lost Tribes" of Florida Amerindians, a painting by Theodore Morris. The tribes that became known as the Calusa and Tocobaga dominated the southwest coast of Florida at the time of the Spanish invasions. (Reproduced with permission of the artist).

U.S. Coast and Geodetic Survey of Siesta Key in 1942 based on air photographs. Note the variations in the roads. (From the American Geographical Society Library, University of Wisconsin-Milwaukee Libraries).

(By Julia Farrell Patton from old postcards and a Google Earth image).

Vintage postcards showing the transformation of Siesta Key from the 1950s *Cottage Era* to the 1980s *Condominium Era*. Note the large areas of land that were undeveloped and jungle-like before the "condo craze" began in the 1970s. (Illustration created by Julia Farrell Patton).

Crescent Beach in its pre-tourism "almost deserted" state during the early 1950s when real estate developers were advertising "cheap land" as in the brochure that featured this cover. Note the two-piece, miniskirt-style, high-waisted swimsuit with limited skin exposure that was in fashion then. (Illustration copied and improved by Julia Farrell Patton).

Overcrowding on Siesta/Crescent Beach increases hazards and challenges for the lifeguards as well as the waste management capacity.

View of the public beach with its famous volleyball nets from the Siesta Sun Deck, a nineteen-foot-high ADA-compliant pavilion.

Midnight Pass during the 1970s when boats traveled easily between the Gulf and Little Sarasota Bay, although it was already narrowing and migrating to the north. Note that the Solomon house on the Gulf shore was about one-half mile north of the tidal inlet at that time. (Photograph courtesy of Nancy Connelly).

The old Stickney Bridge being replaced in 1965 by construction of a new drawbridge to the north after four decades of supporting vehicular traffic and swiveling to allow boats to navigate the Intracoastal Waterway. (Photograph courtesy of Nancy Connelly).

Drummers assemble and begin warming up for the Sunday evening Drum Circle event in front of the Siebert Pavilion.

Sunsets on Siesta/Crescent Beach with taps playing provide a breathtaking, romantic scenario and are routinely accompanied by applause from hundreds of people along the three-mile-long strand of "America's Best Beach."

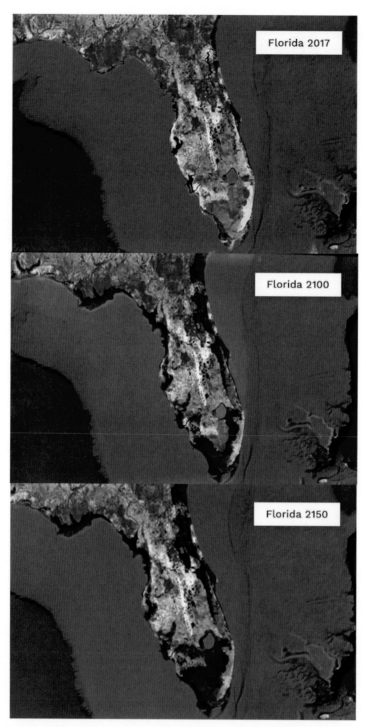

The potential fate of Florida during the next century if global warming continues to raise sea levels and threaten coastal properties. Note the original size of the Florida Platform displayed as the lighter blue color extending as far as 100 miles west into the Gulf of Mexico. (Illustrations created by Julia Farrell Patton based on several Internet-derived sources that speculate on the impact of climate change and rate of sea level increases).

Figure 14.5 The Summerhouse exterior with 10-foot sheets of uninterrupted glass panels (Photograph by John Twitchell)

By the spring of 2004, seemingly out of nowhere on Siesta Key and on the mainland, a strong emotional impetus arose to save the building and its landscaping. Within a few months of the announced sale, a public outcry emerged. A "Save the Summerhouse" group was established and a petition campaign organized that amazingly garnered 4,816 signatures. The advocates for preservation emphasized that customers didn't come to the Summerhouse just to eat dinners or enjoy the ambience. Rather they came for the uplifting experience of the stunning architecture and the family bonding that persisted long after in fond memories. This became increasingly apparent as testimonies emerged. As Harold Bubil

concisely put it, this is a building "where people have marked birthdays, holidays, and anniversaries… and first dates have been followed months later by proposals—all framed by the magnificent setting that is as much a part of the Summerhouse's charm as the building itself."

During the spring and summer of 2004, the "Save the Summerhouse" movement gained momentum. Although it was only twenty-eight years old and the building really couldn't be regarded as intrinsically historic, the community considered it an icon linked to the Sarasota School of Architecture, and the idea of historical designation arose. Interestingly, this Sarasota "School" was never an academic institution. Rather it was

Figure 14.6 The treetops balcony of the Summerhouse

a "school of thought" and represented the style of architecture that evolved in Sarasota and became embraced by many architectural luminaries. Its origins are thought by many to be from Siesta Key itself when Mary Rockwell Hook designed the Whispering Sands Inn in 1937 as "a little tropical paradise" and was followed with Sandy Hook projects by Hook herself and Paul Rudolph, then the work of Ralph Twitchell, Tim Seibert, and others.

The historic preservation movement gained traction with leadership by Mollie Cardamone, mayor of Sarasota in 1996-97.

Lorrie Muldowney, Sarasota County's historic preservation specialist, asked Snaveley to do an assessment of the historical significance of the property, which brought into the evolving drama Marion Almy and her invaluable firm Archaeological Consultants Inc. Among the conclusions in Almy's report was this: "Although less than 50 years of age, the Summerhouse Restaurant is part of the the Sarasota School of Architecture, a recognized modern movement and may meet the criteria for exceptional significance for buildings of the recent past." Almy's views resonated with Lorrie Muldowney in particular, and she further burnished the building's significance in her role with the Planning Commission, emphasizing that the Summerhouse is a "classic example of Sarasota School modernism" and "an absolutely seamless transition between the indoors and out... It embodies the best of the school."

And, thus, the ball was back in the court of Snavely Siesta Associates, and Polly Snavely proved her point about being a "Sarasota local" with extraordinary insight, flexibility, and site planning skills. Instead of three five-story condo buildings, Snavely came back with a proposal to construct two buildings—one of the original five-story structures and a nine-story Summer Cove condo closer to the bay—and to convert the Summerhouse into a clubhouse, as Carl Abbott had suggested. Just one obstacle remained, namely the height of the nine-story condo, which was 35 feet, 10

inches above the acceptable limit. Initially the Planning Commission rejected the revised proposal by a 7-1 vote, concluding that the height issue was more important than saving the Summerhouse. The controversy thus boiled down to a "heart versus head" conflict, to borrow a phrase from President Thomas Jefferson, as ultimately the Sarasota County Commission chairman, Jon Thaxton, said that his "heart and mind were at odds over the issue" but "reluctantly, I'm going with my heart on this one." After twice delaying a vote, all the other commissioners agreed with him and thus, on December 17, 2004, the variance to allow construction of a 113-foot building with two conditions was approved. First, it was stipulated that the Summer Cove's clubhouse had to be made available seventeen times annually for civic and community group functions—i.e., public functions. And secondly, a legal written

Figure 14.7 The Summer Cove buildings B (foreground) and C. Note that the 35-foot higher elevation of building C was the key to a compromise that preserved the Summerhouse

agreement was required between Snavely Siesta Associates and Sarasota County to assure adherence with protections of the building.

The final milestone in the rescue effort was a public hearing on July 27, 2005, "to approve the historic designation of Gregg's Greenhouse Restaurant/The Summerhouse Restaurant ..." This led to approval by the Sarasota County Historic Preservation Board. Thus, the Summerhouse was saved from demolition because of these unique public efforts and the flexibility of Snavely Siesta Associates to convert the building to their clubhouse/office/fitness center at a $1 million expense in exchange for approval to raise their A building 35 feet above the code's requirement—a variance that is hardly noticeable. It was a good decision. Snaveley made significant improvements to the building (although Carl Abbott does not feel positive about the manner in which the building was retrofitted), and the Summer Cove Condominium Association has taken good care of it. Best of all, Siesta Key has preserved an architecturally significant but hidden treasure at 6101 Midnight Pass Road.

CHAPTER 15

Development and Expansion of Villages Transforms Siesta Key

From "everybody knew everybody" to "who are these people?"
—Anonymous interviewee on Siesta Beach, 2017

The north and northwest regions of Siesta Key, despite being platted as early as 1907 and being made accessible by the Higel Bridge, were slow to develop. Even the better North Bridge of 1927 and destination facilities like the Roberts Casino, the distillery and speakeasy on Higel Avenue, and a bordello failed to attract a sustained crowd of tourists. Originally, the half-mile strip along Ocean Boulevard was predominantly residential.

While transitioning in the 1980s from a more residential population to a predominance of touristy short-stay visitors, and following the first best beach award in 1987, Siesta Key's evolution entered a new period of commercial growth. The condo rental potential had increased and was being driven by realtors. Condominium units bought in the 1970s were generally well decorated and appreciated in value with island build-out.

Figure 15.1 Siesta Key Village as seen from the top of the Terrace Condominium during the late 1960s, when Ocean Boulevard was a quieter street

The demand for rental units was soon greater than the supply, so naturally prices rose and owners throughout the key responded accordingly. The previous requirements for two- to three-month leases were abandoned by condo associations as owners were motivated to rent their units short-term—one or two weeks, and eventually even a weekend or less. Sarasota County officials were fine with the transformation from residential occupation to short-term tourist visitors because they made even more money—tax on the rental fees in addition to the property taxes. Moreover, in 1992 Sarasota County imposed a 2 percent tourist tax on business revenues—money that was used for beach maintenance (50 percent), advertising (25 percent), and arts/culture (25 percent).

But the cultural impact of the change from residential to short-stay tourist was disturbing to the longtime residents. No longer did "everybody know everybody." As a result, the friendly, interpersonal pattern of behavior diminished in general around the key.

The Chamber of Commerce Leads the Way Forward

In addition to the Siesta Key Association organized in 1948, visionary business leaders had the foresight to organize the Siesta Key Chamber of Commerce (SKCC) in 1959. It succeeded a travel-related, for-profit business known as Siesta Key Vacations Inc. SKCC had only six members, listed as "directors," in the beginning. Its growth was slow, and it had only thirteen members on April 2, 1987, when a reorganization took place and its mission was clarified. These moves stimulated rapid growth, and 123 paid members came to a meeting on July 2, 1987. Growth has continued, and in 2017 the Siesta Key Chamber of Commerce had 470 members. To achieve increased visibility, SKCC established an office at 5263 Ocean Boulevard and began marketing and business promotions.

An annual holiday parade was organized and well publicized. The Ringling organization even brought elephants to Siesta Key. As the short-stay tourist population increased, the accommodations on the island were collecting about one-third of Sarasota County's Tourist Development Tax by 1993. This provided clout and allowed the SKCC to pressure Sarasota County to assure a daily cleanup of Siesta/Crescent Beach. Other events and campaigns have been organized such as "sandfests" and a sand sculpture contest (annually since 1977). Since 1980 an arts and crafts festival, called "Siesta Fiesta" in recent years, has been held along Ocean Boulevard, and a craft festival has been underway since 1998.

Development and Transformation of Siesta Key Village: Nightlife Returns in the 1990s

During the Roaring '20s and into the 1930s, despite the Great Depression, Siesta Key was a magnet for the young and young at heart seeking nightlife thrills. The "Big Casino" that Captain Lewis Roberts operated and the "Little Casino" known as Mira Mar provided almost every entertainment a man or woman might desire. But during and after World War II, the place to go was Lido Key, whose casino was the "centerpiece" as described by Jeff LaHurd. After the casino was demolished in 1969 ("history wasted," according to LaHurd), St. Armands Circle became the nightlife magnet of Sarasota County. Siesta Key residents and visitors could drive there in about fifteen minutes, the parking situation was much better than today, and there was plenty of upscale entertainment. Few on sedate, peaceful Siesta Key would have expected that Siesta Key Village would become the nightlife capital by the mid- to late 1990s, but so it has evolved.

The development of Siesta Key Village, so named in the mid-1960s, has a fascinating

Figure 15.2 The Beach Club is in its seventieth year of continuous operation

history. During the early to mid-1950s, the half-mile strip along Ocean Boulevard consisted mainly of houses, the Beach Club (a popular bar and grill), the Beach Restaurant (a good place for lunch or dinner), and several small shops operating out of old wood-frame houses. There was also a hardware store and gasoline station. The most prominent of the small shops sold upscale apparel featuring fine clothing for both women and men—e.g., the Conrad Egan boutique. There was no need to go to the mainland for clothes.

Figure 15.3 The cozy Beach Club J-K bar during the 1950s when the artists and writers had their own bar stools and convened daily to enjoy the cocktail hour(s). Note the Boston Red Sox photographs above the bar on the left side; they were probably regular customers during the spring training season

As the village evolved, the anchor business for the nightlife seekers was the Beach Club. It opened in 1947 and is believed to be Siesta Key's longest continuously operating business. The appeal of the liquor was only topped by the atmosphere. It was the ultimate hangout during the eclectic period of the 1950s to 1970s when artists and writers convened there. They each had their own stool and favorite cocktail that was served without being ordered by the always-alert bartenders. These creative types also competed with each other on the bocce ball court behind the Beach Club. When the *Wheel of Fortune* show became popular on television, they also competed with each other at the bar, trying to be the first to answer the question posed to a TV contestant. Everyone obviously felt that the bar food and music were consistently good, as indicated by seventy-plus years

Figure 15.4 Siesta Key Village map made in around 1980 to advertise selected stores, restaurants, and real estate agencies

of successful operations. On the other hand, nightlife then meant that the crowd stayed until 8:00 or 8:30 P.M.

In 1965 John Davidson and Dr. Freeman Epps (see Chapter 9) built the present shopping center. There they attracted very high quality shops such as the Butcher's Block. There were many real estate agencies, just as today, and some clothing stores specializing in upscale women's apparel. There were also some good restaurants—some so good that they didn't need to advertise. A landmark was Anna's Restaurant and Deli, which was established in the village during 1971 by Anna James. All of Anna's sandwiches were, and are still, great thanks to "Anna's Famous Sauce" and fresh bread baked on site. The signature sandwich that became Anna's #1 seller is the "Surfer"—a combination of ham, turkey, Swiss cheese, and cucumber with *the* sauce on freshly baked marble rye bread. It is advertised as "the sandwich that made Siesta Key famous!" Even a half-Surfer is enough for a filling lunch.

Other special eateries opened during the 1970s and enjoyed varying degrees of success. Among the standouts, the Old Salty Dog deserves special mention. It began operations on November 1, 1985, at 5023 Ocean Boulevard. Its location at the north end of the village strip would not seem ideal, particularly with so many nearby residences, and parking can be a problem. On the other hand, everything else has been excellent as its thirty-two year history proves. The Old Salty Dog is advertised as a "British style tavern serving hot dogs," but that's an understatement. The Salty Dog hot dog is a quarter pound, foot long, beer-battered, deep fried frankfurter served with a variety of toppings or fully loaded. It's good and special enough to be featured on TV's Food Network. In addition to the fully loaded Salty Dog, the restaurant's most appealing characteristic over the years has been its

distinctive casual atmosphere and fishing shack motif, with wooden decking that feels like being on the water. It blends a Florida Keys and British aura to create a wonderful environment. The Old Salty Dog's success at the end of the Siesta Key Village has been so amazing that the owners exported their formula to City Island, where breakfast is also available, and to Venice.

Although the four-decade impact of the Old Salty Dog and about thirty other eating establishments along the half-mile strip has been extraordinary, the south end of Ocean Boulevard at 5250 features the attraction that has been the game-changer for Siesta Key Village: the Daiquiri Deck Raw Bar or simply the Daiquiri Deck. It was created in 1994 from three old wooden houses whose front porches could be easily joined together. Its perfect location and casual, seaside atmosphere and great capacity made the Daiquiri Deck an immediate hit as *the* island hot spot. As John Davidson remarked during our interview, "It changed everything... The village has never been the same." Stan McGowan, owner of the Butcher's Block, pointed out that a different, larger, late-night crowd was being attracted to the bars. Store rents were being raised, thus displacing many upscale retail businesses that did not generate high enough profits year-round to cover higher overhead costs. On the other hand, T-shirt shops with their greater volume of sales and high profit margins thrived thanks, in part, to evening shoppers. Even though the Daiquiri Deck was not solely responsible for this rapid evolution, it brought the most successful *modus operandi* in Siesta Key's history. Offering a 3:00 to 7:00 P.M. happy hour, with live music to draw people off the beach and an enticing combination of unique drinks and food, the Daiquiri Deck's business skyrocketed. Customers loved the casual ambience, where beach clothes fit in well, and the large amount of deck seating. It's a place to mix

Figure 15.5 The Daiquiri Deck—Siesta Key Village's game-changer after 1994

and mingle while waiting for the Slurpee-like beverage machines to deliver one drink after another—daiquiris, margaritas, piña coladas, hurricanes, bushwackers, etc. After a few of these specialty drinks, almost everyone agrees that the food is more than good enough. The Daiquiri Deck's raw bar was an early hit, offering a variety of gulf and Atlantic oysters, as well as some from as far away as Japan.

An interesting aspect of the Daiquiri Deck's early history is the reaction of the residents around Siesta Key Village in 1994-95. Many complaints were filed with the Siesta Key Chamber of Commerce about the crowd noise and loud music coming from the many dining establishments with outdoor seating, which mainly those at the south end of Ocean Boulevard. After several Sarasota County meetings to discuss the issue of nightly noise, a compromise was reached on closing time (2:00 A.M.), and the bars became more cautious about live music at night. Frankly, they don't need it to attract crowds, and they can't control crowd noise. These neighborhood issues are all part of the transformation of Siesta Key Village. As with the Old Salty Dog, the success of the Daiquiri Deck led to its opening a second location at St. Armands Circle in 2011 and another in Venice in 2013, where the same formula has worked well. Who would have imagined in the 1940–1990 era that sleepy Siesta Key would develop and export nightlife attractions to the Ringling Isles?

Finally, the great success of the Daiquiri Deck at Siesta Key Village recently led to a second Siesta Key location 2.7 miles to the south at 1250 Stickney Road. Explaining the second site on the key, managing partner Troy Syprett pointed out, "It seems like it is really close, but Siesta Key is kind of divided into two areas... There are a lot of people staying on the south end of the island... They don't come up to the village a lot...."

Quietly and Successfully, Another Village Evolves

The south end of Siesta Key was once a peaceful quiet region that eventually spawned a second village. Like Siesta Key Village, it developed incrementally and continues to do so. John Davidson said he recognized the opportunity in 1970 for a second drugstore, as there was not much commercial development on the southern end of the Key and it was a "different market." Little existed besides the Crescent Club, which was established in 1949, and the Beach Shop, serving groceries to patrons since 1952. The Crescent Club, however, was attracting steady business and, like the Beach Club, became a secondary hangout for some of the artists and writers who otherwise congregated at the Beach Club. For instance, John MacDonald and Gil Elvgren (the pin-up artist) could walk there from their homes less than one mile south. The Crescent Club also served the need for a package liquor store, and still performs that function today, including the unusual feature of drive-up service. By the early 1970s the south-key Davidson Drugs occupied a building in front of the old Siesta Lodge (page 98). In fact, the drugstore was located between an outdoor swimming pool and Midnight Pass Road. John Davidson, always an astute businessman, optimistically took out a ten-year lease. His optimism paid off.

By 1980, it was clear that a variety of stores could successfully operate in a cluster just south of where the new Stickney Bridge was bringing more traffic to the key. Building the bridge slightly north of the old swing/swivel

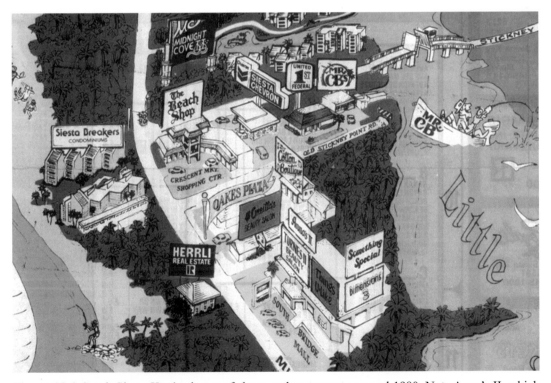

Figure 15.6 South Siesta Key's cluster of shops and restaurants around 1980. Note Anna's II, which opened in 1978, but no evidence of Captain Curt's Clam and Oyster Bar, which moved to Oakes Plaza in 1982

bridge facilitated development of new businesses that in turn helped develop the southern region of Siesta Key. For instance, in 1959 Chuck Berecky ("Mr. C.B.") began to operate a much-needed full-service shop for fishermen, with bait and tackle, boat rentals, fishing charters, etc. Eventually, Mr. C.B.'s offered a broader range of goods and services to customers, such as a full line of diving gear, beachwear, sunscreen, and several boat rental options including Jet Skis and popular pontoon boats. Other shops were opened to expand the cluster. Most noteworthy, Anna's II Restaurant and Deli was established in what was called South Bridge Mall, which became the new home of the relocated Davidson Drugs. Anna's II, started by the second owners Rita and Him Harrigan, was an immediate success and eventually replaced the original Anna's in Siesta Key Village.

The game-changer for the Stickney South Side cluster, however, was the relocation of Captain Curt's Crab and Oyster Bar and its associated Sniki Tiki Tropical Bar. The incredible success of this enterprise, which now owns and has connected all the original Siesta Lodge buildings, effectively led to the key's second tourist/entertainment village which is now designated "Captain Curt's Village."

Captain Curt's World-Famous Clam Chowder Repeats History

The evolution of Siesta Key proves again and again that history repeats itself. One hundred years after the clam chowder of Ocean and Captain Lewis Roberts attracted enough guests to open the key's first hotel, Captain Curt's chowder has had almost as significant an impact. The story of the Stewart brothers' achievement in 2007 with their special, carefully developed recipe for New England-style clam chowder deserves a complete description, along with an explanation of why clam chowder is an excellent food.

The creation of a widely recognized clam chowder occurred through a most interesting sequence of events initiated by another kind of captain—not a boat captain as many have assumed. In 1979, Curt Marsh retired from his position as a captain in the Indiana State Police and moved to Siesta Key. There, he opened Captain Curt's Crab and Oyster Bar near Turtle Bay at 8865 Midnight Pass Road. Among the foods he served, clam chowder became a favorite. But the location was not ideal, although currently the Turtle Beach Grill does well at Captain Curt's original site. And, perhaps the demanding role of a restaurateur was not the best choice for a retired state police captain either, because Curt Marsh sold the restaurant in 1981. A better location was found at the intersection of Old Stickney Point Road and Midnight Pass Road at what was then called the Oakes Plaza. The property at the old Siesta Lodge was available, including the building that Davidson Drugs had vacated, and had the advantage of being close to the entry road for automobiles arriving on the key. Thus, the new Captain Curt's Clam and Oyster Bar was established there in 1982 by another owner who improved the business over the next decade. However, that owner also decided to sell out.

Then, in 1994, the Stewart family bought the restaurant and upgraded both the food and the atmosphere. A new recipe for clam chowder was developed by Brad and Brett Stewart, arguably the best seafood dish on Siesta Key. It was as extraordinary as the Roberts' recipe, but more consistent and loaded with clams (rather than potatoes). The clams are carefully selected from Maine to Maryland. To make their restaurant more accommodating and attractive, as well as to increase its capacity, the Stewarts soon added on a saloon section to the east. In 2005, and the very popular Sniki Tiki bar/restaurant was added. By then, Captain Curt's was

Figure 15.7 Captain Curt's Clam and Oyster Bar, serving thousands of customers with arguably the world's best clam chowder

serving thousands of annual customers, but the most significant achievement of the Stewarts was winning the Great Chowder Cook-Off in Newport, Rhode Island, in 2007. The coveted national award confirmed what Siesta Key residents and visitors had suspected all along about the legendary clam chowder they had been enjoying.

Many restaurants make dubious claims to having award-winning clam chowder, but Newport's Great Chowder Cook-Off is a challenging and meaningful competition that began in 1981. Originally a regional competition, it became a wide-open international event that attracts chefs from all over the U.S. and some from Europe. Approximately 25,000 people attend the event at Rhode Island's Fort Adams State Park. Up to 100,000 chowder samplings may be consumed. Every ticket-purchasing attendee is given a ballot, and anytime during the noon to 6:00 P.M. tasting period, voters may drop their ballots into the bins of the restaurant or company whose chowder they

enjoyed the most. The top vote-getters are announced at 6:00 P.M. sharp and immediately posted on the Newport Waterfront Events website. Clearly, with such a rigorous and well-organized competition, the distinction of serving the nation's best clam chowder secures forever the reputation of Captain Curt's Crab and Oyster Bar.

It is appropriate that the Great Chowder Cook-Off is held in a New England state close to Boston. Original published recipes for New England clam chowder date back to 1751, when this early comfort food was being served in Boston restaurants and homes. Fish and clam chowders were introduced into New England by European settlers who had eaten the nutritious soup on the voyage to the New World. Chowder probably originated in the fishing villages of Brittany, France, and/or Cornwall, England—regions that traded with each other as long ago as 4,000 years, likely sharing food recipes for centuries. Although some might argue otherwise, it is likely that the word "chowder" came from the French—either the word *chaudrée* or *chaudière,* which derive from the Latin word *calderia*—a place for warming things and later referring to a cooking pot or cauldron.

Leaving Siesta Key after a spring break or snowbird season used to mean leaving Captain Curt's clam chowder behind and settling for an inferior recipe elsewhere—perhaps a fish chowder or a predominately potato soup masquerading as clam chowder. The Stewart family, however, resolved the problem of chowder withdrawal symptoms in 2012 when they developed an ingenious and very successful kit with a 15-ounce can of preserved chopped ocean clams and a second can containing all the other "base ingredients" except butter and cream. These kits are now being shipped from Siesta Key to countries around the world.

Clams are nutritious as well as delicious, and are one of the healthiest of all seafoods, especially with regard to their fat and protein quality. Their fat content is especially nutritious because they have relatively low cholesterol levels and provide predominately omega-3 fatty acids. Sound medical evidence has shown that omega-3 fatty acids can improve blood lipid profiles and cardiovascular health, and other research data suggest benefits for the central nervous system. Clams also contain abundant B vitamins like niacin and are rich in essential minerals such as iron, selenium, zinc, and magnesium.

CHAPTER 16

A Tale of Two Beaches

Sarasotans have had a long-term love affair of damaging nature… most of our historical environmental disregard is spurred by arrogance… probably the best example of officialdom's arrogance of the environment is the story of Midnight Pass…

—Paul Roat, *Siesta Sand*

The differences between Siesta/Crescent Beach and Turtle Beach are like night and day, but that has not always been the case. Although separated by only a couple of miles of shoreline distance, they have been subjected to much different environmental impacts since the early 1960s when the Intracoastal Waterway was dredged, and especially since 1983 when Midnight Pass was closed through individual and governmental naïveté. Review of the history of Midnight Pass helps explain the problems of Turtle Beach and is enlightening, sobering, and even frightening. Inextricably intertwined with these issues is the story of Syd Solomon, an artistic genius who has been vilified over the closure of Midnight Pass.

Relevance of Comparing Beach and Key Histories

A comparison of Siesta/Crescent Beach with Turtle Beach is presented below. Most of the differences can be attributed to the erosion-nourishment cycle affecting Turtle Beach, as its recently acquired sand has been pumped in from miles offshore in 2007 and 2015-16 projects. Once erosion begins on a gulf

barrier island, it is usually relentless. The most recent effort to restore Turtle Beach was completed by Weeks Marine on April 30, 2016. This $21.5 million project reclaimed 690,000 cubic yards of sediment from far offshore. In addition, 1.1 acres of dune vegetation was added to protect the shoreline. Sadly, however, erosion at Turtle just one year after the Weeks nourishment project was already significant. In fact, it can be predicted that by 2021-23 another nourishment will be necessary. Consequently, the beach became "the best it can be" during 2016-17. Thanks to Sarasota County's additional improvement project, costing nearly $1 million, the facilities at Turtle Beach have been delightful for visitors.

Although the sand borrowed by Weeks Marine will become a lighter color over time, it will never be white and will remain relatively coarse—contaminated in many places with shell fragments and hot enough to require shoes for afternoon strolls. In contrast, the majority of people walking along Siesta/Crescent Beach are in bare feet. The authors actually measured sand temperatures with a meat thermometer on sunny afternoons during April 2017. On days with ambient

Turtle Beach Compared to Siesta/Crescent Beach

Characteristic	Turtle Beach	Siesta/Crescent
Ownership	Originally private, now public	Public and private
Resiliency	Continuously eroding	Stable or expanding (accreting)
Sediment supply	Sand-starved	Sand-enriched
Current sand source	Offshore transport	Natural through upward shoaling
Sand color	Gray-black	White
Sand temperature	Hot	Cool
Surface stability	Soft	Generally firm

temperatures varying between 84 and 88°F, Siesta/Crescent sand where the crowds were walking was 77-81°F in either the sun or the shade (under an umbrella). Turtle Beach's sand, however, measured 93, 98, or 100°F, depending on its location and color—that is, the darker sand was absorbing and retaining more of the sun's heat, as expected. Surprising to the authors, even the wet sand on Turtle Beach a few feet inland from the water's edge measured 80–89°F on a day when the gulf temperature was reported as 72°F. Obviously, color matters in many ways along a gulf beach.

Recent visitors might ask if the sand at Turtle Beach was ever the equivalent in quality of the Siesta/Crescent Beach sand. The answer is yes. Prior to the 1980s, according to photographs and our interviews, the two beaches had similar characteristics. Usage may have been different, as crowds always flocked to the public beach, but the two showed a similar appearance. Turtle Beach had a much smaller population of strollers and bathers when the southern one-third of Siesta Key was focused on commercial and sport fishing. Among its favorable characteristics for fishermen, Midnight Pass offered easy passage from the Intracoastal Waterway to the gulf and vice versa (see color page 10, top photo). That advantage was important for about five decades.

Factors Explaining How Siesta/Crescent Beach Has Thrived

With all the beach erosion nearby, it seems incredible that Siesta/Crescent has been expanding during recent decades when it became known as "America's Best Beach." Yet, that is indeed the case, as property owners in the vicinity marvel at their good fortune. Many have pointed out to the authors that they have "been lucky." Perhaps luck has played a role in avoidance of a hurricane direct hit, as well as the minimal damage from the 2015 tornado and the 2016 storms. On the other hand, careful assessment reveals that Siesta/Crescent Beach is blessed with a variety of favorable factors.

First and probably foremost, Siesta/Crescent Beach benefits from being situated on the drumstick head of a mixed-energy barrier island where it can continue to be sediment-enriched through the upward shoaling process discussed in Chapter 2. In summary, it can effectively capture the wave energy and create swash bars that promote upward-shoaling effects. Just as significant, perhaps, Siesta/Crescent Beach is also the beneficiary of sand via longshore transport processes from the north (page 12). This mechanism has probably been augmented by sediment enrichment from the beach nourishment projects addressing the barrier islands to the north that suffer severe

Figure 16.1 Turtle Beach picnic area during the 1950s, when the sand there was similar to that of Siesta/Crescent Beach

erosion— Longboat Key, for example. Supporting this conclusion is the fact that Siesta/Crescent Beach expansion has occurred following the nourishment projects of the keys to the north. It seems likely that this advantage is enhanced by the effect of Big Sarasota Pass slowing sediment flow southward as it temporarily retains sand. In fact, impact of this large tidal inlet has been to create a reservoir of sediment in a white sand bar used for gatherings of partying boaters.

Another positive factor that may be quite important is the impact of Point of Rocks acting as a barrier—essentially like a natural groin. As Laird Wreford, Sarasota County's coastal resources manager, explained, "Because of the location of Point of Rocks to the south of the beach along the coast, that acts as a barrier to hold in that fairly unique sand so it doesn't just move along to other beaches… not only do we have a better retention of that beautiful white sand, but it also causes that beach to accrete rather than erode. The beach is actually getting fatter and wider rather than eroding." With regard to groins, it should be pointed out that the arrangement of long, low groins, closely placed along Siesta/Crescent Beach during the 1930s, may be historically significant. Indeed, they seem to have been exceptionally well designed and may have been quite important during the storm surges associated with the seven hurricanes of the 1960s. In retrospect, their proximity, which really annoyed beach walkers, could have been a stabilizing factor and likely would have prevented down-drift erosion.

Figure 16.2 Aerial view of Crescent Beach showing nineteen of the closely spaced groins constructed during the 1930s

Factors That Could Account for the Resiliency of Siesta/Crescent Beach

1. Being situated on the drumstick head of a mixed-energy barrier island
2. Capturing the wave energy conducive to upward shoaling effects
3. Benefiting from sand addition through natural longshore transport processes
4. Probable enrichment of donated sediment from the beach nourishment projects on keys to the immediate north, i.e., Longboat Key and Lido Key
5. Potential effect of Big Sarasota Pass tidal inlet generating an ebb-tidal delta, retarding sediment flow southward, and serving as a sediment reservoir
6. Likely impact of Point of Rocks acting as a barrier
7. Closely placed and properly engineered low, long groins along Siesta/Crescent

Beach during earlier periods of storm exposures
8. Lack of any direct hit storms/hurricanes

South Siesta Key Development

After the original Stickney Bridge was no longer swinging around but was replaced in 1965 with a modern four-lane bridge, better access to south Siesta Key was available to motorists. The Old Stickney Road adjacent to Captain Curt's was replaced in the project by a new pair of two-lane roads for arriving on or departing from Siesta Key. By the early 1970s, with the nation's economy booming and the Vietnam War over, peace and prosperity brought a greater influx of visitors and residents to Florida. Not surprisingly, Sarasota County in general, and Siesta Key in particular, shared in the new boom, which supported many new restaurants such as the Flying Dutchman, the Magic Moment, and the Surfrider.

MIDNIGHT PASS - circa 1940

Figure 16.3 The shell road used in south Siesta Key that became Siesta Road and later was named Midnight Pass Road

As condominiums were rising in mid-key along Midnight Pass north from the Stickney Road, attention turned to the southern one-third of the key. This area offered not only available land, but also many other advantages, including the beautiful, secluded Turtle Beach; the very interesting Mote Marine facility with its fascinating shark tanks; and a more peaceful, relaxing atmosphere with much less traffic than north of Stickney Road.

The old shell road had been replaced by a modern, nearly straight section of what was originally called Siesta Road. Because of the many fishing shacks along the gulf and bay shores, there was plenty of flat, pre-landscaped property available for purchase at bargain prices. Many fishing shacks were modernized with air conditioning. Others were targeted for "knock down" to be replaced by larger, elegant homes.

Figure 16.4 Syd and Annie Solomon on the "bridge" of their Midnight Pass House (Photograph by Alexander Georges and provided thanks to Mike Solomon)

Figure 16.5 The Solomon house on the left being threatened by the "wild and migrating" Midnight Pass

The most significant and ultimately tragic construction project was the home/studio of renowned artist Syd Solomon and his wife, Annie. This award-winning edifice was designed by the outstanding architect Gene Leedy and built in 1970. It was an impressive beach home of what some might call "Florida modernism." To ensure enough land for home, studio, as well as a potential artists' colony, Syd and Annie bought three parcels of contiguous land to save it from the increasingly aggressive developers who were visionary enough to recognize the condo potential of Siesta Key. Ironically, the location of the property, relatively near to Midnight Pass, probably would have precluded a building permit for a

condominium but not for the internationally acclaimed artist and his wife, who had engaged a superb architect and excellent builder. Thus, they constructed a magnificent home/studio and celebrated with the first of many parties on New Year's Eve of 1970.

The Condominium Era was well underway in 1970 and many large construction projects were being completed in south Siesta Key. One of the most impressive condo complexes was the Tortuga Club, which was perfectly named and well located at 8730 Midnight Pass Road, right on the pristine Turtle Beach. Although originally intended to be a gulf-to-bay condo, financial challenges resulted in restricting the construction to the more desirable gulf frontage. This focus led to seventy-seven superb condominiums by 1973 and eventually a thriving community at the Tortuga Club. Residents interviewed for this book emphasized the beauty and resiliency of Turtle Beach at the time with its fine sand, beautiful shells, and abundant shark teeth, similar those found along Caspersen Beach in Venice today. There was also an abundance of wildlife and fabulous fishing. Midnight Pass, the nearby tidal inlet, provided fishermen with the best of both worlds—Little Sarasota bay or the gulf. On the other hand, little did these residents know, including Solomon, that the dredging of the Intracoastal Waterway in the mid 1960s would soon dramatically change Midnight Pass.

The Goal and Impact of the Intracoastal Waterway and Associated Coastal Engineering Projects

Although the 54-mile long Intracoastal Waterway (ICW) is now used almost exclusively for recreational activities, its original purpose was to facilitate transport of goods and services along the southwest coast through more navigable waters that were sheltered by the many barrier islands. In 1895, as settlements proceeded and populations increased, commercial interests and local citizens requested federal support and persuaded Congress to appropriate $5,000 for the U.S. Army Corps of Engineers to dredge a 5-foot deep by 100-foot wide channel from Tampa Bay to Sarasota Bay. This was a very successful project, leading to significant industrial benefits without apparent harm. Sarasota and Tampa were connected by a safe, secure waterway that served the commercial interests well. It was recorded that in less than twenty years nearly 4,000 tons of goods were transported on the ICW between Tampa and Sarasota. Few apparently realized that the developing railway systems and improved roads for truck traffic would soon replace the much slower steamships with their limited geographic reach. Extension of the ICW to Venice occurred in 1907, cutting through and destroying the ecologically important area known as "the Mangroves."

Although it must have been obvious that the commercial value of the ICW was limited after World War II, Congress nevertheless appropriated funds in 1945 for a more ambitious 100-foot wide, 9-foot deep dredging operation along the 54-mile route. In retrospect, the purpose other than improving navigation further seems unclear, because recreational boating had not yet become popular. Whatever the rationale, the Corps of Engineers dredgers arrived at Sarasota Bay in 1962 with heavier equipment. By 1964 they were dredging around the tidal inlet to Little Sarasota Bay at Bird Key—that is, the channel from the gulf known as Midnight Pass. In conjunction with their dredging work the engineers dumped 225,000 cubic yards of sediment on the Bird Islands and thus not only damaged the ecology but also upset the tidal inlet equilibrium with the nearby beaches.

The Saga of Midnight Pass

Midnight Pass has a very interesting, complex, and controversial history that illustrates the vagaries of tidal inlets—those channels between barrier islands through which gulf-derived tidal currents flow. There can be no doubt that Midnight Pass had a high-volume tidal flux for several decades. In 1955 it was measured as more than 13 feet deep and 500 feet wide—about half the size of Big Sarasota Pass—so it was obviously exchanging a huge volume of water between the gulf and Little Sarasota Bay and ensuring a healthy estuary in Little Sarasota Bay. Our interviews with Siesta Key residents of the 1950s and 1960s, especially those who were teenagers and young adults at that time, reveal that the water flow through Midnight Pass was so fast that it became Florida's first water park. They describe delightful stories of how they would drive their cars down the Blind Pass "roller-coaster road" hauling large, truck-tire inner tubes and arrive at the beach north of Midnight Pass as the gulf tide was rising. Then, groups of thrilled youngsters would enjoy a wild trip to the bay.

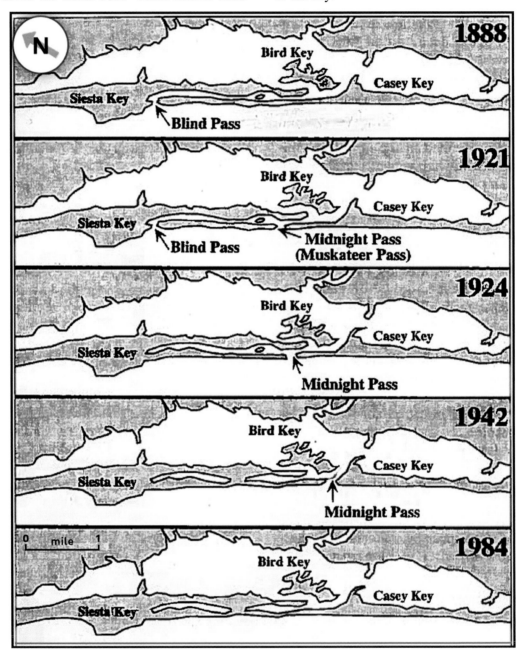

Figure 16.6 The history of Midnight Pass: opening as a wide tidal inlet during 1924 due to storms and closed completely by 1984 after an order from Florida Governor Graham and bulldozing the original inlet without success in opening a new pass (Modified from maps in *Barrier Islands of the Florida Gulf Coast Peninsula* by Richard A. Davis)

The tidal inlet between south Siesta Key and Casey Key has a history of instability that was not fully appreciated by architects and builders who wanted to develop the area. The earliest documentations of a connection between the Gulf of Mexico and Little Sarasota Bay are government survey charts from 1883. At that time the inlet mouth was located just south of Point of Rocks on Siesta Key. It was originally named Little Sarasota Pass, presumably to differentiate it from Big Sarasota Pass, and later was referred to descriptively as Blind Pass. Connected to Little Sarasota Bay by a long, deep waterway that entered the bay by the Bird Islands about two miles to the south, Blind Pass was a tenuous inlet at best that was unlikely to continue, and indeed it closed in 1942. The remaining remnants of this historic waterway are Blind Pass Lagoon, which leads to the public boat launching facility at Turtle Beach and Heron Lagoon, a 15-foot deep land-locked body of water in the Sanderling section of Siesta Key. Early navigation charts show that Casey Key extended north almost to Point of Rocks, more than two miles north of its current boundary. Siesta Key was east of Casey Key, with the above-described gulf-to-bay waterway in between.

Time Line of South Siesta Key's Tidal Inlet

1888: Inlet from gulf to bay is located just south of Point of Rocks and is known as little Sarasota Pass or Blind Pass. Casey Key extended more than two miles farther north than at present and overlapped the more easterly situated south Siesta Key.

1921: A hurricane opens another inlet about two miles south that is originally called Muskateer Pass, but in 1924 its name is changed to Midnight Pass.

1924: Little Sarasota Pass inlet closes naturally (spontaneously), creating a long lagoon system between Point of Rocks and Midnight Pass. Siesta Key acquires the northern tip of Casey Key.

1942-48: Midnight Pass inexplicably migrates north by about 1,200 feet. The Intracoastal Waterway (ICW) system, planned in 1889 and initiated in 1895 at Lower Tampa Bay, was fully funded by Congress.

1955: At its peak size Midnight Pass is more than 500 feet wide and has a maximum depth of 13 feet.

1960: Hurricane Donna alters sediment boundaries and flows to partially fill in the more northern channel, resulting in a shallower Midnight Pass.

1964: Dredging nearby in Little Sarasota Bay upsets tidal inlet equilibrium by changing water circulation.

1972: Hurricane Agnes deposits more sediment in the north channel, Midnight Pass.

1983: A relatively quick increase in the northern migration of Midnight Pass moves it about 300 yards to the north in three months while shrinking it in width to 50 feet with a 4-foot depth at mean high tide. The new location of the Pass threatens the homes of Syd Solomon and Pasco Carter.

1983-84: The Solomons and Carters obtain approval to close Midnight Pass and open a new pass to the south.

1983: Three attempts by these homeowners to create a new pass by dredging fail.

The Bird Islands have retained their basic shape and location throughout recorded history and are essentially a bay-mouth flood-tide delta created by the flushing action of the active tidal inlet. The size and configuration of the Bird Islands provide clear evidence for the existence of a large, natural tidal inlet at the Midnight Pass site long before recorded history—perhaps for as long as the barrier islands themselves have existed. From some time prior to 1883 until 1921, this waterway configuration survived several hurricanes. Then, in October 1921,

Figure 16.7 South Siesta Key aerial view in 1948 showing the wide tidal inlet named Midnight Pass in equilibrium with Little Sarasota Bay and the Bird Islands (Courtesy of the University of Florida George A. Smathers Libraries with thanks to Suzanne Stapleton and Pamela Handley)

a severe storm breached the Casey Key northern extension, creating a new inlet near what is today the northern end of Blind Pass Lagoon. By 1924 it was officially recognized as Musketeer's Pass and retained that name until 1937. Soon after its creation, however, Musketeer Pass began a steady migration to the south. By 1943 it was below the eastern finger of Siesta Key (the present location of The Pointe condominium complex). The southern migration was apparently caused by the restoration and influence of ebb tidal flow through the northern channel. By 1948 the tidal inlet, now being called Midnight Pass, had found equilibrium opposite the lower half

of the Bird Islands and was a wide waterway. A 1955 hydrographic survey chart identifies Midnight Pass as one of the strongest inlets along this part of the Florida coast, and it had become a stable, natural tidal inlet integrated with the southern tip of Siesta Key. However, the dredging of Little Sarasota Bay around the Bird Islands, along with other factors, had upset the equilibrium as described above.

By 1972, Midnight Pass had begun to slowly migrate northward and shrink in both size and flushing influence. In 1983, apparently due to prevailing littoral current from the south, the pass quickly migrated northward so as to pose a serious threat to two gulf-front homeowners, the Solomons and the Carters. After a number of appeals by the Solomons over the summer of 1983 with no response by local authorities, the governor himself finally responded by issuing emergency authorization to close the now un-navigable inlet and to relocate it south of the affected properties. The tidal inlet was closed by a large bulldozing operation on December 4, 1983, with every intention of effectively rerouting Midnight Pass to the south by opening a new tidal inlet. Unfortunately, however, Sarasota County did not plan and execute the closing/relocating maneuvers well. After at least three failed attempts at relocation, the "new pass" restoration effort was abandoned following a thirty-three-day effort. Thus, Midnight Pass resisted human attempts to relocate it. The problem, as coastal geologists later said, was the current wasn't strong enough to push the water through the newly dug pass.

In summary, what had happened in December 1983 was an attempt to thwart nature through a poorly planned relocation of Midnight Pass by inserting a man-made plug between the two barrier islands, Siesta Key and Casey Key, and re-opening a small inlet hundreds of yards to the south. Because of a lack of flow, the new inlet never had a chance of staying open. Solomon originally had won approval to relocate the pass on the condition that it would be kept open for two years. After failed attempts, the Solomons cited financial hardship and successfully petitioned the government to give up Midnight Pass restoration efforts.

The Triumphs and Tragedies of Syd Solomon

Syd Solomon is forever linked to the Midnight Pass closure and the thus the damage to Turtle Beach. He has in fact been vilified for the loss of the tidal inlet. During the 1950s through the 1970s, Solomon was famous for other reasons on Siesta Key, throughout Sarasota County, and indeed internationally. Best known eventually for his abstract expressionist art, Master Sergeant Syd Solomon was a World War II hero who arrived in Europe to serve during the Normandy invasion. He was decorated with five Bronze Stars for his service. Solomon was raised in Pennsylvania, learned to paint in high school, studied informally at the Art Institute of Chicago in 1938, and enlisted in the U.S. Army in July of 1941. His great skill on behalf of wartime operations was as an aerial *camofluer*—a designer of camouflage to disguise military installations from air attacks. While working in London on assignment to the Royal Engineer Camouflage Corps, he developed an interest in abstract art—partly as a result of images he visualized in aerial reconnaissance missions. After the war he studied at the French art school, L'Ecole des Beaux-Arts, and then returned to the United States. Because Solomon suffered from frostbite acquired during the early stages of the Battle of the Bulge, he was required to live in warm climates for the rest of his life. Thus, he and his wife, Annie, moved to Sarasota, arriving on New Year's Day, 1946. They lived a simple life while he developed his unique style as an abstract artist, creating vibrant, multilayered paintings that soon were being shown in national exhibitions. Solomon's style was heavily influenced by nature, which he thoroughly enjoyed on Siesta Key. His paintings illustrate his fascination with the climatic and overall environmental conditions of land, sea, and sky. By 1959 the Solomons had developed the ritual of spending winter and spring in Sarasota and then summers and early autumn in East Hampton, New York. They continued this dual lifestyle for over the next thirty-five years, and both settings served as inspiration for his paintings.

In the 1960s, Solomon started using polymer tempera as a base in his painting and would

Figure 16.8 Master Sergeant Syd Solomon with camouflage designs in approximately 1942. During World War II, Solomon was awarded five Bronze Stars and fought in the Battle of the Bulge, where he suffered frostbite of both hands during record-breaking, below-zero weather, which the U.S. Army was not prepared to endure in the five-week battle. (Photograph Courtesy of Solomon Archive with thanks to Mike Solomon)

then combine it with various colored inks and oils. Eventually he became one of the premier artists to use acrylic paint. Although he used a range of colors in his paintings, the color black was generally prominent. By then, Solomon's reputation had grown, and his work was being shown at many of the finest museums in the world, leading to several awards. This popularity made him a larger-than-life, very influential personality in both his Hamptons and Sarasota communities. He was an intellectual giant on Siesta Key who influenced all the area's writers and other artists.

Syd Solomon was also an avid fisherman and loved the area around Midnight Pass, where he had been fishing by boat since the late 1940s. He discovered Blind Pass Road in the mid-1950s and developed a vision and plans for an artist colony in south Siesta Key. He and Annie would prevent further condo development by buying land adjacent to Midnight Pass. There, in 1969-70, the Solomons built a home/studio that their son Michael referred to as "his version of Monet's Giverny… where the views of the gulf and the pass from his studio and home became the subject of his painting." In fact, the home/studio was spectacular, but it was not well rooted in the sand as buildings are today. Consequently, the "wild, migrating" Midnight Pass endangered the Solomon property as well as the neighboring and Carter property.

Mote Marine Lab, which was positioned much closer to the pass than the houses, was already well aware of the real cause of the migrating tidal inlet and had moved to City Island in 1978. As the Midnight Pass issue became increasingly contentious, the stress of it all had led to the death of Pasco Carter due from cardiovascular disease. After the "debacle of the pass," as Solomon once called it, health issues began to develop for him as well. He began to show signs of depression and then dementia, so the Solomons put the house up for sale. Eventually a buyer for the property was found in the early 1990s.

Tragically, therefore, within thirteen short years nature was taking back the treasure it had given Syd and Annie Solomon in south Siesta Key, as well as taking human casualties. "There was just no saving it," Annie Solomon said in an interview published in the *Sarasota Herald Tribune*. "And I think that is what started Syd on his slide. He was broken-hearted. He just loved that house." The "slide" she refers to is Solomon's gradual development of Alzheimer's disease. His son, Michael, commented, "The stress triggered something in Syd, and he was never the same. Living and working in that house had been the culmination of his life, and its loss plunged him into a depression that soon became dementia, from which he never returned." During the past decade, sound medical evidence indeed has revealed that depression in the elderly is one of the triggers for Alzheimer's disease. Consequently, the closure of Midnight Pass was doubly or triply tragic for Syd Solomon. In the same year as his death, 2004, beach erosion was so severe that Sarasota County condemned and demolished his house after it had partially collapsed into the gulf.

Figure 16.9 The Solomon home is demolished in 2004, having been condemned by Sarasota County after it partially collapsed into the Gulf of Mexico

Figure 16.10 Turtle Beach before (left) and after nourishment (right) by Weeks Marine during 2016 (Photograph courtesy of Emy Stein from the Sarasota County website and *Siesta Sand*, May 2017)

Midnight Pass and Turtle Beach

Over the ensuing years, there has been much debate over the impact of human intervention around Midnight Pass. Many experts and casual observers believe that the bulldozing that closed Midnight Pass was the critical factor in the deterioration of Turtle Beach and the need for repeated nourishment, which has been expensive but effective. That may be true, but the underlying cause of disequilibrium was likely the U.S. Army Corps of Engineers' dredge-and-fill work of 1964 at the bay end of the tidal inlet adjacent to, and involving, the Bird Islands. Some have vilified Syd Solomon for leading the charge to close Midnight Pass, while others have argued that it was "wild and migrating" and probably would have closed soon anyway. Certainly, the handwriting was on the wall when Corps of Engineers dredgers aggressively altered the integrated tidal inlet further. Consequently, we believe that Syd Solomon should be remembered on Siesta Key for what he achieved as a World War II hero and uniquely talented artist, as well as for what he loved. Frankly, no one ever achieved more on Siesta Key and no one loved it more than Syd Solomon. Unfortunately, however, due largely to the closure of Midnight Pass, south Siesta Key has not had stable beaches since the 1980s while Siesta/Crescent Beach just a few miles to the north has become "America's Best Beach."

CHAPTER 17

Spring Break Haven

Spring is nature's way of saying, "Let's party!"
—Robin Williams

The spring break vacation for high school and college students has become an American tradition that is valued at least as much as summer vacations. Generally occurring in March or April, it developed because U.S. schools at all levels since the 1930s have designated a week, or even two weeks, for suspending classes in the spring. Other countries also have spring breaks, but Americans use it as welcomed opportunity for a beach vacation that features social diversions and relaxation, particularly somewhere with a warm climate. For students, the main goal of spring break is often considered nonstop partying— ideally on Florida's Atlantic or gulf coast beaches, although other venues in Alabama, Mississippi, and Texas have also become popular. Not surprisingly, among Florida sites, Siesta Key with "America's Best Beach" has become spring break haven.

The Origin and Evolution of Spring Break Vacations in Florida

Ft. Lauderdale is the origin of the spring break beach vacation for students, dating to the 1930s when the Colgate University men's swim team traveled there in a much-publicized trip during Christmas week of 1934 to practice for spring competitions.

After a lull during the Great Depression and World War II, university students rediscovered Ft. Lauderdale in the 1950s. About 20,000 students gathered in Ft. Lauderdale annually throughout that quiet decade. Although not low profile, they were relatively well behaved on the beach and in the city, particularly in comparison to what was on the horizon.

The game-changer was the combination of a clever novel, a record-breaking movie, and a hit song—all entitled *Where the Boys Are*. The seminal event in the modern spring break was the publication in 1958 of Glendon Swarthout's book, originally entitled *Unholy Spring*. It was inspired by his two weeks on the beaches of Ft. Lauderdale during a break from teaching English at Michigan State University. Escaping from a bitter cold winter in East Lansing, Michigan, his trip with some of his English Honors students provided experiences and personal observations that soon led to the influential novel. Published in the same year that oral contraceptives were approved by the FDA, the book tells the story of four girls who are students at a midwestern university taking a spring vacation in Florida. In the opening act, the assertive leader of the quartet expresses her opinion in class that premarital sex might be something young women should experience. Soon after arriving in Ft. Lauderdale on

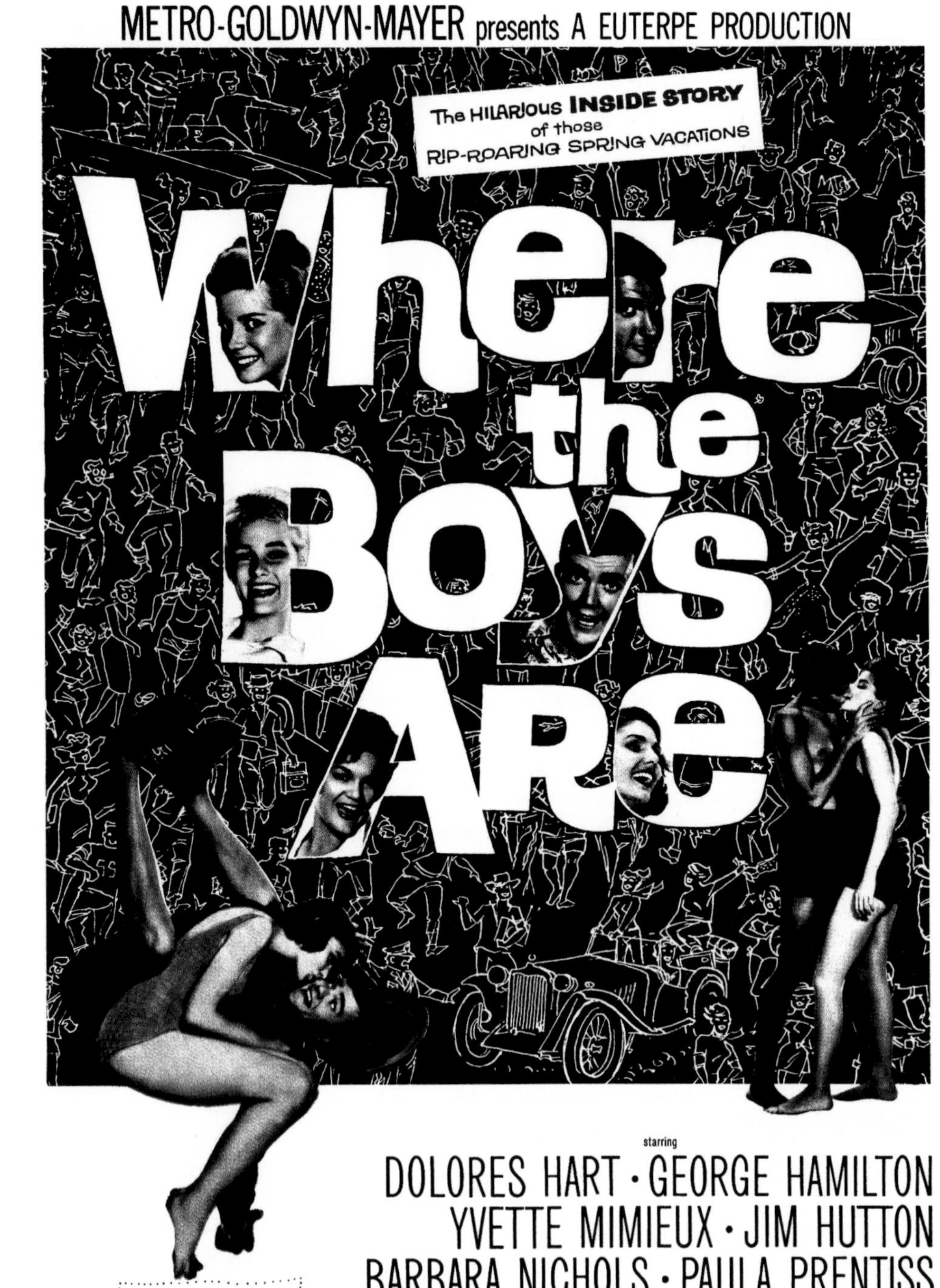

Figure 17.1 Videotape case of the 1960-61 blockbuster movie, *Where the Boys Are*

spring break, this speech results in one of the girls losing her virginity when they go to the beach and find out *where the boys are*, with the rest of the story the relations between boys and girls. The book was already a national phenomenon when MGM persuaded Swarthout to change the title and subsequently released the blockbuster movie *Where the Boys Are*. It, and its theme song by actress/singer Connie Francis, were strategically released on December 28, 1960, to attract the Christmas crowds. It became a national phenomenon. Undoubtedly, the song, which was translated that year into six other languages, helped the movie become the highest grossing low-budget movie in MGM's history. The long-term economic boost for Florida is incalculable.

In spring of 1961, university students on spring break increased to over 50,000 vacationers. By the early 1980s, Ft. Lauderdale was attracting 250,000-350,000 students annually during spring break weeks. The disruption for residents and snowbirds invested in the Ft. Lauderdale area became intolerable. The trash left behind and damage done by these young intruders spurred the local government to pass laws restricting parties in 1985. In addition, the National Minimum Drinking Age Act now required Florida to raise the minimum drinking age to 21. Consequently, Ft. Lauderdale increased surveillance during spring break and discouraged annual visitations. By 1989, the number of students visiting Ft. Lauderdale had dropped to 20,000, but other beaches, particularly the gulf beaches as far away as South Padre Island, Texas, were discovered by the students for their annual spring break partying.

Daytona, already well known for its Daytona 500 NASCAR race, became one magnet. Interestingly, to bolster its economy and feature its excellent beaches, Panama City leaders initiated a campaign in the early 1990s with an advertising campaign promoting Panama City Beach as *the* spring break destination in an effort to attract the student vacationers. They were successful beyond their expectations as an estimated 300,000 spring breakers began traveling there annually. In fact, using social media and digital marketing, Panama City Beach was indeed transformed into *the* spring break mecca for the entire month of March. Security is difficult on 27 miles of beaches and not surprisingly, Panama City saw the same downside as Ft. Lauderdale. After a series of widely publicized shootings and a gang rape in 2015, several new ordinances were enacted prohibiting drinking on the beach and establishing a bar closing time of 2:00 A.M. Since then, reports describe a decrease in Panama City Beach's spring break turnout, and family tourism is being promoted. Nevertheless, Panama City Beach still welcomes the spring break travelers, has a devoted website (www.springbreakfunplace.com), organizes fun events with numerous sponsors such as Victoria Secret and Banana Boat, and annually receives a "Spring Break Capital" award for its variety of entertainments.

The March weather of Panama City Beach is much cooler than south Florida, so communities along the southwest gulf coast are drawing large spring break crowds. These resort communities, including Siesta Key, need to learn from the experiences of Ft. Lauderdale and Panama City Beach. It's important to keep in mind the nature of the challenges—why students come, what risks prevail, and how to prevent serious calamities.

The Attractions of Spring Break

Spring break beach vacations have evolved into an annual ritual and are now considered a second semester entitlement by university students. Breaks during the autumn semester are for family gatherings at Thanksgiving and Christmas, but spring travel means "Let's party!" At least one-third, and probably closer to one-half, of university students—two to three million—take a spring break trip. The number of high school students also participating is large but incalculable.

The popularity of spring break beach vacations has coincided with widespread air conditioning, emergence of better resorts with enticing advertisements, a growing and wide variety of restaurants, and inexpensive deals for air travel to and automobile rentals in Florida. In addition, spring break trips are liberating experiences for students that provide an atmosphere conducive to intensive and intimate social interactions. They are attracted to the beaches of Florida as the ideal place for socializing and for showing off the latest in swimwear fashions

The pleasure and entertainment of spring breakers relates as much to what they see as to what they do on the beach. Because Sarasota County has never had prohibitions affecting beach attire, Siesta/Crescent Beach is one place where the evolution of swimwear can be photographed and appreciated, especially during spring break periods. And, there is no topic of conversation more frequent on the beach than comments about the fashionable and avant-garde swimwear. The latest fashions are displayed in the Swimsuit Issue of *Sports Illustrated,* published annually since 1964 in February for spring break season, and they provide evidence of how swimsuit fashions have changed dramatically during recent decades.

Women's Swimwear Evolves to Make a Big Splash on Spring Break

Women's swimwear evolved during the past century as beaches became more popular and changes in the social climate allowed new styles to become fashionable. Briefly, at the turn of the nineteenth century, women wore bathing dresses—a beach frock buttoned up to the neck and covering the length of the legs. About the time of Bertha Palmer's first visit, progress began as the billowy, heavy layers of the earlier swimsuits were reduced by a couple of inches to a light dress instead. Even though the suits still resembled dresses right down to the collars and buttons, a smaller silhouette signaled that the culture was changing.

The first major advance in women's swimwear can be attributed to a courageous woman born in 1887, Annette Kellerman—a polio survivor, internationally acclaimed Australian swimmer, diver, and ultimately a popular swimmer/actress foreshadowing Esther Williams. Annette's impact was huge and her connection to spring break was recognized in 1974 when she was honored

Figure 17.2 Annette Kellerman in her revolutionary form-fitting swimsuit that led to her arrest in Boston in 1907

by the International Swimming Hall of Fame at Fort Lauderdale. Annette's story illustrates how swimwear reflects social changes and the needs of athletes. Female athletes in the early 20th century showed a special interest in swimming, especially in Australia, but were hampered with dresses or wool pleated skirts. At the age of six, severe weakness in Kellerman's legs due to polio required her to use steel braces for walking support. When the acute phase of polio subsided, Annette was left with weak, bowed legs. To help her overcome this disability, her parents wisely enrolled Annette in swimming classes in Sydney. Soon, she was walking without leg braces, and by age ten had become a competitive swimmer. To improve her swimming performance and help overcome leg weakness, Annette wore a form-fitted one-piece suit with neither collars nor buttons. This allowed her to cut through water without being impeded, and it also started a fashion and cultural revolution.

Beginning in Australia and while performing in Europe and the United States, Annette became famous for advocating the right of women to wear a one-piece bathing suit rather than the cumbersome dress and pantaloon combinations other female swimmers wore at the time. In 1907, at the height of her popularity, Kellermann was arrested by two policemen for "indecency" on Revere Beach, Massachusetts, as she was wearing one of her fitted one-piece swimsuits. After a public outcry, the charges were dropped as the Bostonians decided that their planned court case was going nowhere. This publicized harassment only served to make Annette even more famous and impactful. The popularity of Annette's risqué

Figure 17.3 Beach patrolman measures above-the-knee length of a suspect swimsuit around 1925 when the Bathing Suit Regulations of the American Association of Park Superintendents required a maximum of six inches of leg showing below the skirt

one-piece suits soared and resulted in her developing a line of women's swimwear that became known as the "Annette Kellermans." According to *Smithsonian* magazine, "Her form-fitting suit paved the way for a new kind of one-piece, and over the next couple decades, as swimming became an even more popular leisure-time activity, beachgoers saw more arms, legs, and necks than ever before."

The next breakthroughs in women's swimwear developed during the Roaring '20s when reckless, pleasure-seeking behaviors naturally stimulated swimwear expressions of the new culture with sleeves eliminated, hemlines up, and the form-fitting upper section tighter. On the other hand, the Bathing Suit Regulations of the American Association of Park Superintendents were being enforced in the United States. In 1922, if a bathing suit was too short, it could result in receiving a warrant from the police. Beaches even had "bathing suit" patrolmen who would measure to see if a bathing suit was of proper length standards, as they could not be more than six inches above the knees. In the 1930s, knee-length bathing dresses were discarded, legs and shoulders were bared, and suits were even tighter with the advent of stretchy synthetic fabrics. During the 1940s, hems rose further and bathing suits appeared with spaghetti-strap tops.

Although two-piece swimsuits existed, they were high-waisted, covering up the belly button and resembling a miniskirt, while the top was usually a modest halter/bra hybrid that was popular on American and many European beaches. After World War II, the next revolution occurred with introduction of the four-fabric triangle bikini in Paris. Soon, thereafter, they were on beaches everywhere, despite the objections

Figure 17.4 Movie star Joan Collins models the fashionable high-waisted swimsuit with halter/bra hybrid during the 1950s

Figure 17.5 Ursula Andress wearing an iconic bikini she designed for the 1962 James Bond movie *Dr. No*

of religious organizations. Hollywood was very influential as Brigitte Bardot popularized the bikini in 1953. Later, the first "Bond Girl," Ursula Andress, made an everlasting impact when she emerged from the surf wearing an iconic bikini she herself designed for the 1962 James Bond movie *Dr. No*. This became the rage of the 1960s and beyond on Siesta/Crescent Beach. Now, the twenty-first century is the "anything goes" era with thongs, fishnet, and gladiator styles, as well as extra-extra cheeky and monokini (topless) designs for European beaches.

Evolution of Men's Swimsuits

The history of male swimwear is a simpler story then women's, although trends are parallel. The Bathing Suit Regulations enforced during the 1920s also applied to men, stating that "all-white and flesh-colored suits were discouraged as anatomical details were too clear. Nothing of the chest below the armpits could be shown on the chest. Men's suits needed a skirt or skirt effect, worn outside the trunks." The first men's swimsuits were made from knitted wool that

made swimming difficult because it absorbed water easily and a swimsuit weighed up to nine pounds when wet. Early in the twentieth century, most male swimmers wore tank suits in dark, solid colors reaching to the elbow and below the knees. As the beach became a more popular destination, designs for men's swimwear became more body-conscious and athletic.

During the 1930s, a more fitted, high-waisted design in swimwear emerged with new fabrics heralding a new era in swimwear for men but they still weren't allowed to have a bare chest. Fortunately, Hollywood intervened again. Two handsome actors who were world-class swimmers with enviable physiques appeared on the scene, Buster Crabbe and Johnny Weissmuller, and both appeared bare-chested. Soon thereafter, views of bare-chested men were acceptable, and shorts became the standard swimwear. Companies producing swimwear for men were inspired and tried to design their trunks with a more tailored look to make them more publicly acceptable with a fly front and a buckle belt. In recent years, male swimwear has highlighted masculinity and athleticism

Figure 17.6 Men's swimwear displayed on Siesta/Crescent Beach in the 1920s

as sports activities on the beach such as volleyball became prominent on beaches like those of Siesta Key.

The Current and Future Challenge of Becoming a Spring Break Haven

After Siesta Key was awarded "America's Best Beach" designation in 2011 and the transformation from residential to visitor dominance had taken place, Siesta/Crescent Beach became one of the destinations replacing Ft. Lauderdale as a spring break

Figure 17.7 The 1940s style of high-waisted wool swimsuit for liberated men, with a belt that was buckled tightly to keep the heavy-when-wet suit up

haven. Of course! The weather is warm and even hot, while the gulf water is warm. The three-mile beach is spectacular and relatively compact in contrast to the 27 miles at Panama City Beach, where finding the right companion can be challenging. Siesta's volleyball courts beckon players. Moreover, police surveillance is limited though effective thus far. Beer is sold at concessions stands. There are numerous showers and bathrooms.

If those features were not enough, Siesta Key Village is only minutes away by foot. After a quiet breakfast period, the village action continues through the day and night until 2:00 A.M. Joining the Beach Bar, a mainstay since 1947, the Daiquiri Deck became the anchor for spring break frolicking in 1994. Its daily advertising, which hardly seems necessary, is high in the sky as slowly moving airplanes fighting headwinds pull banners advertising the deals and events, including happy hour, two-for-one pricing of drinks, ladies' nights, and so on.

The beach serves all interests well. Some university students soak up the sun, protected by the many high sun protection factor (SPF) sunscreens available. Observations of the past few years suggest that the spring break period on Siesta Key has become more than two months long, and a good time for partying. The explanation is that some colleges have spring break in mid-February, while others designate Easter week, which can be as late as the last week of April. Consequently, the hard partying is now prolonged beyond what was ever envisioned in the *Where the Boys Are* era. This has resulted in greater personal health risks such as sexually transmitted diseases and outbreaks of viral diseases such as influenza when the students return to college.

CHAPTER 18

Battle of the Keys

Those who cannot remember the past are condemned to repeat it.
—Jorge Agustín Nicolás Ruiz de Santayana y Borrás (George Santayana), *The Life of Reason*

The tidal/coastal equilibrium among the Sarasota County keys has been disrupted over the past few decades, just as has happened to about half of Florida's seashores. Recognizing the challenging situation, the Florida Department of Environmental Protection has pointed out on its website (http://www.dep.state.fl.us/beaches/programs/becp/restore.htm) the following:

> Over 485 miles, or approximately 59% of the state's beaches, are experiencing erosion. At present, about 387 of the state's 825 miles of sandy beaches have experienced *critical erosion*, a level of erosion which threatens substantial development, recreational, cultural, or environmental interests. While some of this erosion is due to natural forces and imprudent coastal development, a significant amount of coastal erosion in Florida is directly attributable to the construction and maintenance of navigation inlets.

Except for Siesta/Crescent Beach, all of the Sarasota County beaches have experienced erosion as they became densely developed. There are several possible explanations for the variations in response to tidal currents, wave energy, and storms. Much of the erosion has been caused by housing developments and some by alteration of tidal inlets such as the closing of Midnight Pass, which disrupted Turtle Beach's equilibrium. Sea-level rise has and will continue to accelerate erosion because when the gulf level is higher, it takes more sand with every wave. In addition, what happens on one of Sarasota County's keys can influence the resiliency of the adjacent barrier island.

Efforts to Retain or Renew Barrier Island Beaches: A New Gulf Coast Way of Life

With the multimillion-dollar tourism industry at stake, along with billions of investment dollars also at risk, the barrier island beaches have been given top priority as clearly the crown jewels of the gulf coast. Nowhere is this more obvious than in Sarasota County. During the post-World War II tourism boom, and especially the past few decades, all of the keys have invested millions of dollars in maintaining their treasured beaches.

There have been two basic strategies employed to maintain the gulf barrier island beaches facing relentless erosions, but neither of them addresses the underlying causes of erosion. In the first strategy, efforts are devoted to retaining sand by installing a variety of artificial barriers on the beaches. These include structures such as shoreline seawalls, breakwaters that are either parallel or perpendicular, and groins. Because seawalls only protect upland property while preventing the favorable effects of upward shoaling, they must be considered long-term failures with regard to beach preservation. Similarly, breakwaters have produced mixed results and are eyesores. To create effective groins, complex coastal engineering is required, as well as a thorough understanding of marine forces. Groins that are too long or too high can actually trap too much sediment and increase down-shore erosion and become ineffective. Groins that are too short, too low, or too permeable are also ineffective because they retain too little sediment. In addition, a groin of improper length may not meet the challenge of tidal variations (e.g., high tides and storm surges might flow past a groin that is too short on the landward end and cause nearby shoreline erosion).

Nevertheless, groins became the favored structure of the first strategy in Florida. In fact, they were a very prominent and aesthetically undesirable feature of many beaches such as Crescent Beach during the Interlude. Theoretically, groins should counteract longshore transport processes and dampen attrition of sand by wave energy. In practice, however, many if not most have been poorly designed or constructed and thus have had limited effectiveness on the gulf coast. Groins have been customarily constructed of concrete, but other materials, including automobile tires, have also been used as on Lido Beach. The instability of tires exposed to waves and tides makes them undesirable, as Siesta Key found out when numerous tires from its northern neighbor were washed ashore on Crescent Beach a few decades ago. Most recently, groins are geotextile—i.e., large, linear sandbags—but their effectiveness is also variable. Based on the solid evidence

of their negative effects, especially on downdrift shorelines where they have been shown to accelerate erosion, North Carolina law (G.S 113A-115.1) now prohibits the use of groins. The United States Army Corps of Engineers' Coastal Engineering Manual describes groins as: "…probably the most misused and improperly designed of all coastal structures… Over the course of some time interval, accretion causes a positive increase in beach width updrift of the groin. Conservation of sand mass therefore produces erosion and a decrease in beach width on the downdrift side of the groin."

Beach Nourishment: An Expensive But Necessary Strategy

Inability to retain sand along the precious beaches with artificial structures such as groins has led gulf coast communities to adopt the second, more expensive strategy known by the term "beach nourishment" (a.k.a. "beach renourishment"). In a more common context, nourishment refers to food that encourages growth and health, but when applied to beaches, nourishment is defined by Richard Davis, in his book *Barrier Islands of the Florida Gulf Coast Peninsula,* as "the addition of sand to the beach to widen it." The Florida Department of Environmental Protection's description is as follows:

In a typical beach nourishment project, sand is collected from an offshore location by a dredge and is piped onto the beach. A slurry of sand and water exits the pipe on the beach and once the water drains away, only sand is left behind. Bulldozers move this new sand on the beach until the beach matches the design profile. Beach nourishment is a preferred way to add sand to a system that has been starved by the

Figure 18.1 Bulldozer moving borrowed sand that was just pumped in from offshore toward the east end of Turtle Beach. Note the many birds feasting on shellfish arriving with the sediment. (Photograph courtesy of Martha Kramer)

Figure 18.2 Bulldozer elevating borrowed sand to build up an eroded section of Turtle Beach (Photograph courtesy of Martha Kramer)

altered inlets because it provides a significant level of storm protection benefits for upland properties and is the least impacting to the coastal system.

During the past twenty years since the Florida Legislature dedicated a portion of the Ecosystem Management and Restoration Trust Fund for beach management, over $600 million of state money has been appropriated to cost-share with local governments on local and federally authorized projects. Each of three governmental sources contributes about one-third of the cost of the entire program, and thus more than $100 million per year is being spent on Florida's beach nourishment projects. This has resulted in the restoration of over 200 miles, or about half, of the state's 407 miles designated as critically eroded beaches. Beach nourishment is the only engineered shore protection

alternative that restores a beach while directly addressing the problem of erosion. The result is a wider beach that improves natural protection while also providing additional recreational area. The process of "addition" can involve enormous volumes of sand. Projects in Sarasota County have typically required 600,000–900,000 cubic yards of sediment, and a current Lido Key proposal envisions 1.2 million cubic yards of reclaimed sand. These volumes of sand would typically replenish 4- to 10-foot natural erosions along beaches 1 to 4 miles long.

There have been at least seven such projects on the keys of Sarasota County, and certainly more will follow. In 2016 alone there were two nourishment projects totaling about $50 million in the county. These addressed severe erosions of Longboat Key and Turtle Beach on Siesta Key. The "addition of sand to the beach to

Figure 18.3 A hazardous, 3- to 4-foot erosion on Turtle Beach that was repaired by a 2016 nourishment project at a cost of $21.5 million (Photograph courtesy of Martha Kramer)

widen it" has been accomplished in all but one project by dredging up sediment from one to nine miles offshore, pumping it by a large pipeline system to the eroded beach, and then using heavy equipment such as bulldozers to mold the gray sand into the design desired by the beach renovators. One can reasonably argue that these massive nourishment projects have been good for the economy in the short term. After all, a renovated beach continues to attract tourists during seasons of spending exuberance like spring break, property values are at least maintained if not increased, tax revenues continue to expand, and the beach nourishment industry thrives with the multi-million dollar contracts available repeatedly. This kind of business must be especially desirable to the marine engineering companies specializing in nourishment projects because as soon as they finish, the erosion resumes. Just as Arnold Schwarzenegger said in *The Terminator*, the foreman of a recent nourishment project mentioned to one of the authors on the day his project finished, "I'll be back," as we stood above the beach and watched the rising tide and waves assault his beautifully renovated beach and initiate erosion all along the shoreline.

Recognizing the recurrent nature of these projects, Thomas Becnel wrote in the *Sarasota Herald Tribune* on May 24, 2014, that "beach renourishment is Gulf Coast way of life." Since Sarasota County's large keys are so close to being almost contiguous, it should come as no surprise that major projects on one beach can have significant impact on the others. With so much money at stake, it's also no surprise that controversies and conflicts have also surfaced as a "gulf coast way of life." To gain perspective, however, one needs to appreciate the magnitude of the beach erosion problem, acknowledge that it is not only inexorable but actually accelerating,

and recognize that what happens to one key or its tidal inlet can affect other keys.

Sources of Sand for Beach Nourishment Projects

One interesting aspect of the gulf coast beach nourishment strategy is that it generally takes advantage of the Florida Platform's original western extension into the Gulf of Mexico, which provides somewhat similar Appalachia-derived quartz sand that was part of the original mainland beach. In fact, out to as far as about ten miles west of the current gulf coast there may be abundant sand for dredging and pipeline transport to the shore. In view of this valuable resource, it is remarkable that the 2016 beach nourishment project on Longboat Key introduced an overland, more expensive method of obtaining and delivering sand. This project cost at least $25 million and was managed efficiently from April to July with as many as 100 to 180 truckloads per day of sand being hauled over more than one hundred miles from Immokalee's pristine reservoir of snow-white sand. Despite the trucking costs, this component of the Longboat Key project ensured a white sand veneer in contrast to the gray beach with shells resulting from previous projects. In addition, the $25 million cost pales in comparison to the estimate of more than $500 million for Atlantic Coast nourishment projects currently being considered.

The Lido Key Challenge

Lido Key presents a more difficult challenge for beach nourishment projects. Most of the land was originally fragmented south of Longboat Key to Siesta Key. The spits of sand there were aggregated by the massive Burns/Ringling dredge-and-fill operations of the 1920s that are described in Chapter 8. Thus, Lido, St. Armands, and Bird Key are

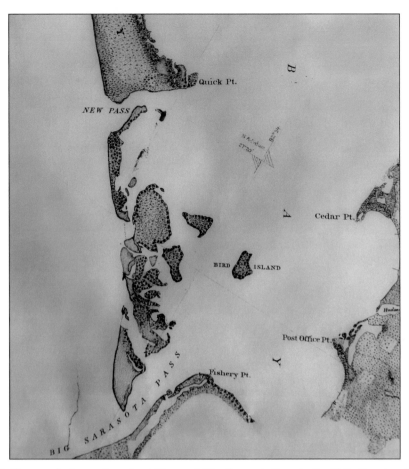

Figure 18.4 The area between Longboat Key and Big Sarasota Pass in the U.S. Coast and Geodetic Survey of 1883 (Section VI, Sarasota, Florida)

not natural barrier islands but man-made bodies of unstable land prone to erosion and poor drainage. The frequent flooding of St. Armands Circle is largely attributable to its geologic/geographic history, while the lack of resiliency at the Lido beaches is also attributable to the Burns/Ringling aggregations. In addition, Lido Key became populated earlier than the adjacent keys because of the Lido Casino near the shoreline, and it is now very densely developed. Even during the heyday of the Lido Casino, erosion was a major problem, as demonstrated by the shrinking beach and groins in 1959. Its beach is also much more intrinsically susceptible to erosion due to its configuration and other unfavorable factors

described elsewhere in this book and by Richard Davis. Consequently, Lido beach preservation and restoration initiatives began as long ago as 1964 but have been only temporarily successful.

Irrespective of the challenges, Lido Key leaders and owners have proposed an estimated $22 million project to create a "beefier beach" in collaboration with the U.S. Army Corps of Engineers (USACE) and the City of Sarasota. They requested approval in 2013 from the Florida Department of Environmental Protection (DEP) for dredging from Big Sarasota Pass at least 1.2 million cubic yards of nearby sand needed to replenish 1.6 miles of erosion and extend the beach westward. In fact, Big Sarasota

Figure 18.5 The Lido Casino beach eroding in 1960 despite two "dog-bone" groins constructed in 1959

Pass has never been dredged and thus is not actually an eligible site for borrowing sand, according to the Sarasota County Cmprehensive Plan. Moreover, it was learned during a court hearing in Sarasota from December 12 to 18, 2017, that the huge project proposed would require at least 1.7 million cubic yards of sand, which would likely be the largest such beach initiative in Florida history—larger than a recent nourishment project for the entire City of Miami. It was also testified that the USACE's two-dimensional modeling was flawed and deceptive, with some estimates off by 495 percent due to omission of relevant data. Finally, an expert witness, R. Grant Gilmore from Coastal and Ocean Science, Inc. of Vero Beach, testified that the Lido/USACE permit application "basically ignored three sections of the Florida Statutes," omitting issues related to the ecology such as impacts on "critically endangered" fish species.

The proposed massive dredging of Big Sarasota Pass and the installation of two or three groins for presumed stabilizing would just be the first round. The work would need to be repeated about every five years for the next fifty years, with escalating costs. The inclusion of groins in the proposed plan is surprising because studies done in New Jersey and North Carolina determined that "using groins in conjunction with beach nourishment projects is of dubious value as well. When big storms occur, groins direct strong currents that carry large amounts of sand seaward, in an offshore direction parallel to the groins."

But on a more fundamental level perhaps the most disturbing aspect of the Lido/USACE proposal is their naïve goal to combat Mother Nature by repeatedly attempting to reverse the longshore transport processes occurring for many centuries and thus capturing sand that would otherwise

Figure 18.6 Longshore transport of sand from Lido Beach to Siesta Key through Big Pass during the 1950s

flow south toward Siesta Key while the tidal inlet equilibrium and local ecology are being disrupted. This would surely damage Siesta/Crescent Beach equilibrium. It brings back memories of what occurred with the 1964 USACE dredging that was followed by disruption of Midnight Pass and irreversible damage to Turtle Beach and local fishing. It is not surprising, therefore, that the Siesta Key Association and others such as Save-our-Sand 2 have objected to this proposal, retained legal counsel, and brought the issue to court. The outcome of the "battle of the keys" remains uncertain at this writing and may require many more months of legal actions. In the meantime, the inexorable erosion of Lido Beach will continue. A more modest nourishment project with sand hauled in from inland sources would have been a better alternative, as Longboat Key demonstrated convincingly in 2016.

CHAPTER 19

Future Threats for America's Best Beach

We have met the enemy and he is us!
—Pogo (Walt Kelly), on Earth Day, 1971

While drafting this chapter during 2016-17, it became increasingly apparent that what we originally envisioned as *future* threats are already evident and must be considered *current* threats. Any unbiased observer cannot deny the impact of some risks such as climate change and rising sea levels. Siesta Key has been able to celebrate its booming tourist era as a destination resort with "America's Best Beach," while overpopulation and climate change threaten the future way of life. The threats listed below and discussed thereafter need to be addressed to protect past investments and for the sake of progress. Some are associated with overpopulation, as Siesta Key has become a magnet for those who seek a spectacular beach vacation, and half of the threats listed relate to climate change.

Challenges Facing Siesta Key Currently and in the Foreseeable Future

1. Increasing motor vehicle traffic density with speeding and irresponsible driving
2. Increasing risks for pedestrians and bicyclists
3. Overcrowded beaches creating more hazards

4. Dredging Big Sarasota Pass and elsewhere
5. Other human misbehaviors on the island and its beaches
6. Rising gulf temperatures along with overheated oceans everywhere
7. Increased risks of tropical storms and surges
8. Rising gulf levels with continued climate change
9. More red tide harmful algae blooms
10. Increasing insurance costs.

Many residents feel that Siesta Key has been lucky to avoid severe tropical storms in recent years. Others invoke a sacred, mysterious protective force. An idea has surfaced that Amerindian blessings help protect the key—a notion that Nancy Connelly attributes to "Texas Jim Mitchell." He ran a reptile farm in Sarasota from the mid-1930s to the mid-1960s and befriended Native Americans as a youngster. Many of his Native American friends would visit him when tropical storms threatened and together they would do away with the evil spirits. More recently, after Hurricane Irma, some grateful citizens again suggested that the area is blessed and voiced a legend that Amerindians who lived on this land may have granted it special powers and made it safe by dispersing their burial grounds around the area and thereby warding off storms in the process. An objective assessment via a historical hurricane database reveals that Ft. Myers has been affected or brushed by a hurricane or tropical storm approximately once every three years, whereas Sarasota's frequency is once every four and one-half years. For a direct landfall, which is defined as within forty miles, the data show that the likelihood is once every thirteen years for Ft. Myers and once every twenty-six years for Sarasota. Thus, the statistics reveal that the relative frequency is lower for Sarasota County, and thus Siesta Key, but they are based on historical data when the Gulf of Mexico was cooler.

Increasing Motor Vehicle Traffic Density with Speeding and Irresponsible Driving

The list above includes a number of interrelated threats, some identified for decades. *Pelican Press* articles in the 1970s described severe traffic problems and suggested that a third bridge might become necessary. No bridge planning is currently underway, however, and rightly so, because other options should be considered to improve traffic flows and/or decrease traffic. For instance, the Coast Guard decision to reduce the number of drawbridge openings may help. The free trolley service is another step in the right direction, but it is regrettable that SCAT needed seven years to launch "Siesta Key Breeze." Yet while alleviating some vehicular traffic on Midnight Pass Road, Beach Road, and Ocean Boulevard, the trolley has caused new problems such as traffic jams at the Canal Road and Ocean Boulevard intersection, i.e., in the center of Siesta Key Village. Dangerous driving, such as inappropriate use of lanes, can cause car accidents, injuries,

and potentially more fatalities. Even with Siesta Key Breeze, automobile traffic will increase on the key, especially during the long spring break season. One interviewee said empathetically, "Wow, so much has changed. Driving to the beach was quick, easy, and safe twenty years ago. Now, it can be a nightmare just to drive across the Stickney Bridge and turn right."

There are intersections on Siesta Key that have been hazardous for decades but have thwarted attempts to resolve their deficiencies. The most notorious is "Dead Man's Curve" where Siesta Drive intersects with and turns into Higel Avenue at Faubel Street. From 2012 to September 2017, there have been twenty-one known motor vehicle accidents at the Siesta-Higel curve. Poor adherence to the 40 mph speed limit along Siesta Drive and Higel Avenue is undoubtedly one of the causes of the numerous traffic accidents. Most drivers and certainly the bicyclists have welcomed recent attention to this issue.

Increasing Risks for Pedestrians and Bicyclists

Another particularly dangerous intersection is the junction at Midnight Pass and Beach Road. This was demonstrated tragically on January 7, 2012, when a 53-year-old resident of Siesta Key, Donna Chen, was jogging along the sidewalk peacefully with her dog and suddenly was hit and killed by an inebriated motorist. Her dog panicked, ran to the beach, and was found in the gulf. Tragically, the driver had been identified by the Sarasota County police as probably drunk and certainly causing a disturbance; law enforcement deputies ordered him to leave the Public Beach parking lot, but allowed him to carry a bottle of liquor to his vehicle and drive away. Just as surprising, in the aftermath, efforts by the Siesta Key Association and others to persuade the Florida Department of Transportation (FDOT) to install more signage and safety features at this dangerous intersection were rejected. Requests for something as simple as blinking lights failed because of "*potential* complaints from nearby residents." Lastly, a request to lower the speed limit on Midnight Pass Road was also rejected.

Lowering the speed limits and enforcing them is obviously necessary to anyone who regularly walks, jogs, or bikes along Midnight Pass Road or Higel Avenue. Moreover, Beach Road is also hazardous at any speed. The imperative to intervene with safety measures seems to be finally accepted for "Dead Man's Curve," as a result of the June 2017 fatality. Other stretches of these roads, however, need similar attention. For instance, motorists occasionally use Midnight Pass Road south of Stickney as a drag racing track.

Overcrowded Beaches Creating More Hazards

The strategy of deploying four unique lifeguard stations on Siesta Public Beach and employing EMT-trained lifeguards with backups is an investment that has paid huge dividends for "America's Best Beach." As the crowds increase, however, the lifeguards and the trash collectors might be overwhelmed. The density of beachgoers must make rapid identification of problems nearly impossible for the lifeguards. During the 2017 Memorial Day weekend, the beach was seriously overcrowded and trashed. With a concerted effort and proper receptacles, trashing Siesta Key's beaches can be prevented, as demonstrated during the next summer holiday—2017 Fourth of July holiday weekend. This was accomplished by a heroic "Pack-In-Pack-Out" campaign with distribution of trash bags.

On the other hand, the hazards on the beach and in the water remain challenging.

Figure 19.1 Overcrowding of Siesta Beach during the Fourth of July holiday

Figure 19.2 Children doing what they enjoy the most on a beach—digging holes

One problem that can become serious is the many holes dug in the sand. The poor illumination of the beach during turtle season adds to the challenge. Obviously, as more people are on the Siesta/Crescent Beach, more holes are being dug. When there are many swimmers and the winds are brisk and the gulf is turbulent, the risk of rip currents makes any swimming potentially risky. Fortunately, the lifeguards fly flags that are changed during the day to show the degree of hazards, and warnings and lifesaving instructions are provided on the blackboards of each station. It is a tribute to the Siesta Public Beach lifeguards that drownings and near drownings are being prevented very successfully. Their heroic work as first responders should be deeply appreciated. In the future, however, more swimmers will increase their challenges. One wonders if a fifth or sixth lifeguard station will be needed—perhaps an orange or white shack along the half-mile long public beach. Undoubtedly, the crowds on Siesta/

Crescent Beach will continue to increase as its fame spreads far and wide. As one long-term resident said, "I wish Dr. Beach never heard of this place." No matter what residents wish, however, the many awards as "America's Best Beach" will increase the magnetic attraction of Siesta Key. Clearly, the days when "everybody knew everybody" are long gone.

Dredging Big Sarasota Pass and Elsewhere

The most immediate and potentially devastating threat for "America's Best Beach" would undoubtedly be the dredging up of 1.2 million cubic yards of sand from Big Sarasota Pass as proposed by Lido Key leaders and the U.S. Army Corps of Engineers. The lessons learned from other experiences, as described in Chapter 16, make it clear that the result of a massive dredging could convert Siesta/Crescent Beach from an expanding beach to an erosional beach like Turtle Beach. As Richard Davis pointed out, "the tidal inlets that separate them [barrier islands] are an essential part of the barrier island system… [because] tidal inlets and barrier islands are an integrated coastal system." History shows that the gulf tidal, wave-related, longshore currents and tropical storms are powerful forces that have unpredictable impacts.

The City of Sarasota has initially supported the poorly conceived proposal to dredge up so much sand and thereby radically alter the tidal inlet that has always been crucial for Sarasota Bay. The U.S. Army Corps of Engineers denied Sarasota County's request for a more rigorous environmental study. In fact, the Corps of Engineers defended the superficial assessment it conducted on the environmental impact of dredging the 1.2 million cubic yards of sand from the Pass to restore more than 1.5 miles of Lido Key beach. Moreover, the Corps of Engineers expressed support for the entire project, which includes two groins, even though their manual criticizes the use of groins with strong language ("…probably the most misused and improperly designed of all coastal structures").

Other Human Misbehaviors

One only needs to recall Ft. Lauderdale's experiences during the 1960s and those of Panama City Beach more recently to realize the potential for severe damage in overcrowded beach communities. Spring break periods are especially risky, of course, but with the 2017 awards achieved by Siesta/Crescent Beach, the tourist impact will be more profound year-round. The misbehaviors seen elsewhere are already evident on Siesta Key—drinking, drugs, assaults, thefts, damaged buildings, graffiti on public monuments, etc. In addition to the beach awards and publicity, there are many causes of the key's overcrowding and associated damage. The first and possibly foremost explanation relates to the cultural changes associated with the transformation on Siesta Key—the change from a residential to a resort community for short-term visitors/tourists. Allowing, and even promoting, stays as short as one night or one weekend brought a different kind of visitor—one with a "living for the moment" mentality. That attitude diminishes accountability and is conducive to human misbehavior. Heavy drinking on the beach and/or in Siesta Key Village also exacerbates misbehaviors.

Lessons from the past as well as the availability of drugs in Sarasota and Manatee Counties make more drug trafficking inevitable with the well-known negative consequences likely to follow. During the nation's opioid crisis, some states have found that retirees can be even more susceptible to substance abuse than the younger age groups. This surprising observation has been attributed to opioid overuse for pain control among senior citizens. Studies show that Florida physicians have contributed to this problem. Unfortunately, Siesta Key retirees could become prime targets for all drug dealers.

Climate Change and the Gulf of Mexico

Rising gulf temperatures, greater risk for tropical storms and storm surges, and rising sea level in the gulf because of climate change/global warming: These three problems are so closely related that they can be discussed together as Florida's greatest twenty-first-century challenge with regard to beach vacations and statewide tourism. The following list summarizes the sequence of events that have already been seen elsewhere along the Atlantic and Texas coasts.

Potential Impact of Rising Gulf Temperatures and Sea Levels

1. Shoreline erosion: rising sea levels allow waves to penetrate farther inland, increasing the potential for more erosion.

2. Amplified storm surges as coastal storms and high winds push water farther inland over Florida's very flat terrain with potentially catastrophic damage to homes and infrastructure.

3. Permanent submerging of low-lying coastal land areas by rising sea levels—thus eliminating many beaches, especially on barrier islands, and jeopardizing property values.

4. Saltwater intrusion as the rising gulf penetrates coastal groundwater sources, increasing the salinity of freshwater used for drinking and agriculture.

Global warming can affect weather patterns, sea levels, coastlines, ocean currents, seawater composition, sea temperatures, tides, and the sea floor. The impact was obvious in September 2017 when a record number of tropical storms formed in the gulf and beyond. The magnitude of sea-level increases around the world is measured by two methods: tide gauges and satellite laser altimeters. The latter method determines the height of the sea surface by measuring the return speed and intensity of a laser pulse directed at the ocean, as observed from space. The consensus from many studies of coastal tide gauge records is that during the past century, sea level has risen worldwide at an average rate of 1–2 mm per year or about one inch every decade. Studies based on satellite altimetry, however, show that this rate has increased to closer to 3.4 mm per year during the more completely monitored last twenty years.

Thus, global average sea level has increased at least eight inches since 1880, but regional variations occur. Several locations along the East Coast and Gulf of Mexico have experienced more than eight inches of local sea level rise in the past fifty years. But peninsular Florida has an advantage due to how it was formed during its carbonate factory period, as discussed in Chapter 2. As Richard Davis stated, the "rate of sea-level rise on the Florida peninsula will remain relatively low compared to most other regions because it is based on limestone, which does not compact." In some East Coast and other gulf regions, land is also subsiding gradually due to erosion, which allows the ocean to penetrate farther inland. These regions are experiencing a phenomenon of "sinking due in part to compression of the thick sediment under them," to quote Davis again.

Scientists have developed a wide range of scenarios for future sea-level rise based on estimates of growth in heat-trapping emissions and the potential responses of oceans and ice. They have also concluded that our past emissions of heat-trapping gases will largely dictate sea-level rise through 2050—that is, we appear to be trapped by our history of altering the atmosphere. But our present and future emissions will have great bearing on sea-level rise from 2050 to 2100 and beyond. Even if global warming emissions had decreased to zero by 2016, sea-level will continue to rise in the coming decades as oceans and land ice adjust to the changes already made to the atmosphere. The greatest effect on long-term sea-level rise will be the rate and magnitude of the loss of ice sheets, primarily in Greenland and Antarctica, as they respond to rising temperatures caused by heat-trapping emissions in the atmosphere. Although the shrinking land ice—glaciers, ice caps, and ice sheets—accounted for about half of the total global sea-level rise between

1972 and 2008, its contribution has been increasing since the early 1990s as the rate of ice loss has accelerated.

The Increasing Hazard of Harmful Red Tide Algae Blooms

Ever since the Spanish explorers "discovered" red tide in the sixteenth century, its potential to cause massive kills of fish has been known, especially in Florida but also along the Georgia and North Carolina coasts. The effect on commercial fishing has been variable depending on the specific region and intensity of toxic exposure. In the current era of booming tourism, a greater problem for southwest Florida in general, and certainly for Siesta Key, is the impact of red tide on the respiratory system of beachgoers. Despite decades of research by several institutions such as Mote Marine, beginning on south Siesta Key in 1973, many aspects of this problem remain mysterious. From several discussions with long-term Siesta Key residents, we learned that the red tide threat is not well understood by the public. Consequently, our goal is to provide a thorough understanding of Florida red tide and its increasing threat for Siesta Key and elsewhere in Southwest Florida.

Red tide is a peculiar and confusing name used in Florida for high concentrations of the harmful marine algae, *Karenia brevis,* when it is in the blooming stage. Because the blooms occur ten to forty miles offshore, the clusters of the red coloration are not generally seen from the beaches, but aerial observations show them as bright red and dense. *Karenia brevis* is especially prevalent along the southwest Florida coast and generally lives a harmless life on the floor of the gulf. When the algae begin to bloom on the sea bottom and rise to the surface, however, *Karenia brevis* causes severe

harm to fish, marine mammals, turtles, sea birds, and humans due to naturally produced toxins. Among the victims have been hundreds of dolphins and manatees. Hence the term, *harmful* algae blooms or HABS applies well. Toxic *Karenia brevis* outbreaks vary from minor, short-lived blooms to severe, intensive blooms that may persist up to eighteen months. They occur almost every year in the gulf and travel with the current in patchy clumps that give the red color. With the warming of the gulf, the blooms appear to be lasting longer. There may also be a shift underway from a peak period of August to December toward a pattern of higher prevalence in September to March.

Although always present in low concentrations throughout the gulf with no apparent adverse effects, high concentrations (blooms) of *Karenia brevis* produce sufficient toxins called brevetoxins to cause the ecological and human impacts. Research has revealed that the toxicity is attributable primarily to their binding to cellular sodium channels and disrupting essential ion transport processes to interfere with nerve transmission. In addition to being sodium channel blockers, brevetoxins may also act on the immune system to promote release of histamine, which has profound physiologic effects.

Massive fish kills are a common result of Florida red tide in high concentrations—leaving beaches and bays full of dead, decaying carcasses. The decomposing fish add to the environmental stress by depleting oxygen from the water, they cause a foul odor all along the shore, and they also attract flies and snakes. Fish accumulate brevetoxins by ingestion of viable *Karenia brevis* cells and contaminated prey, and by absorption of toxins across gill membranes, while shellfish, such as mussels, clams, and oysters accumulate toxins as they filter-feed on algae.

Human health effects include intoxication from neurotoxic shellfish poisoning and

Figure 19.3 Fish killed by Florida red tide and washed ashore on Siesta Key beaches where they attract flies and cause a rotten stench (Photograph courtesy of Martha Kramer)

respiratory tract irritation. The most serious risk in humans is neurotoxicity resulting from ingestion of contaminated shellfish. Symptoms include gastrointestinal disorders, tingling sensation of lips and extremities, reversal of hot and cold sensation, rapid heartbeat, loss of balance, and impaired neuromuscular functions such as the ability to walk. Fortunately, Florida monitors commercial shellfish beds and will close them when *Karenia brevis* levels rise beyond the threshold.

On Siesta/Crescent Beach, the most frequent impact of HABS relates to the respiratory system. There are periods in which the aerosolized toxins are too irritating for residents and tourists to enjoy beach activities—even strolling along the shoreline without a mask can cause intense symptoms that include coughing, sneezing, tearing, and an itchy or sore throat. Beach walkers seem to assume that there are tiny particles in the breezes being blown in from

the gulf. In fact, the brevetoxins are arriving as invisible aerosols. The toxic aerosol is created when *Karenia brevis* in the bloom stage is broken apart by wave action. Their cell walls collapse as they die, and this releases the toxins into the water.

Then, through transport into the atmosphere as tiny bubbles, the toxins are subsequently incorporated into the airborne salt spray produced by the wind and waves. The aerosols are next blown for miles to the seashore and beyond. A significant increase in self-reported respiratory symptoms and visits to emergency and urgent care centers among beach vacationers have been described after recreational exposures to Florida red tide. The density of the toxin-containing aerosols will determine the severity of respiratory symptoms. Tracy Fanara of Mote Marine elaborated: "It's a combination of where the bloom is and the wind —it has to be the right combination for people to see all of those effects." With the increasing incidence of asthma and chronic obstructive pulmonary disease in the elderly, Florida red tide effects are a greater concern. In a severe asthmatics, environmental exposures that trigger asthma attacks may even be fatal.

Increasing Insurance Costs

Natural disasters like tornadoes, hurricanes with high storm surges, and floods can be catastrophic for homeowners, and insurance companies can be bankrupted by payoffs after a widespread massive event. Experience with Hurricane Katrina revealed the limits of insurance coverage and the severe impact on insurers. More recently, Hurricane Harvey with its fifty inches of rainfall causing massive flooding reminds us that flood insurance coverage, if available at all, is often inadequate. Even federal flood insurance is limited, with no temporary housing expenses reimbursement, no coverage for outdoor property (i.e., patio, septic system, trees, swimming pool, etc.), and only up to $250,000 for a house. In the case of private insurance, a mixture of windstorm, homeowners, and flood protection is necessary, but some companies avoid the flood provision and all of them are increasing the deductible.

Although Hurricane Irma diminished in force to maximum sustained winds in Sarasota County between 40 and 50 mph with gusts up to 70 mph at Sarasota-Bradenton airport, it still caused significant damage. Premiums may also increase as the costs of hurricanes, such as Hurricane Irma, are imposed on the state. Estimates of Irma-related claims calculated during October 2017 predict 300,000 claims for wind damage and 150,000 claims for flood damage—for example, the devastation caused by storm surges. The current total for insurance claims is more than $40 billion according to the Consumer Federation of America. This organization warns that "insurance companies may try to wriggle out of covering homes with both wind and water damage through bizarre anti-concurrent-cancellation clauses that remove coverage for wind damage if an insured flood occurs at the same time." Robert S. Hunter of the Consumer Federation further pointed out that "these egregious clauses are impossible for consumers to comprehend as most people cannot believe that their insurance company would sell them a policy with wind coverage that could disappear through a trap door hidden deep in the policy language." Avoiding liability and imposing long delays on payments are two of the tactics that have sometimes been used, as the Crystal Sands condominium in the mid-key region learned after the 2016 tornado. With global warming and more tropical storms expected, insurance companies will undoubtedly need to review their business models, potentially increasing their deductibles further, as well as the annual premiums.

CHAPTER 20

The Fate of Siesta Key

Predictions about the Impact of Relentless Global Warming

Our keys off Sarasota County are older, and for the most part, except for the transient later deposits at the ends and on the beaches, are as solid as the mainland. These gross whims of nature, in a mindless turbulence, created this particular piece of the world we now celebrate, made it a place of bays and inlets, beaches, and vistas. We have been here a hundred years. In geological time the waters will again cover the peninsula and again recede, only to return again. So let us cherish this moment of paradise, relish these years of sun, and beauty, and do what we can to keep it pristine...Siesta Key.
—John D. MacDonald, quoted in *Journey to Centennial Sarasota* by Janet Snyder Matthews

None of who live in the present can relate to the situation predicted for coastal living in the United States by 2050–2100. Coastal areas are six times more crowded than the inland counties, and the population in coastal areas will continue to increase in the future. Currently, although counties directly on the shoreline constitute less than 10 percent of the total U.S. land area (excluding Alaska), they account for 39 percent of the total population. In Florida, about three-quarters of the residents, or approximately fifteen million people, live in a coastal county—the highest population density of all the states. Ironically, the flight to the coasts during the past half-century may reverse into a flight from the coasts by 2050 unless the rate of climate change slows.

Although Florida's peninsula has less susceptibility to sea-level rise due to its limestone base, its many barrier islands will eventually be in jeopardy. It's a question of when and not if the gulf will flood them. On Siesta Key, the loss of "America's Best Beach" would be a tragic outcome. This was demonstrated dramatically in October 2016 when the organization known as This Spaceship Earth assembled local residents for a demonstration that we recommend to readers (https://www.youtube.com/watch?v=2jdyfKtJ0SI). After lining attendees up in front of the red lifeguard station at high tide, the moderator backed them up to where the shore line would be in 2030 if a sea-level rise of eight inches occurs by then as predicted by the National Oceanic and Atmospheric Administration (NOAA) in its worst-case scenario. That increase eliminates about two-thirds of Siesta Public Beach—that is, from a depth of 600 feet to about 200 feet west of the Seibert Pavilion. Next, the line moved all the way back to Beach Road to simulate the water's edge in 2040 assuming a twenty-four-inch rise—again, in accordance with NOAA's projections. In other words, if climate change continues unabated, and NOAA is correct, there will be neither Siesta Public Beach, nor a parking lot by 2040.

It should be noted that the range of predicted sea-level rise is wide and described as follows on the NOAA website (https://www.climate.gov/news-features/understanding-climate/climate-change-global-sea-level): "Scientists are very confident that global mean sea level will rise at least 8 inches but no more than 6.6 feet by 2100." On the other hand, using a more conservative estimate of a sea-level rise of 3 mm per year and taking into account peninsular Florida's limestone bed advantage, Davis predicted, "It is likely that Florida's barrier islands will remain stable from sea-level change at least through the end of this century—*if* the rate of sea-level rise does not increase significantly." This "if" is crucial because there is a consensus that the rate of global sea-level rise has doubled from 1.7 mm/year throughout most of the twentieth century to 3.4 mm/year since 1993.

Of course the rate of deglaciation could slow. A massive volcano could erupt and darken the skies globally and cool the Earth. Or, much less likely, a large meteor could strike the Earth again. Or, industrial nations might begin to limit their greenhouse gas emissions. The last possibility, however, also seems unlikely as Asian countries like China are poised to surpass the United States after our century of world dominance. Frankly, unless effective international management of climate change is underway soon, prevention of global warming will be hopeless.

If the worst-case scenario applies, Florida will lose its barrier islands and is likely to shrink drastically during the next century (see color page 12). If so, the beach vacation era and reign of tourism will have been more than a century in fact. Readers might prefer to dismiss such pessimism, but the dire predictions of all unbiased scientists studying this issue should not be ignored as "fake news." Thus, we should heed the advice of John MacDonald and "cherish this moment of paradise, relish these years of sun, and beauty, and do what we can to keep it pristine… Siesta Key." Breathtaking sunsets, as shown on color page 11, will continue to be enjoyed on Siesta/Crescent Beach for many more years.

Bibliography

Balsera, V. D., and R. A. May. *La Florida*. Gainesville, FL: University Press of Florida, 2014.

Cassell, Frank A. *Suncoast Empire*. Sarasota, FL: Pineapple Press, 2017.

Coolidge, M. C. *Sideways in Sarasota*. Sarasota, FL: Bardolf & Company, 2008.

Davis, R. A. *Barrier Islands of the Florida Gulf Coast Peninsula*. Sarasota, FL: Pineapple Press, 2016.

Diamond, J. *Guns, Germs, and Steel*. New York: W. W. Norton & Company, 1997.

Dobyns, H. F. *Their Number Became Thinned*. Knoxville: University of Tennessee Press, 1983.

Grismer, Karl H. *The Story of Sarasota*. Sarasota, FL: M. F. Russell, 1946.

Halligan, J. J., et al. "Pre-Clovis occupation 14,550 years ago at the Page-Ladson site, Florida, and the peopling of the Americas." Sci Adv. 2016; 13;2(5):e1600375.

Hayes, M. O. "Barrier Island Morphology as a Function of Tidal and Wave Regime." In Leatherman, S. P. (ed). *Barrier Islands*. New York: Academic Press, 1979.

Hine, A. C. *Geologic History of Florida*. Gainesville, FL: University Press of Florida, 2013.

Holloway, J. C., and N. Taylor. *The Business of Tourism,* 7th edition. Upper Saddle River, NJ: Financial Times Prentice Hall, 2006.

LaHurd J. *Hidden History of Sarasota*. Charleston, SC: The History Press, 2009.

LaHurd, J. *Quintessential Sarasota*. Sarasota, FL: Clubhouse Publishing, Inc., 1990.

Leatherman, S. and J. Williams. *National Geographic Field Guide to the Water's Edge*. Washington, DC: National Geographic Society, 2012.

MacDonald, J. D. *Condominium*. New York: Random House, 1977.

Patterson, D. *A Tour of the Islands of Pine Island Sound, Florida*. Gainesville, FL: University of Florida, 2017.

Purdy, B. A. *West of the Papal Line*. West Conshohocken, PA: Infinity, 2002.

Purdy, B. A. *Florida's People During the Last Ice Age*. Gainesville, FL: University Press of Florida, 2008.

Redfern R. *Origins: The Evolution of Continents, Oceans, and Life*. Norman, OK: University of Oklahoma Press, 2001.

Stapor, F. W., T. D. Matthews, and F. E. Lindfors-Kearns. "Episodic Barrier Growth in the Southwest Florida: A Response to Fluctuating Holocene Sea Level." *Memoir 3*, pp. 149-202. Miami Geological Society, 1988.

Index

Note: page numbers in **bold** refer to illustrations. **CP** refers to a page in the color section.

Here are some other books from Pineapple Press. For a complete list, visit our website at www.pineapplepress.com.

Suncoast Empire by Frank Cassell. The story of Bertha Palmer, one of the richest and most famous socialites in the early 20th century, who came to southwest Florida and tried her hand at agriculture and cattle raising. She turned the small settlement of Sarasota into a thriving town.

Myakka by Paula Benshoff. This book takes you into shady hammocks of twisted oaks and up into aerial gardens, down the wild and scenic river, and across a variegated canvas of prairies, piney woods, and wetlands—all in Myakka River State Park, the largest state park in Florida.

Florida's Past: People and Events That Shaped the State by Gene Burnett. Three popular volumes of collected essays by a history-teller extraordinaire.

The Florida Chronicles by Stuart B. McIver. A collection of essays on Florida's famous and infamous people, divided into three volumes. Volume 1: *Dreamers, Schemers, and Scalawags*. Volume 2: *Murder in the Tropics*. Volume 3: *Touched by the Sun*.

Historic Homes of Florida by Laura Stewart. Houses tell the human side of history. In this survey of restored residences, their stories are intertwined with those of their owners from the days of Spanish occupation to the Rawlings House in Cross Creek, Vizcaya in Miami, and President Harry S. Truman's "Little White House" in Key West.

A Land Remembered by Patrick Smith. Ranked #1 Best Florida Book eight times, *A Land Remembered* tells the story of three generations of the MacIveys, a Florida family who battle the hardships of the frontier to rise from a dirt-poor Cracker life to the wealth and standing of real estate tycoons—turning the precious land into a land remembered.

Marjory Stoneman Douglas: Voice of the River by Marjory Stoneman Douglas, author of *Everglades: River of Grass*. The voice that emerges in this autobiography is a voice from the past and a voice from the future, which has truly become the voice of the river.

Nature's Steward by Nick Penniman. This book documents how the Conservancy of Southwest Florida grew land acquisition into regional advocacy and education, and how it adapted its tactics to the changing environmental climate in Tallahassee and Washington.